METALLIC
Textile Designs

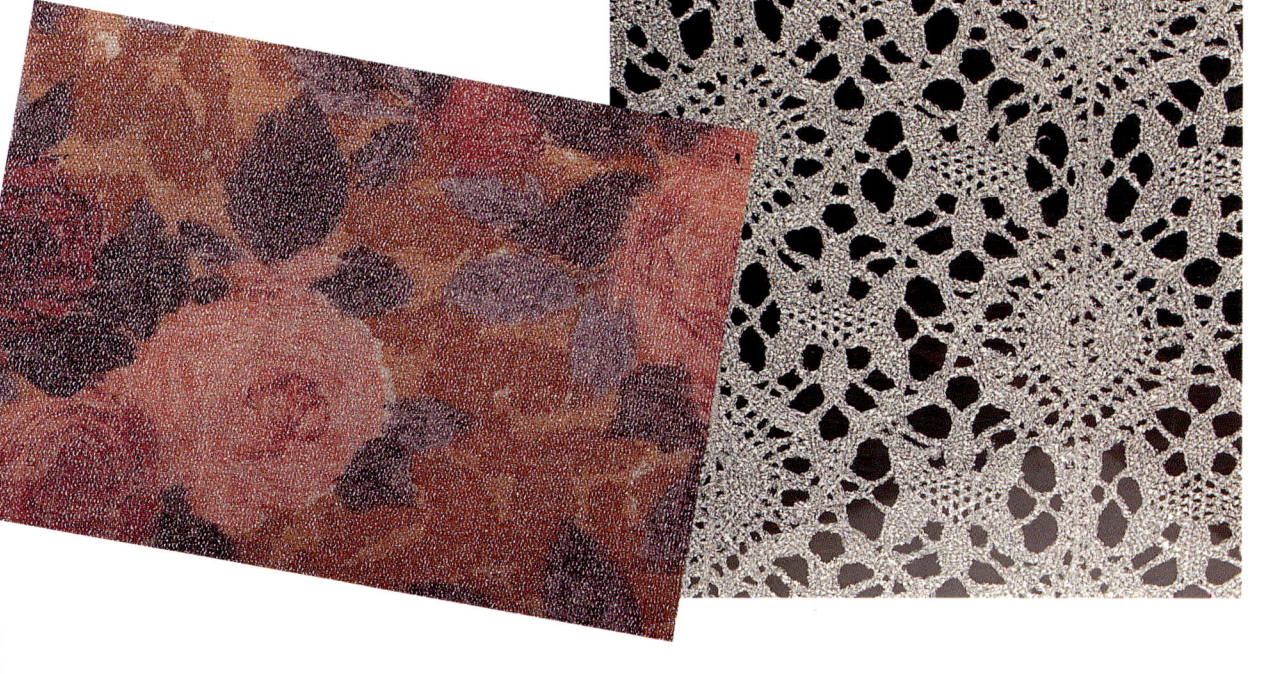

Schiffer Publishing Ltd

4880 Lower Valley Road, Atglen, PA 19310 USA

Tina Skinner

ACKNOWLEDGMENTS

The following couture houses in Europe provided pieces from their lines for inclusion in this book:
   Bouton-Renaud of Vaulx-En-Velin, France.
   Desseilles Textiles of Calais, France.
   Gartex International of Busto Arsizio, Italy.
   Houlé Dentelles of Calais, France.
   Tessitura Taiana Virgilio of Olgiate Comasco, Italy.
   TexStile Team of Milano Italy.
   Textil Hof Denim of Hof, Germany.
   We feel privileged to share them with readers.

Also, special thanks to Jerry Fronefield for his sparkling assistance in this glittery undertaking.

Copyright © 1998 by Schiffer Publishing Ltd.
Library of Congess Catalog Card Number: 98-86019

All rights reserved. No part of this work may be reproduced or used in any form or by any means—graphic, electronic, or mechanical, including photocopying or information storage and retrieval systems—without written permission from the copyright holder.
   "Schiffer," "Schiffer Publishing Ltd. & Design," and the "Design of pen and ink well" are registered trademarks of Schiffer Publishing, Ltd.

Designed by Bonnie M. Hensley
Typeset in Korinna BT/Korinna

ISBN: 0-7643-0635-9
Printed in China

Published by Schiffer Publishing Ltd.
4880 Lower Valley Road
Atglen, PA 19310
Phone: (610) 593-1777; Fax: (610) 593-2002
E-mail: Schifferbk@aol.com
Please write for a free catalog.
This book may be purchased from the publisher.
Please include $3.95 for shipping.

In Europe Schiffer books are distributed by
Bushwood Books
6 Marksbury Avenue Kew Gardens
Surrey TW9 4JF England
Phone: 44 (0) 181 392-8585; Fax: 44 (0) 181 392-9876
E-mail: Bushwd@aol.com

Please try your bookstore first.
We are interested in hearing from authors
with book ideas on related subjects.

CONTENTS

Introduction *4*
Solids *5*
Stripes *12*
Plaids *28*
Florals *35*
Paisley *65*
Geometric *77*
Exotics *91*
Lace *96*
Miscellaneous *105*

INTRODUCTION

An apology, for starters, because no photograph can capture the gleam, the living sparkle, that metallic cloth casts when fashioned into a garment and draped on a live body. Even passing a swatch across splayed fingers makes lights twinkle and colors transform. Still, life offers the designer few opportunities to see and handle so many fabric swatches in one place at one time as a photo album, so we've settled for that. And to do the best we could with it, we used three lights to help pull out the glimmer and glow, along with the best film and camera equipment money can buy.

That work done, we now turn this work over to our readers' fertile imaginations. We'll leave it to you to picture a stretch of glittery lace trimming a bolero jacket at the Academy Awards, that shimmery stretch denim on the mile-long legs of a supermodel, the psychedelic paisley gracing the windows of a rock star's white limousine, and the shiny black threads gleaming in the upholstery of an exclusive restaurant. Isn't it a pretty picture? The kind of which fantasies are made.

Metallics are the fabrics of fantasy, the jewels of the wardrobe. This perceived value isn't based solely on sparkle, either. Metallics are tricky fabrics to manufacture. These threads, whether knit or woven into a fabric, are not as elastic or flexible as other standard textile threads. It takes a lot of experimentation and practice to make metallic mesh with wool, cotton, silk, polyester, or rayon without creating an unintended stressed look.

This book will help designers and historians see how it's done, and trace the highlights in metallics' history. Enjoy!

Chapter One

SOLIDS

Metallic gray stretch fabric. Viscose, nylon, and elastic. *Courtesy of Gartex International, Busto Arsizio, Italy.*

Shimmery viscose/linen blend. *Courtesy of Gartex International, Busto Arsizio, Italy.*

Gray and silver. Cotton, rayon, and polyester. *Courtesy of Gartex International, Busto Arsizio, Italy.*

Viscose, lurex, and polyester. *Courtesy of Tessitura Taiana Virgilio, Olgiate Comasco, Italy.*

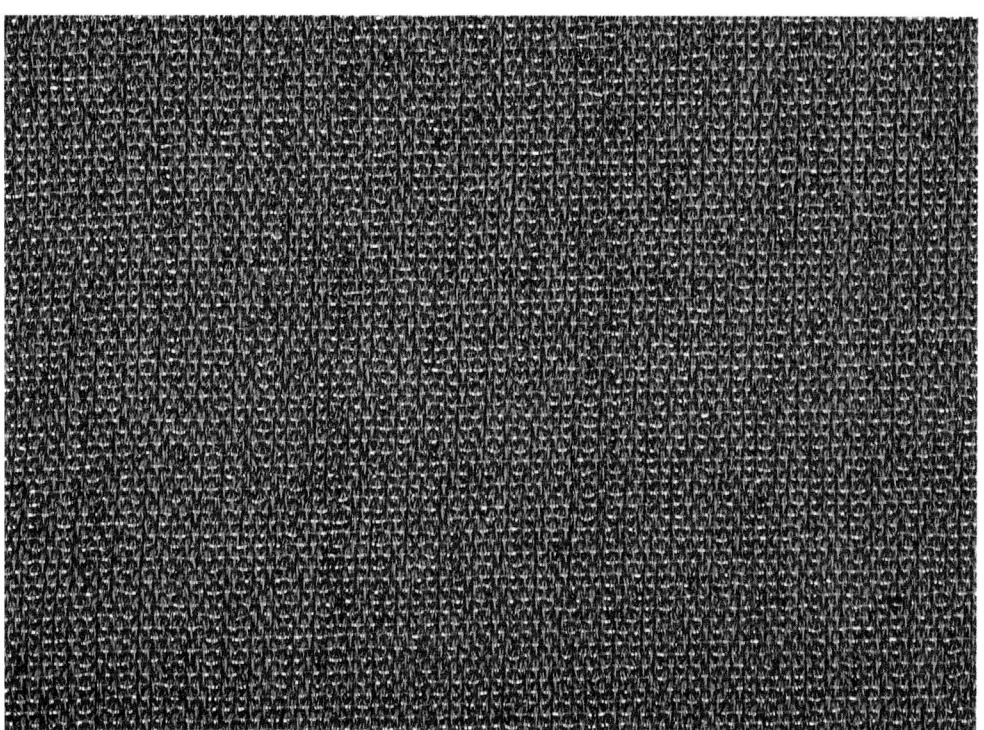

Silver lamé knit. *Courtesy of TexStile Team, Milano Italy.*

Pokane Blue. *Courtesy of Textil Hof Denim, Hof, Germany.*

HighTec Denim. Silver. *Courtesy of Textil Gruppe, Hof, Germany.*

Pokane Yellow. *Courtesy of Textil Gruppe, Hof, Germany.*

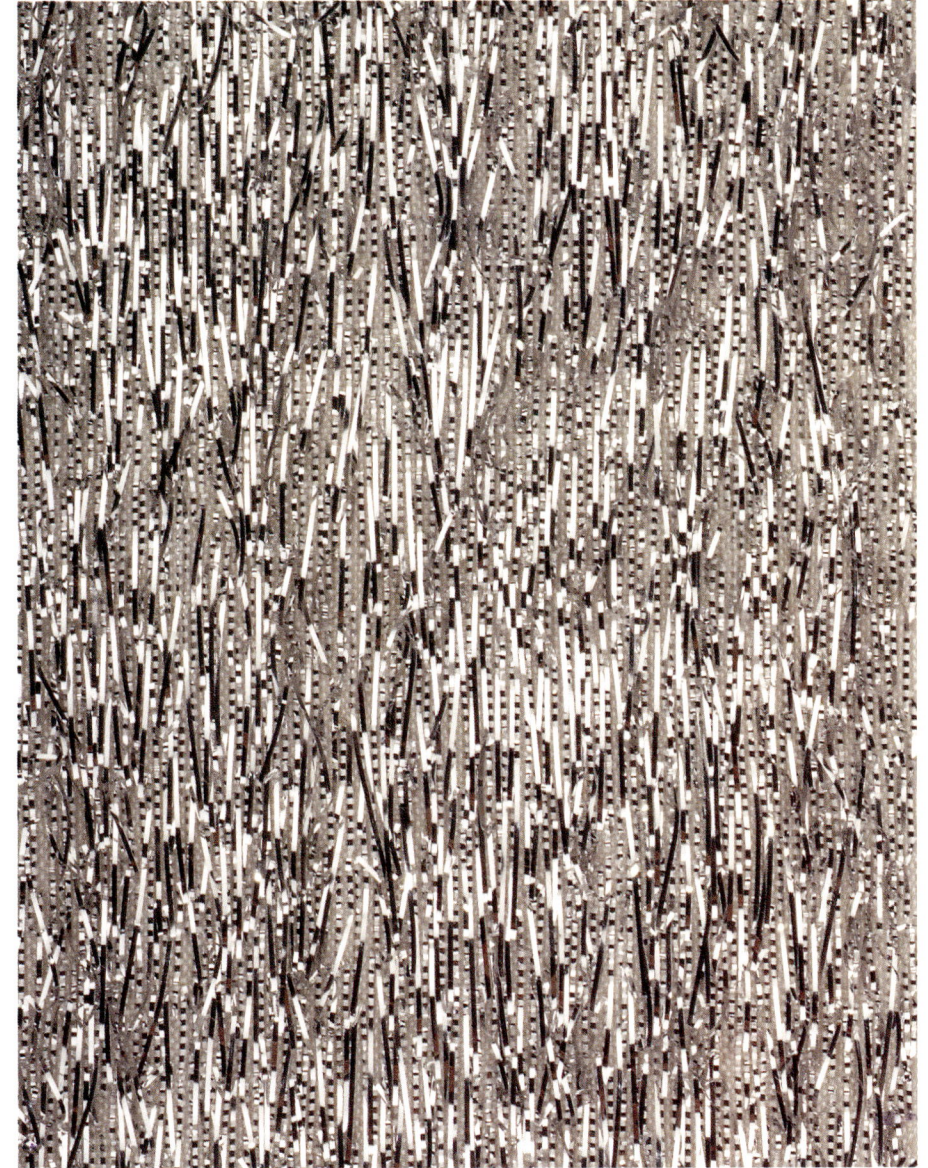

Silver spongy metallic cloth. Japan, 1950s.

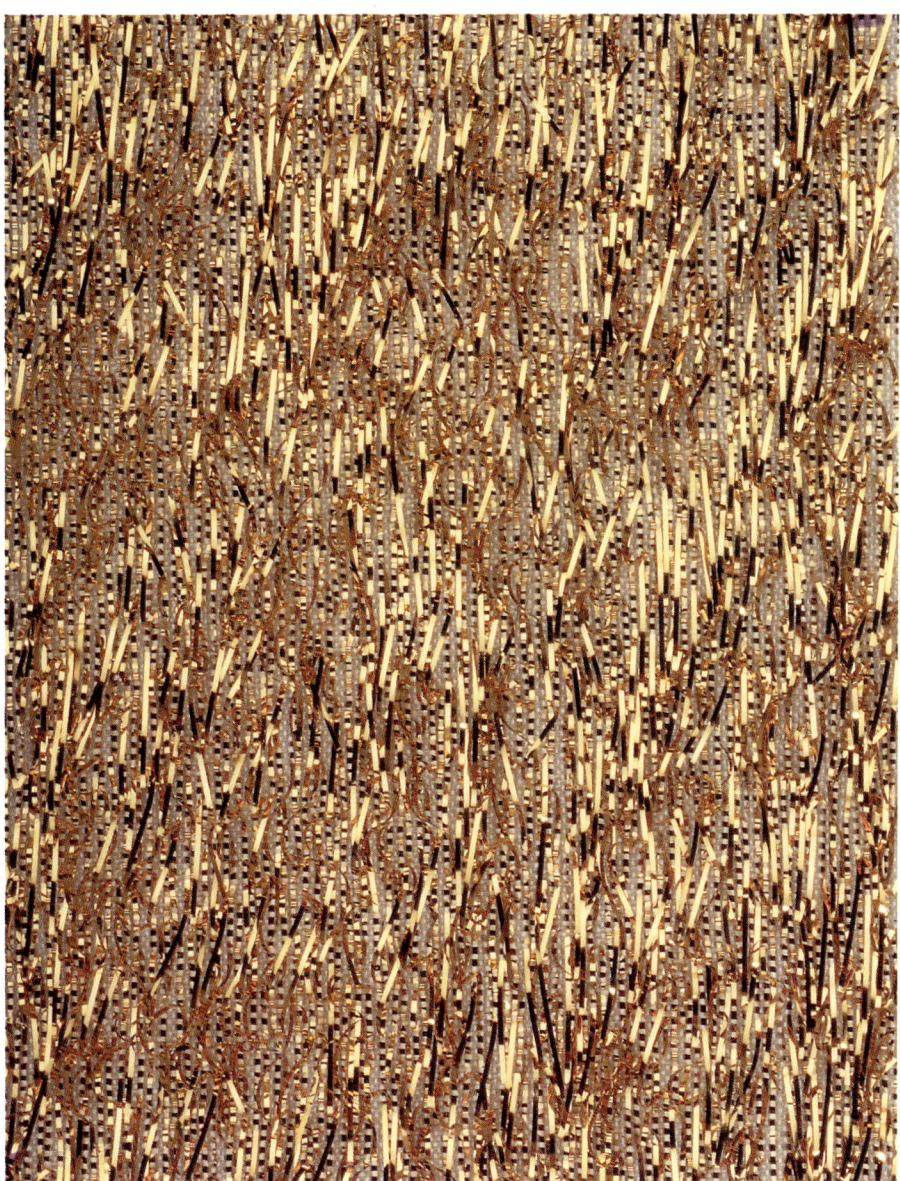

Gold spongy metallic cloth. Japan, 1950s.

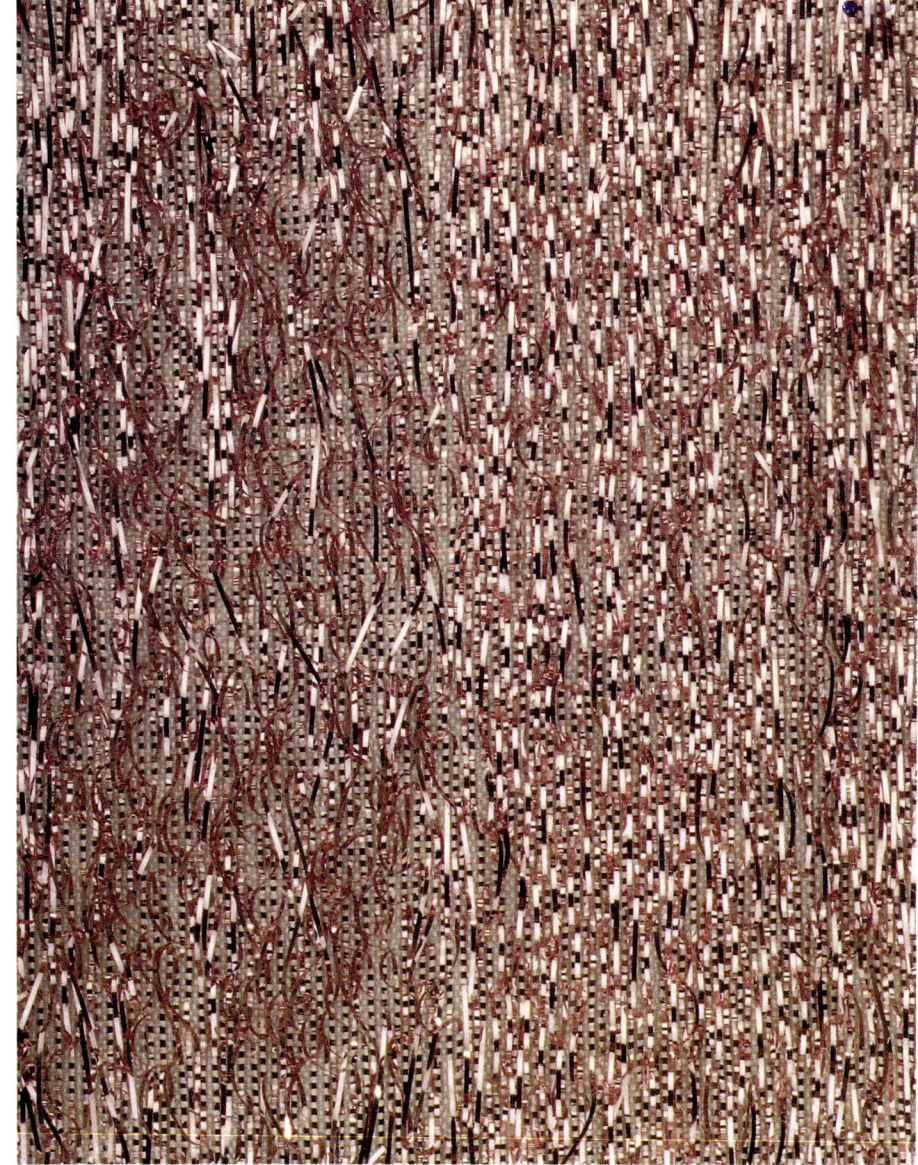

Pink spongy metallic cloth. Japan, 1950s.

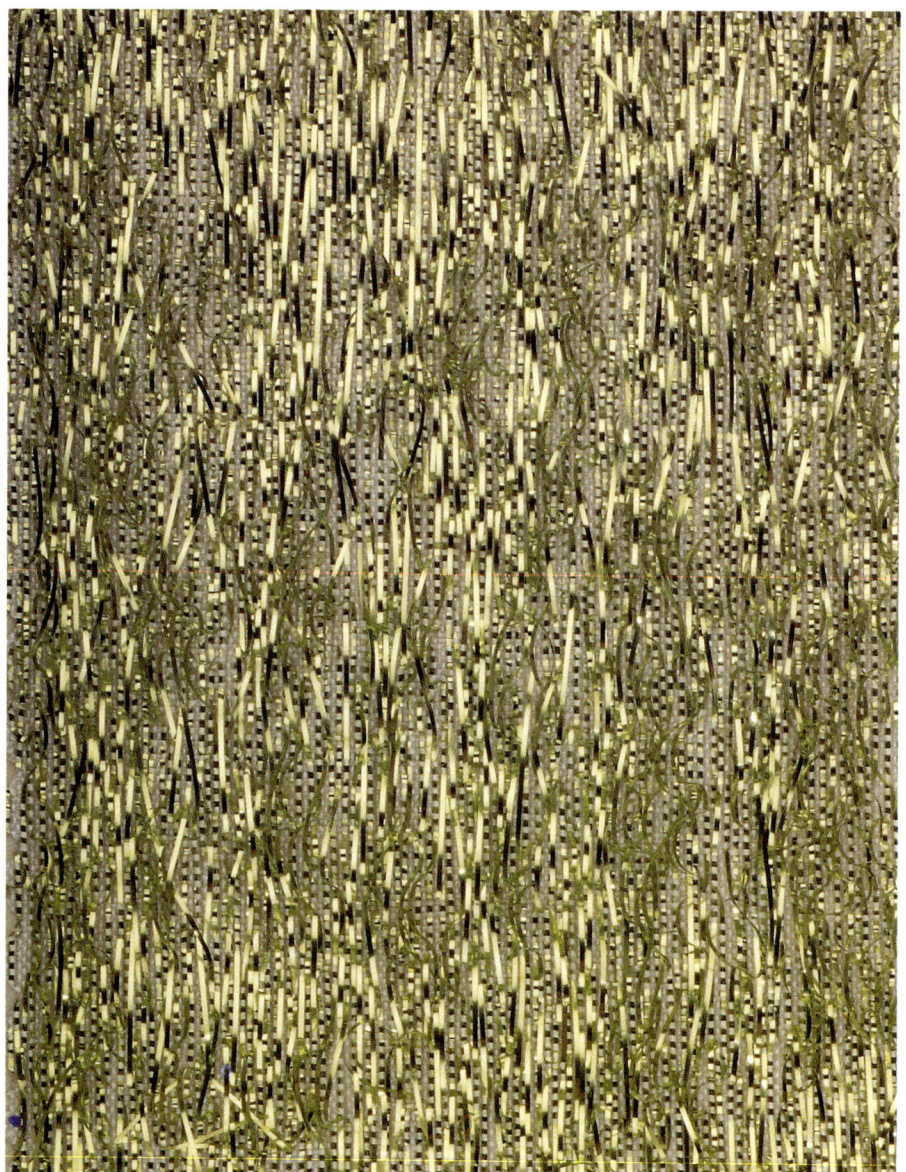

Green spongy metallic cloth. Japan, 1950s.

Spongy silver metallic. Japan, 1950s.

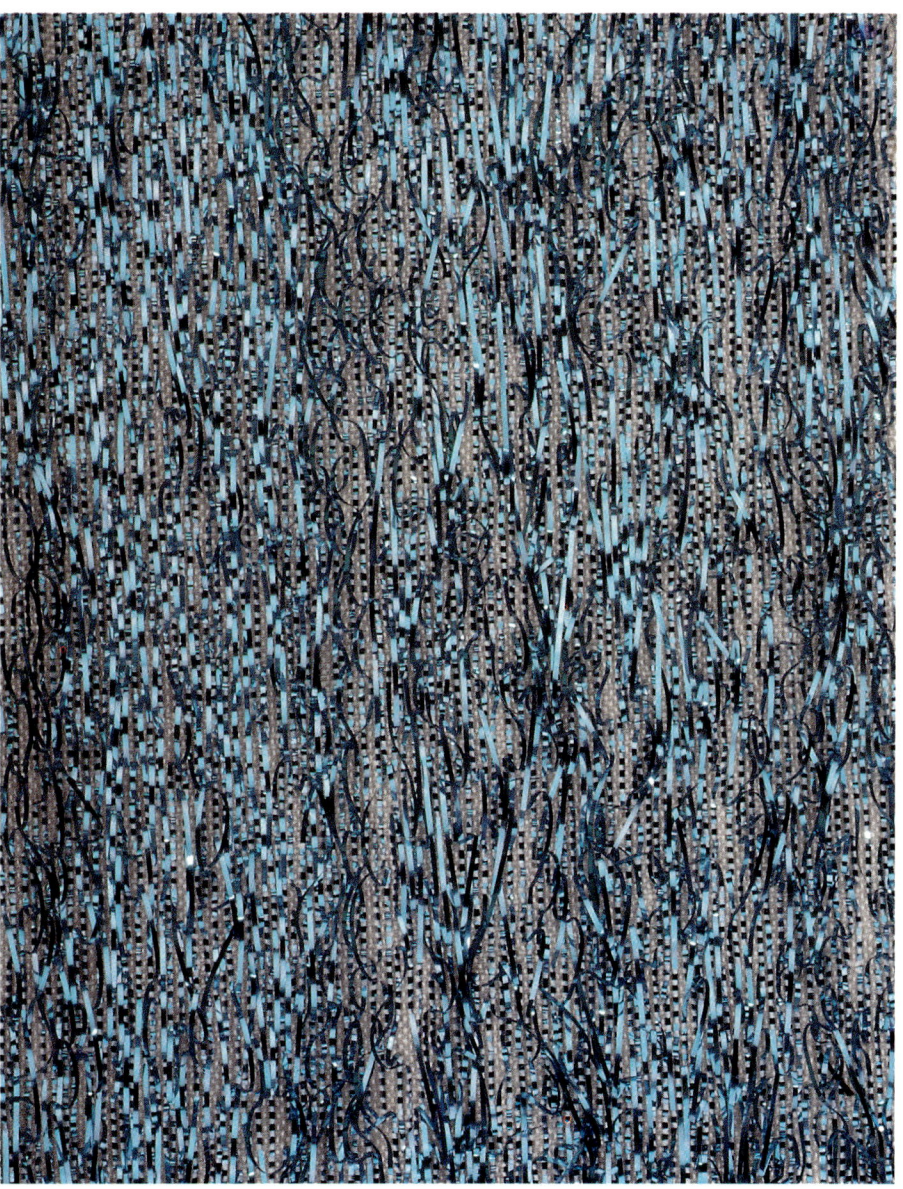

Blue spongy metallic cloth. Japan, 1950s.

Chapter Two

STRIPES

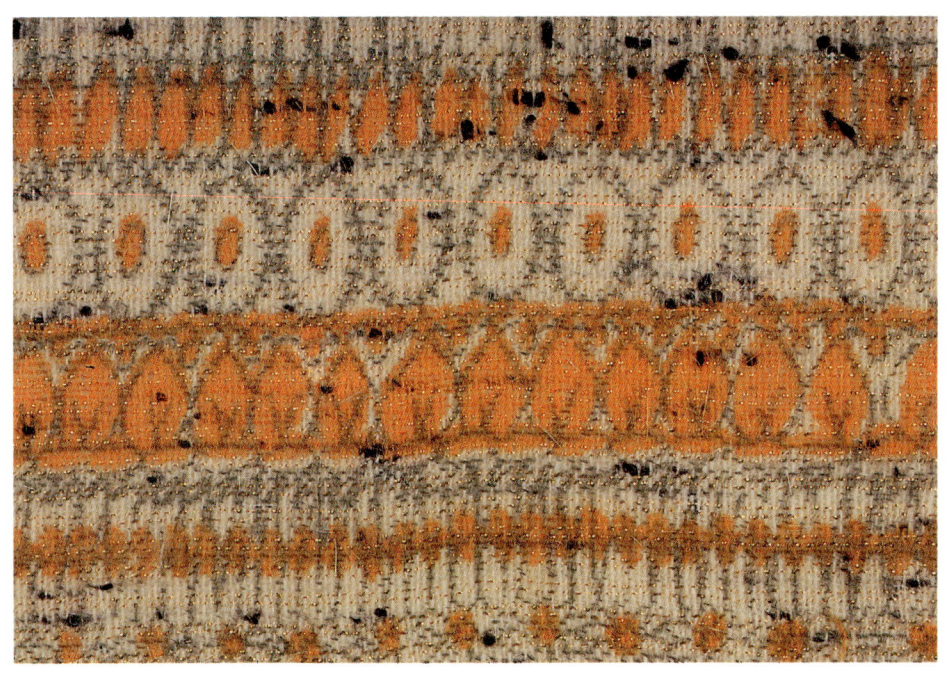

Horizontal design of orange and gray on bone, with gold threads. Wool/nylon/angora, France, 1963.

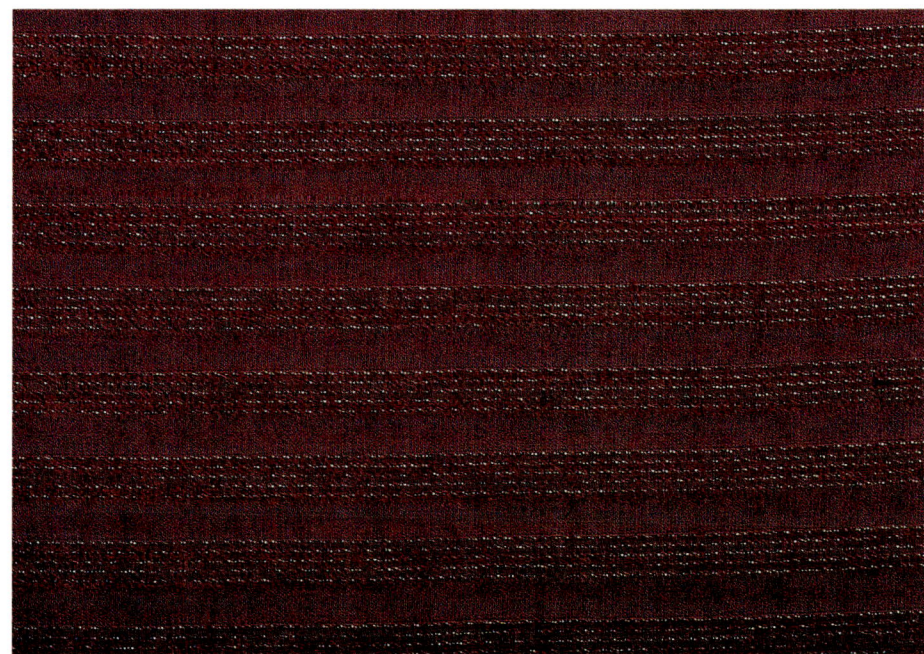

Burgundy film with velour and silver horizontal stripes. *Courtesy of TexStile Team, Milano Italy.*

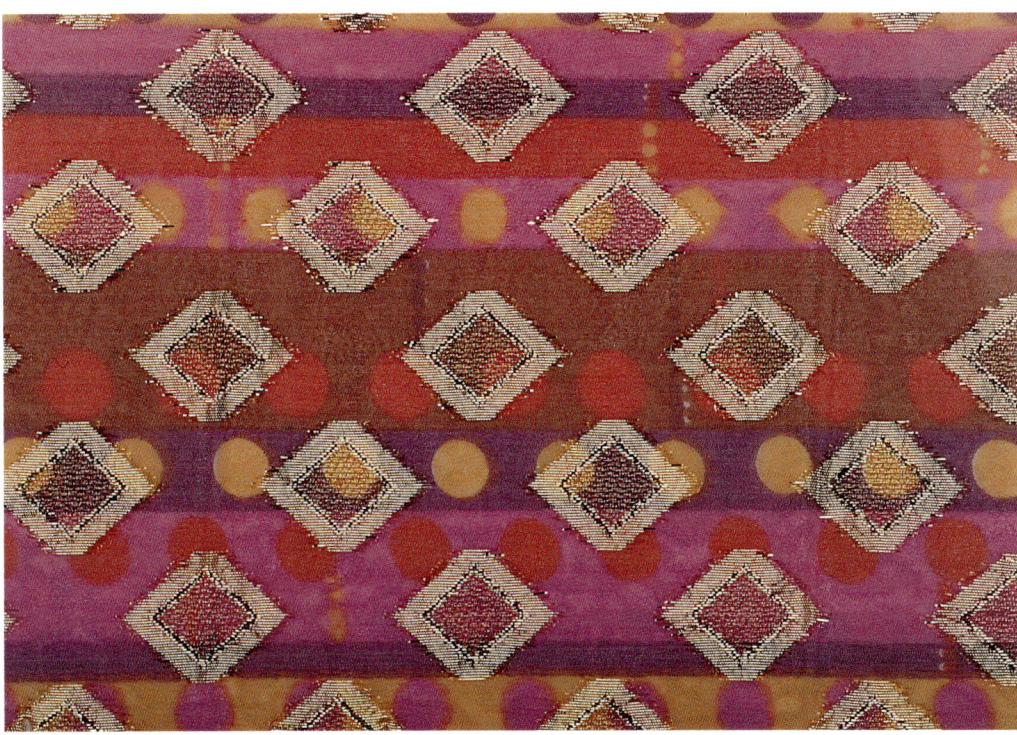

Hot colors form stripes punctuated by gold diamonds. Hand printed nylon/polyester film, Japan 1960s.

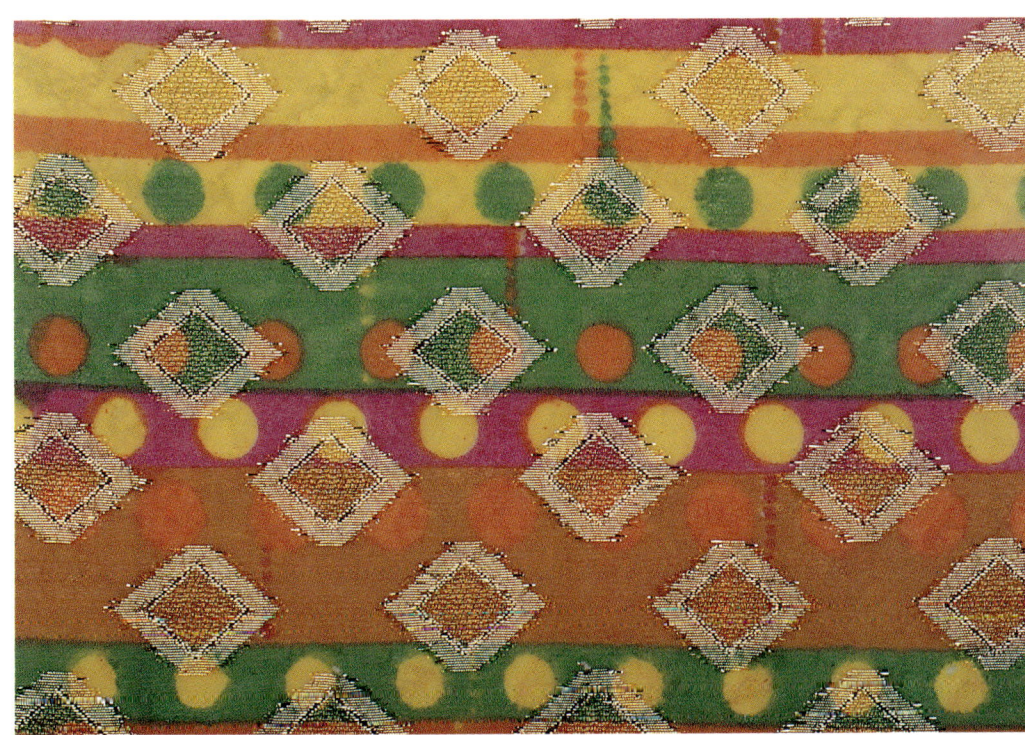

Hot colors form stripes punctuated by gold diamonds. Hand printed nylon/polyester film, Japan 1960s.

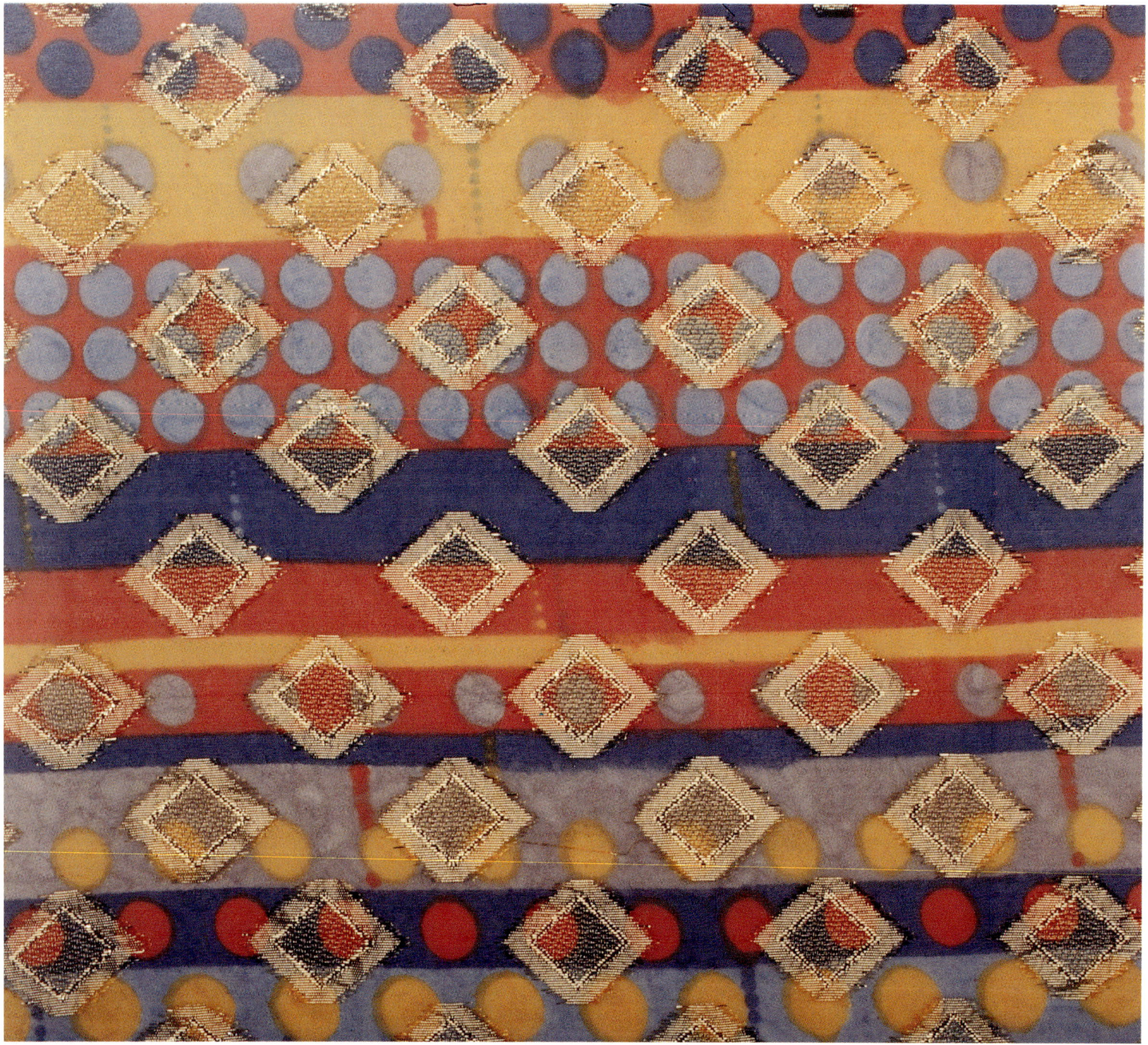

Hot colors form stripes punctuated by gold diamonds. Hand printed nylon/polyester film, Japan 1960s.

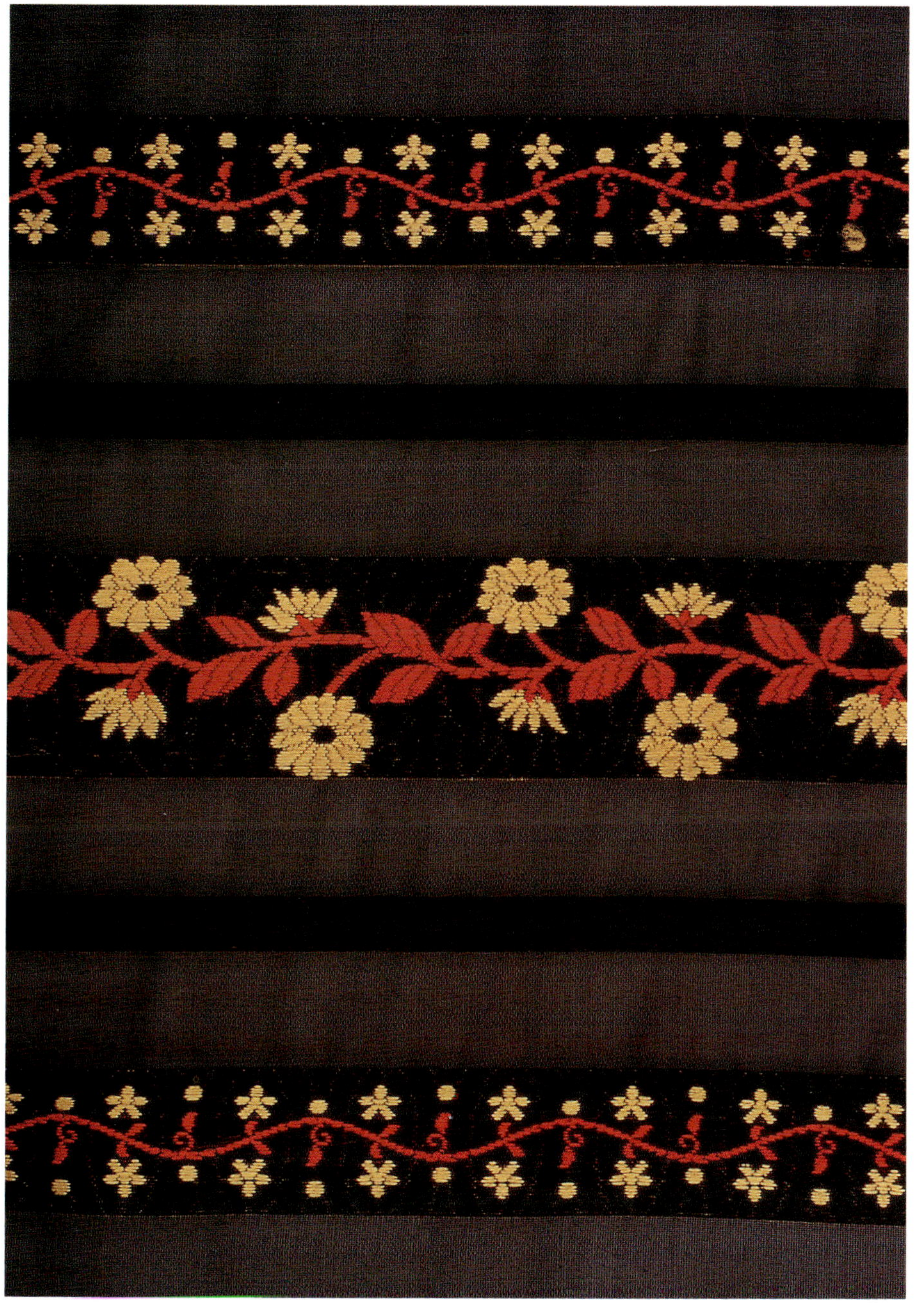

Floral stripes in metallic red and gold wend their way across black film. Polyester/acetate, Japan, 1960s.

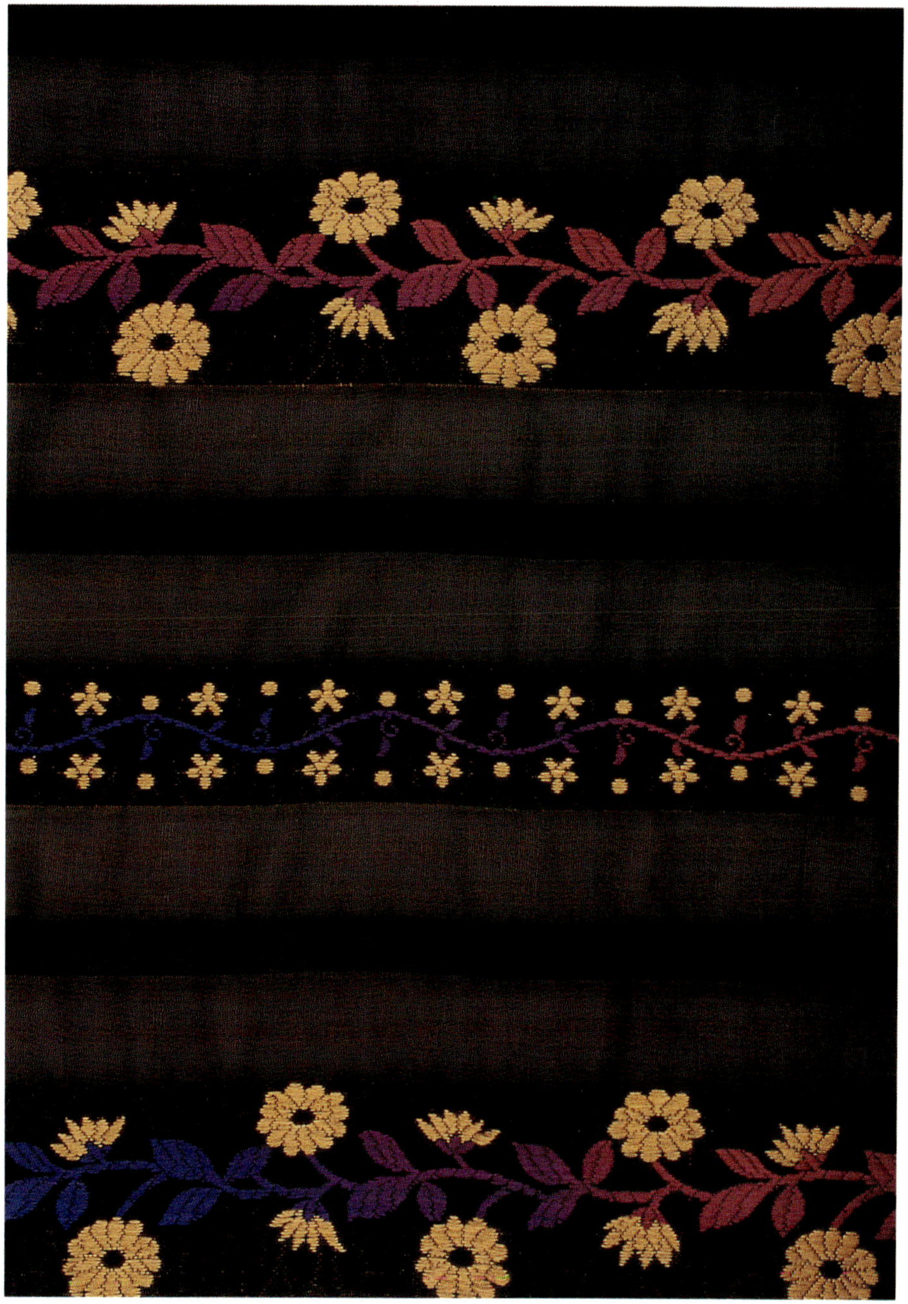

Floral stripes in metallic grape and gold wend their way across black film. Polyester/acetate, Japan, 1960s.

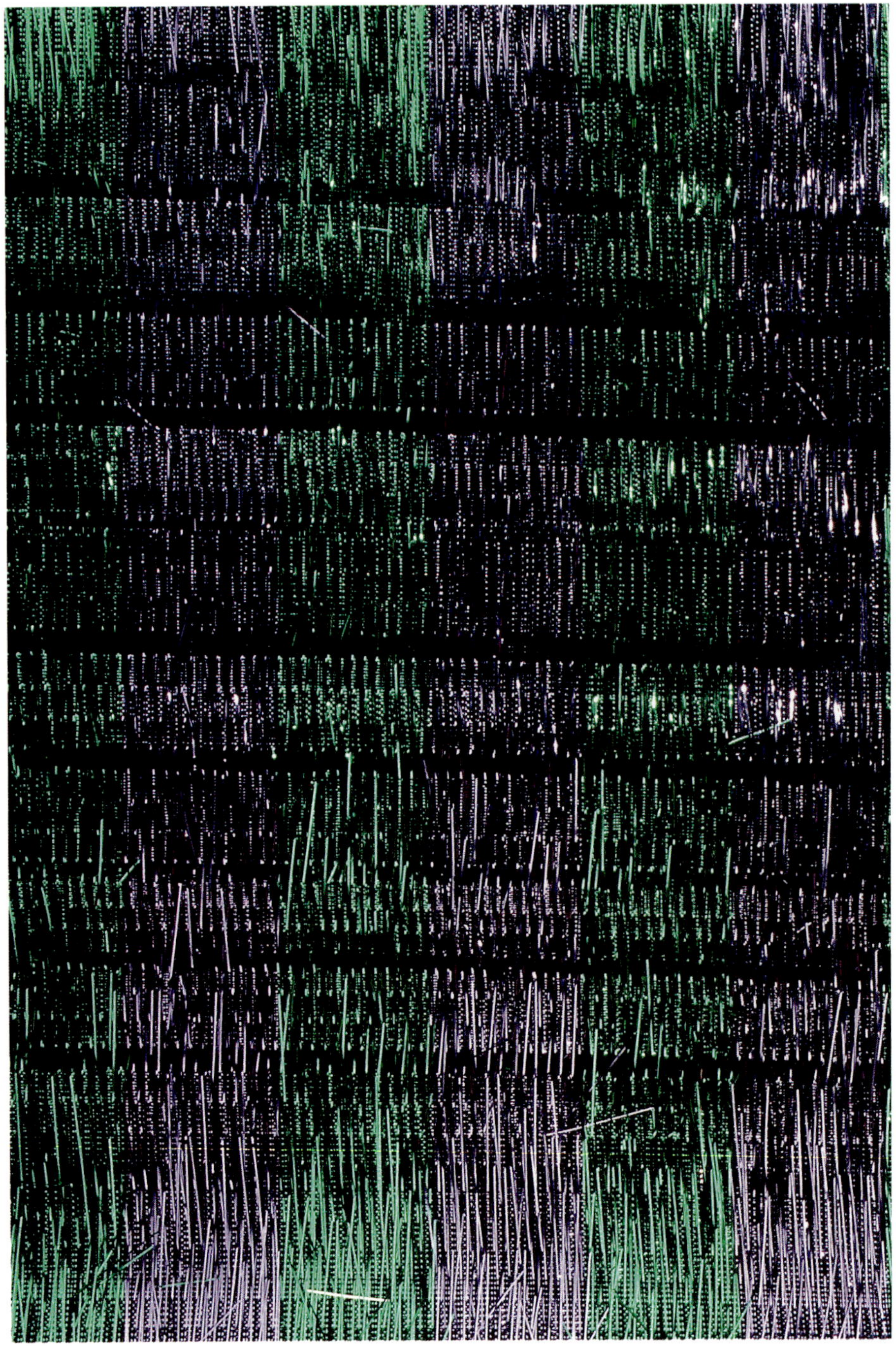

Green and purple lamé stripes. Japan, 1960.

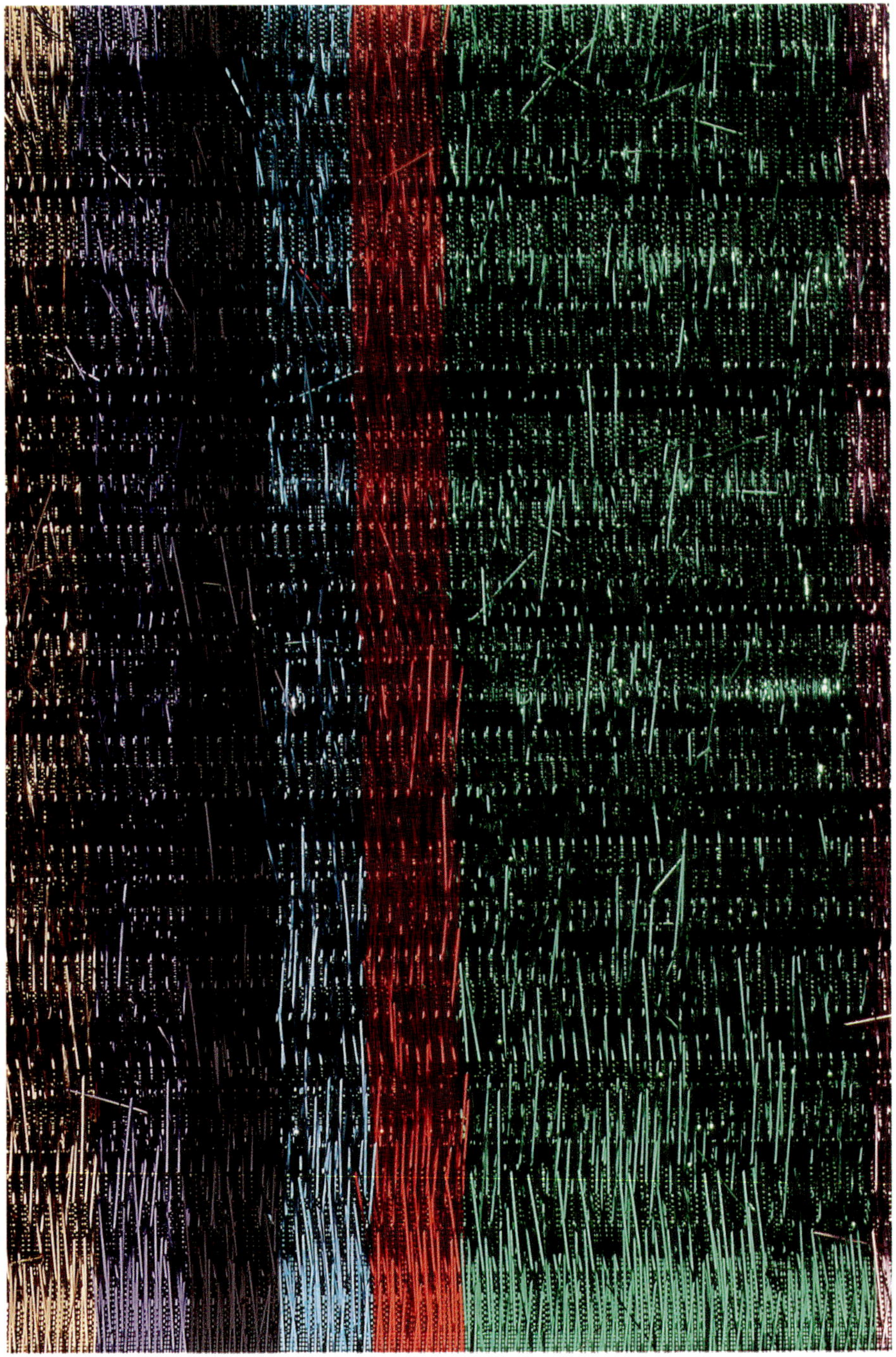

Multi-color lamé stripes. Japan, 1960.

16

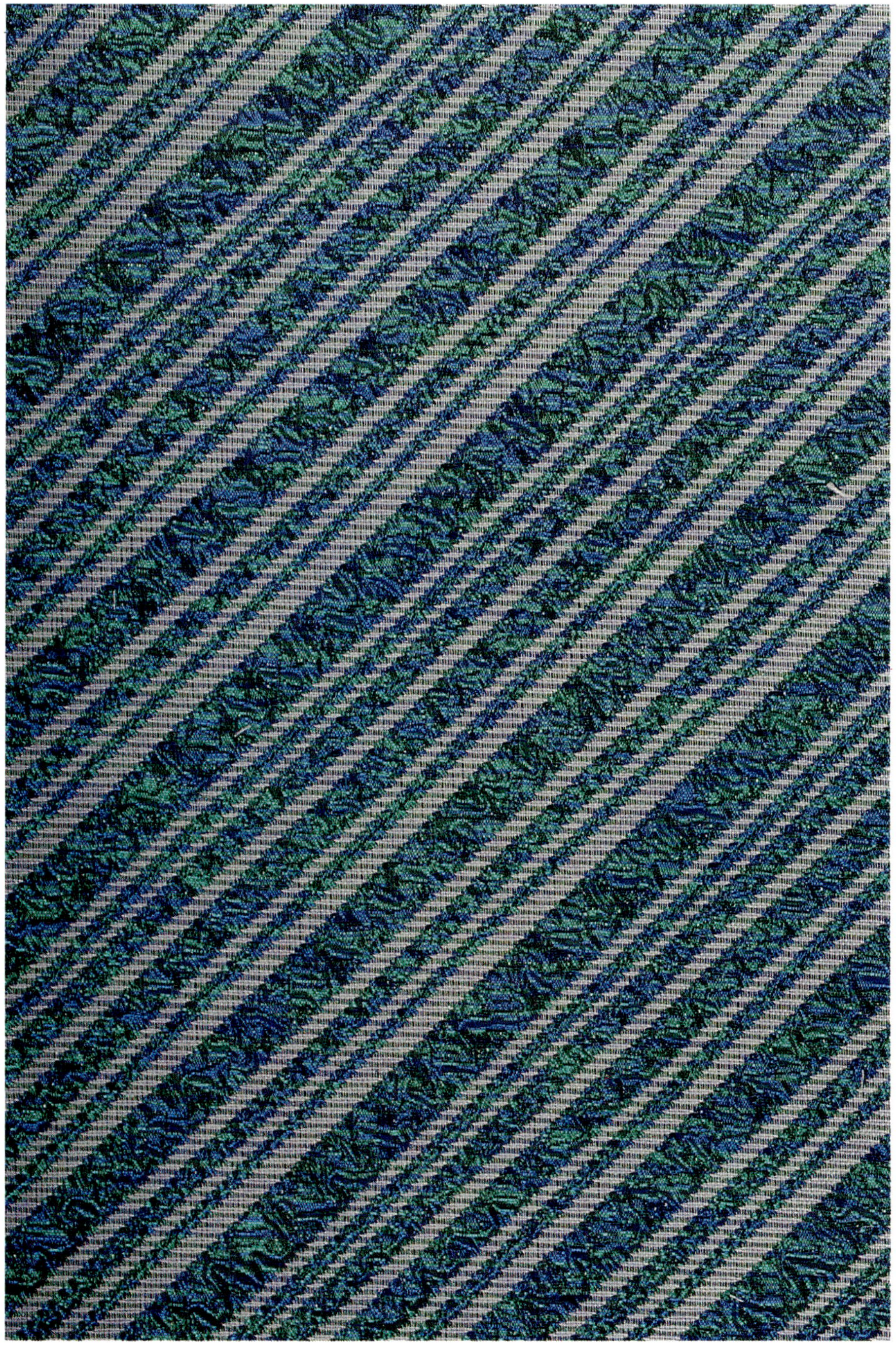

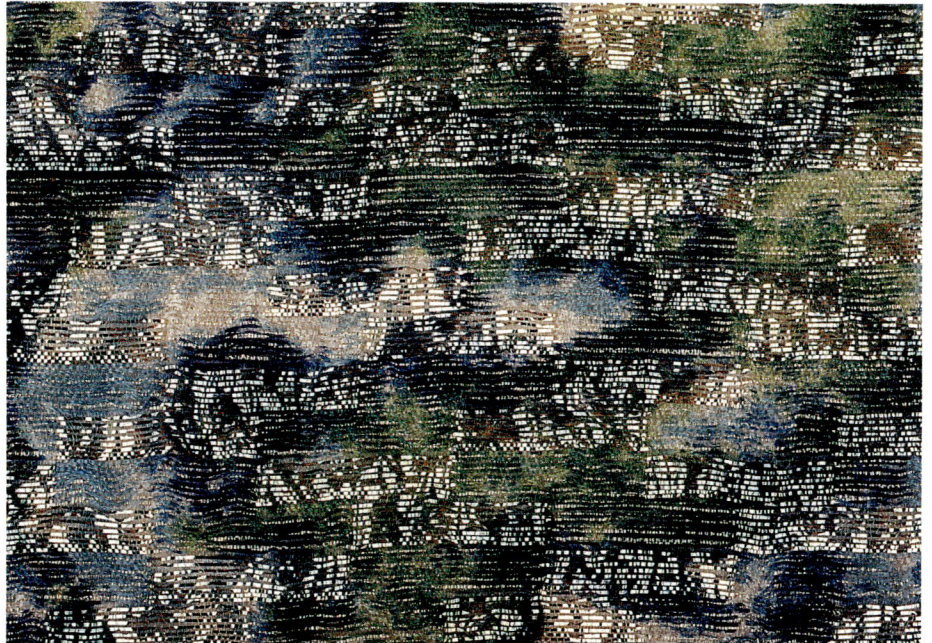

Waves of silver on abstract blue, green, and white. Silk blend, France, 1964.

Green and blue team up for diagonal stripe pattern. Japan, 1970s.

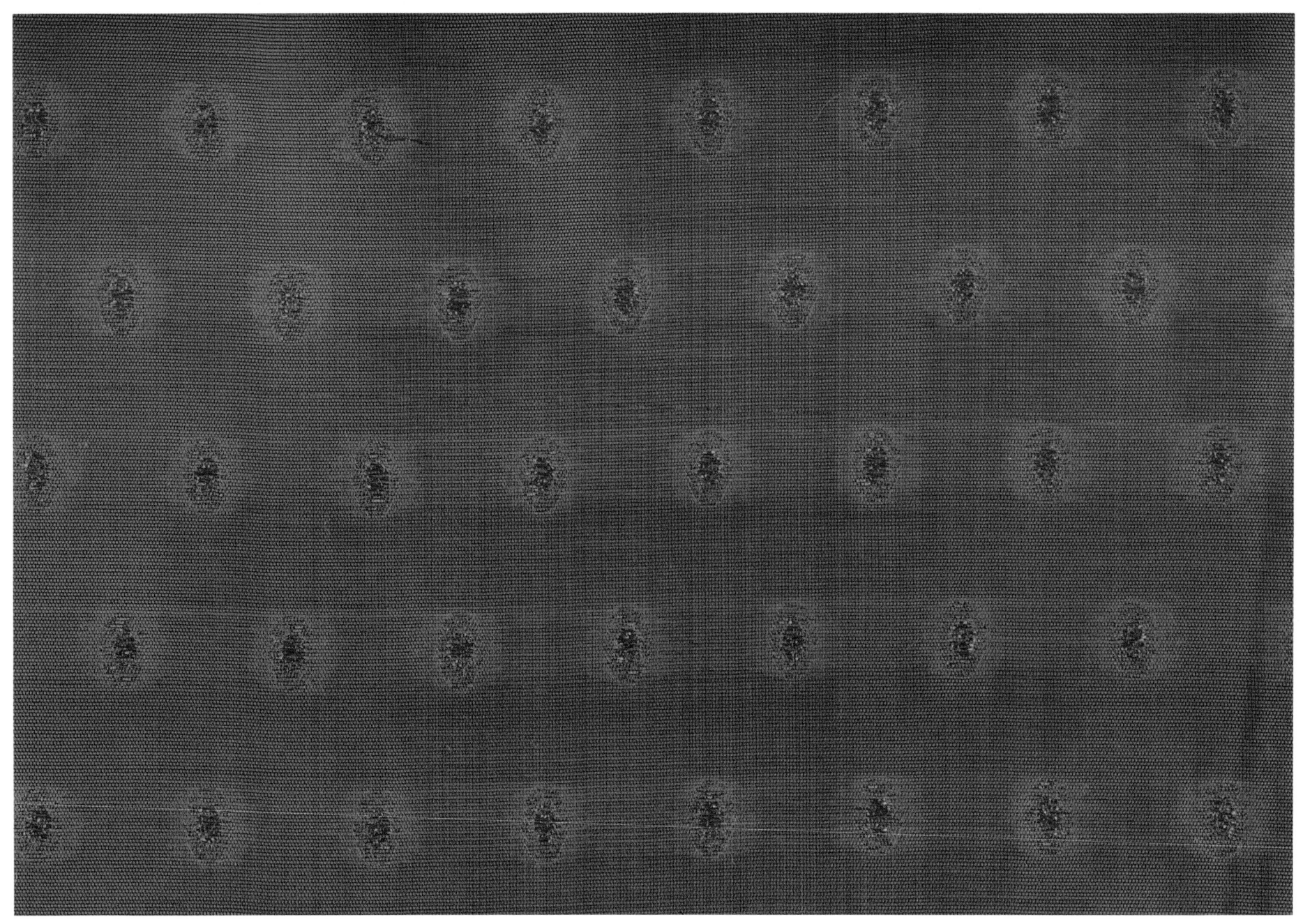

Peach film with glittering polka-dots. *Courtesy of TexStile Team, Milano Italy.*

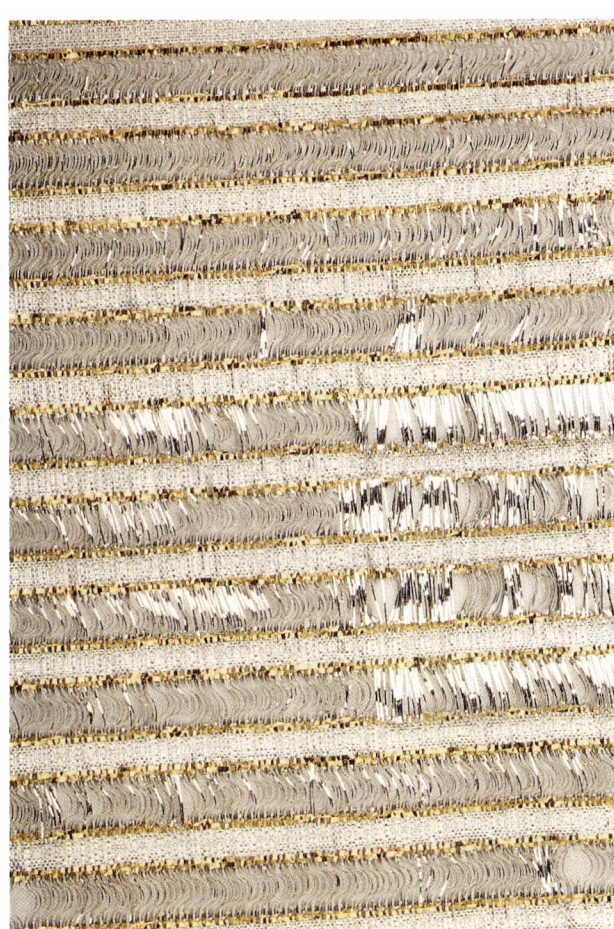

Metallic wave, silver. Japan, 1950s.

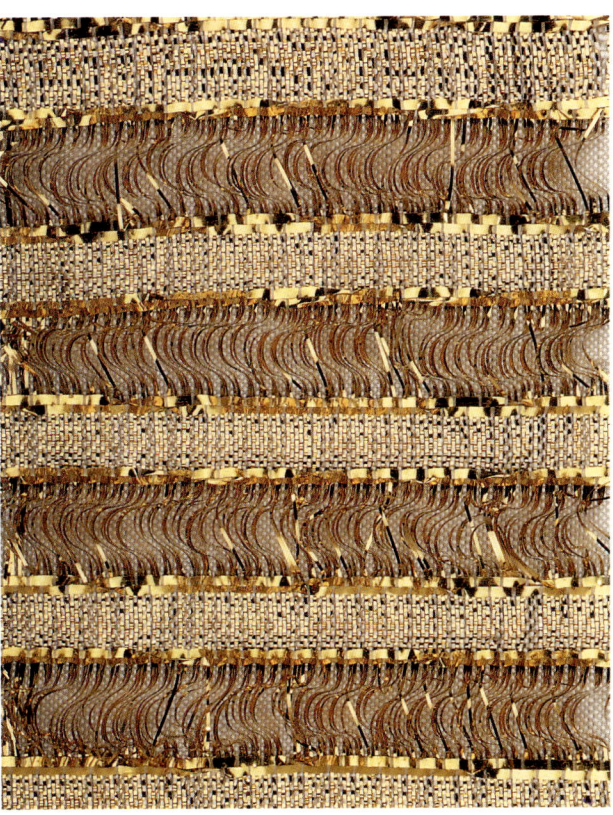

Metallic wave, gold. Japan, 1950s.

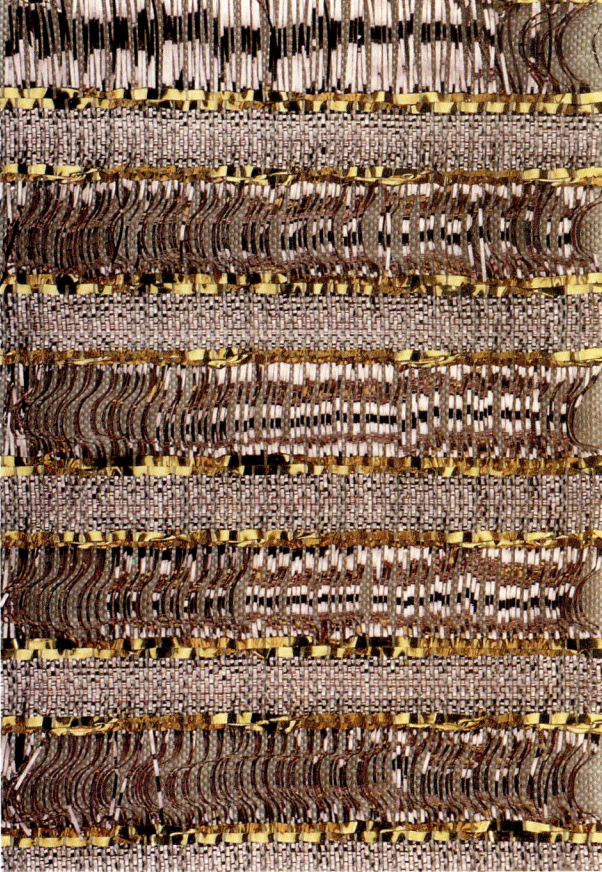

Metallic wave, pink. Japan, 1950s.

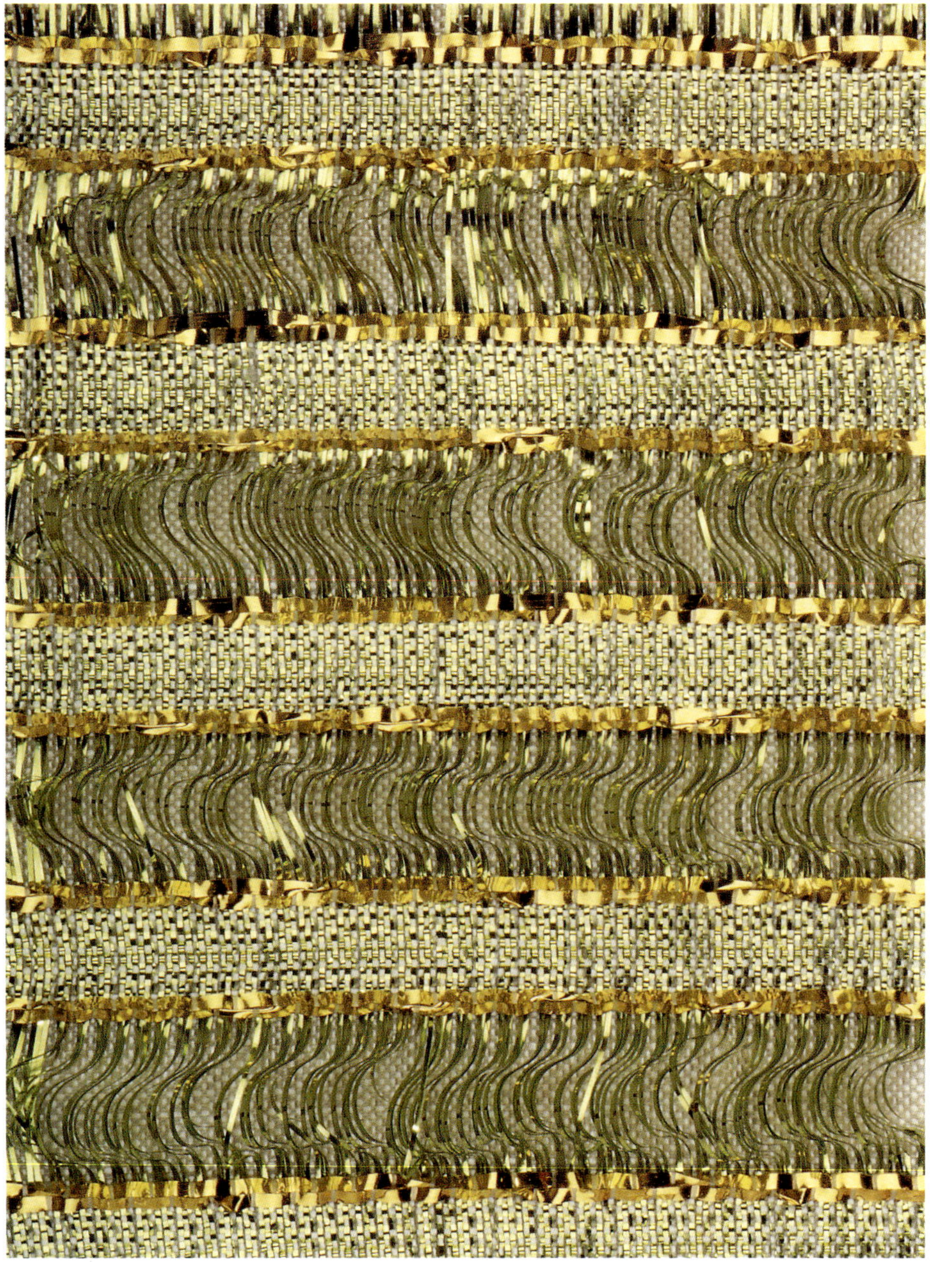

Metallic wave, green. Japan, 1950s.

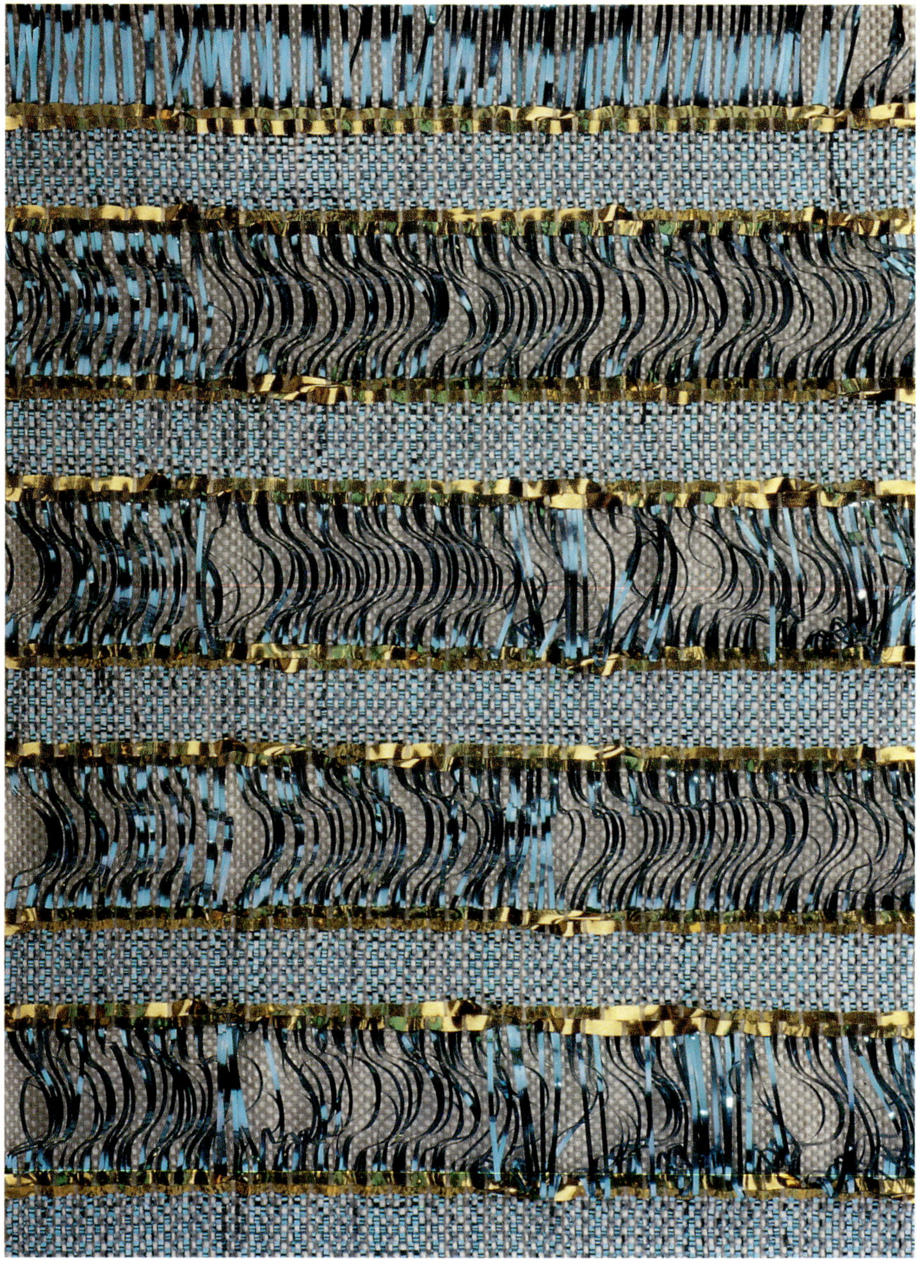

Metallic wave, blue. Japan, 1950s.

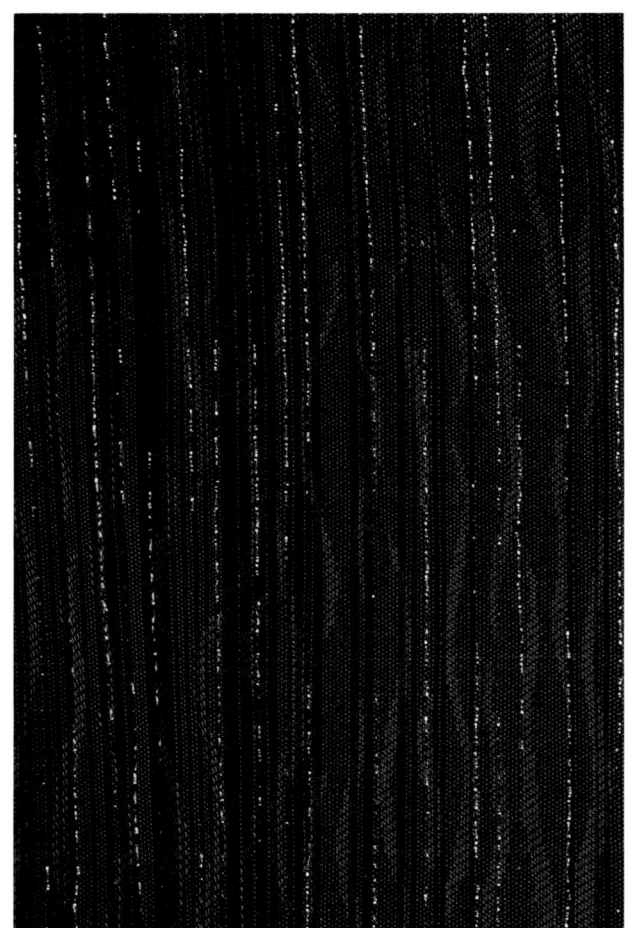

Brown and gray, "Barocco" pattern. Acetate, viscose, and lurex. *Courtesy of Tessitura Taiana Virgilio, Olgiate Comasco, Italy.*

Reds, "Barocco" pattern. Acetate, viscose, and lurex. *Courtesy of Tessitura Taiana Virgilio, Olgiate Comasco, Italy.*

Blues and greens, "Barocco" pattern. Acetate, viscose, and lurex. *Courtesy of Tessitura Taiana Virgilio, Olgiate Comasco, Italy.*

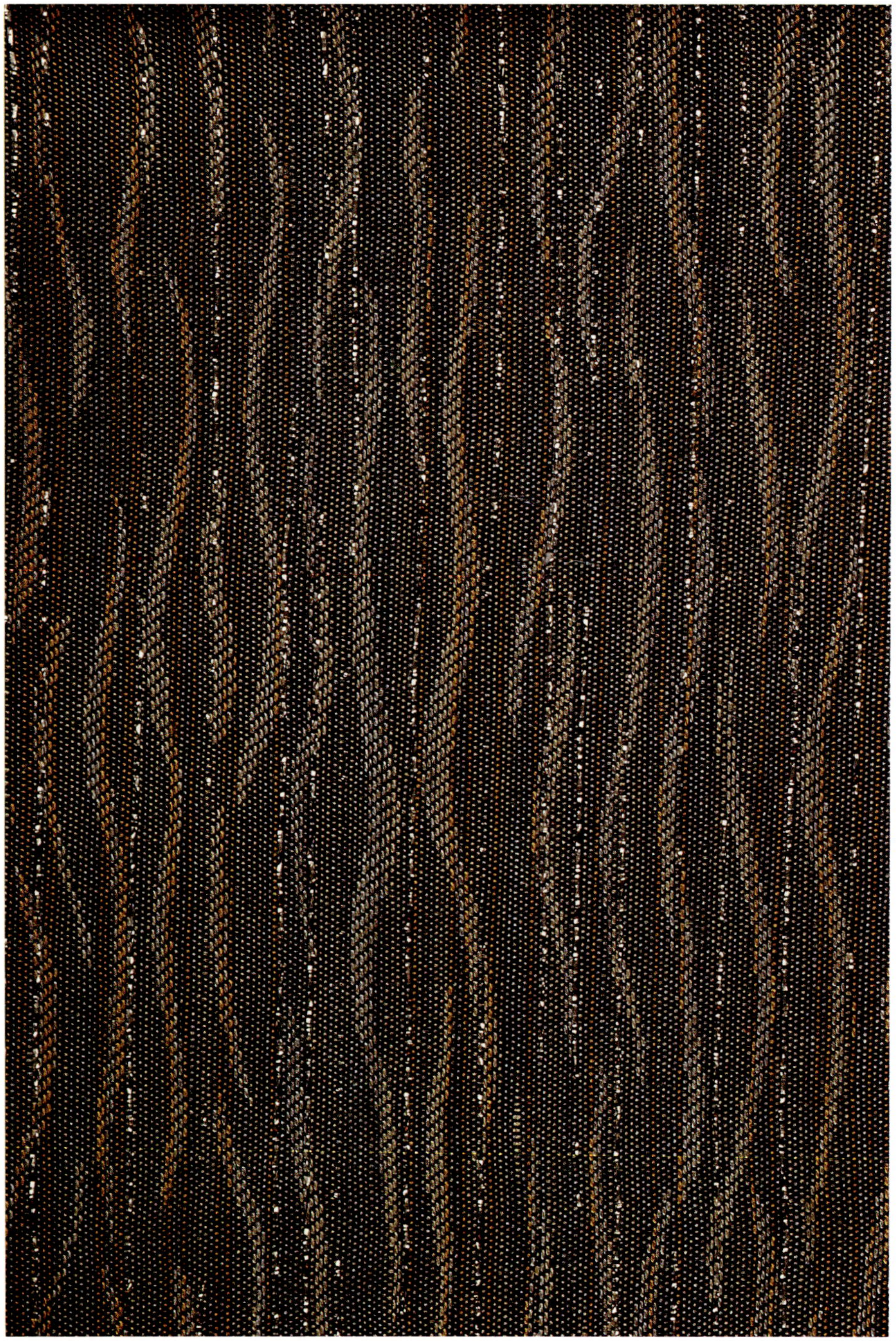

Gray and olive, "Barocco" pattern. Acetate, viscose, and lurex. *Courtesy of Tessitura Taiana Virgilio, Olgiate Comasco, Italy.*

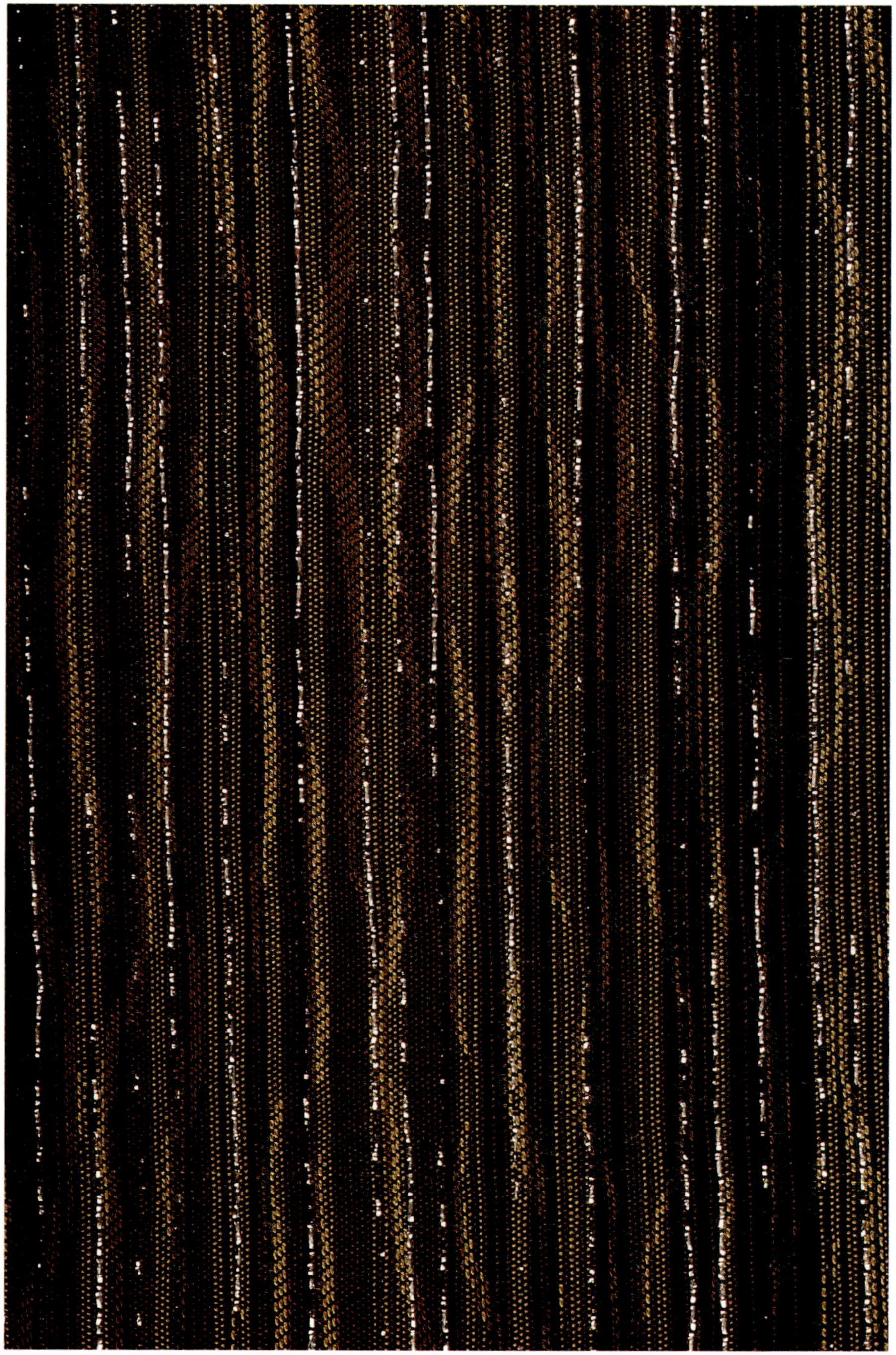

Greens, "Barocco" pattern. Acetate, viscose, and lurex. *Courtesy of Tessitura Taiana Virgilio, Olgiate Comasco, Italy.*

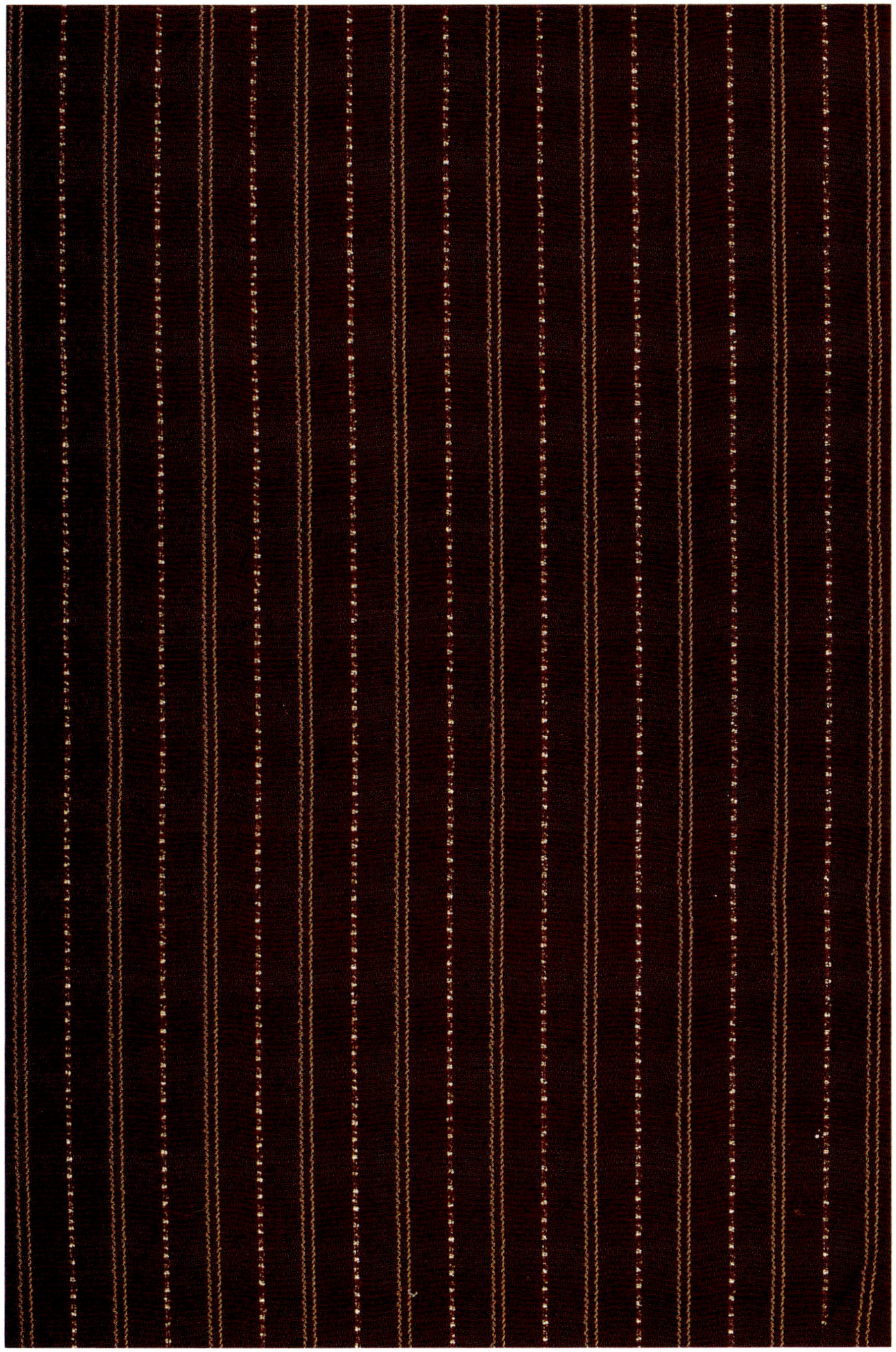

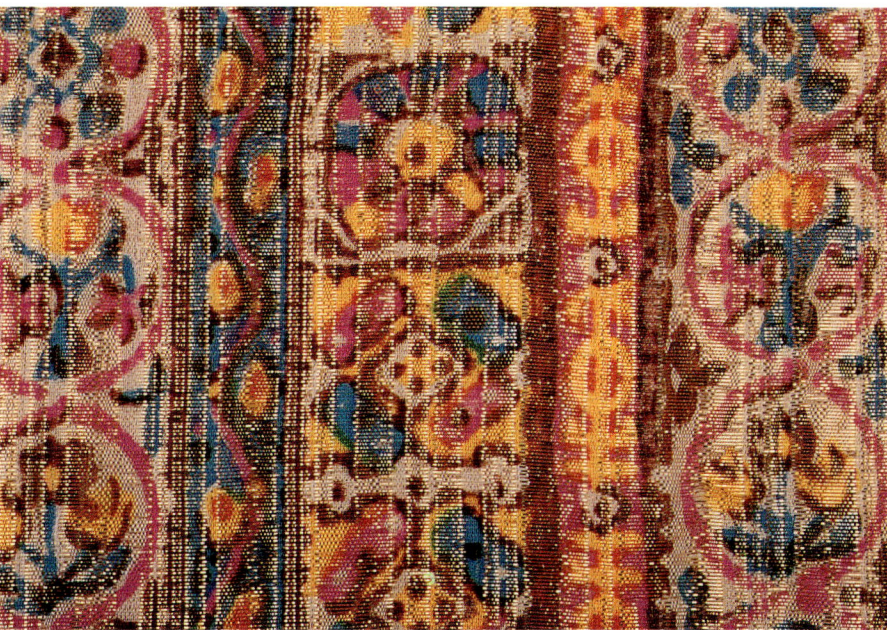

Gold creates vertical stripes of shine on brightly colored, Pennsylvania Dutch-inspired vertical stripe pattern. Silk blend, France, 1964.

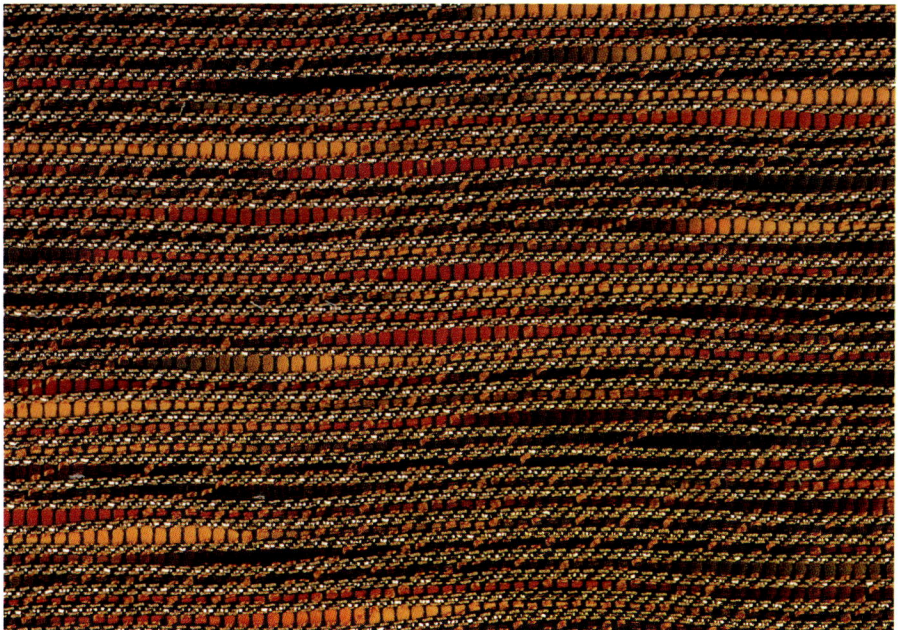

"Esprit." Vertical stripes. Viscose, polyester, and lurex. *Courtesy of Tessitura Taiana Virgilio, Olgiate Comasco, Italy.*

Natural tones with gold horizontal stripe pattern. *Courtesy of TexStile Team, Milano, Italy.*

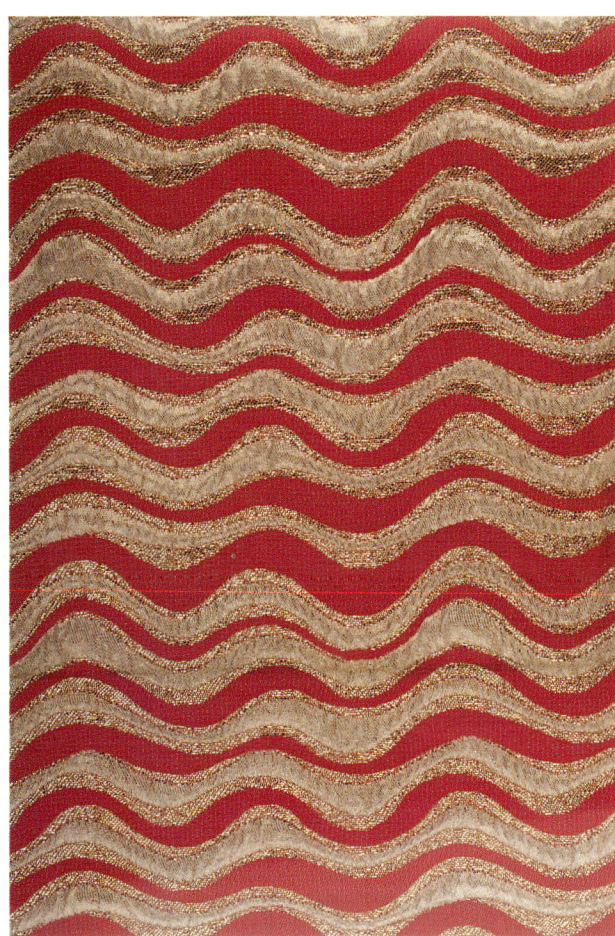

Mixed brocade of metallic-outlined stripes. Beige on hot pink. Yarn dyed acetate/nylon/polyester film/polyester, Japan, 1960s.

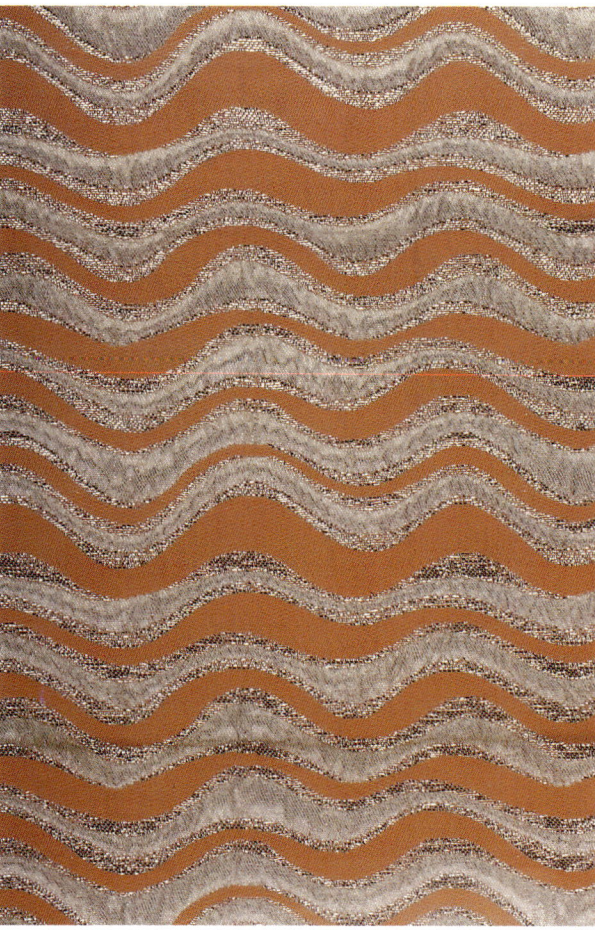

Mixed brocade of metallic-outlined stripes. White on peach. Yarn dyed acetate/nylon/polyester film/polyester, Japan, 1960s.

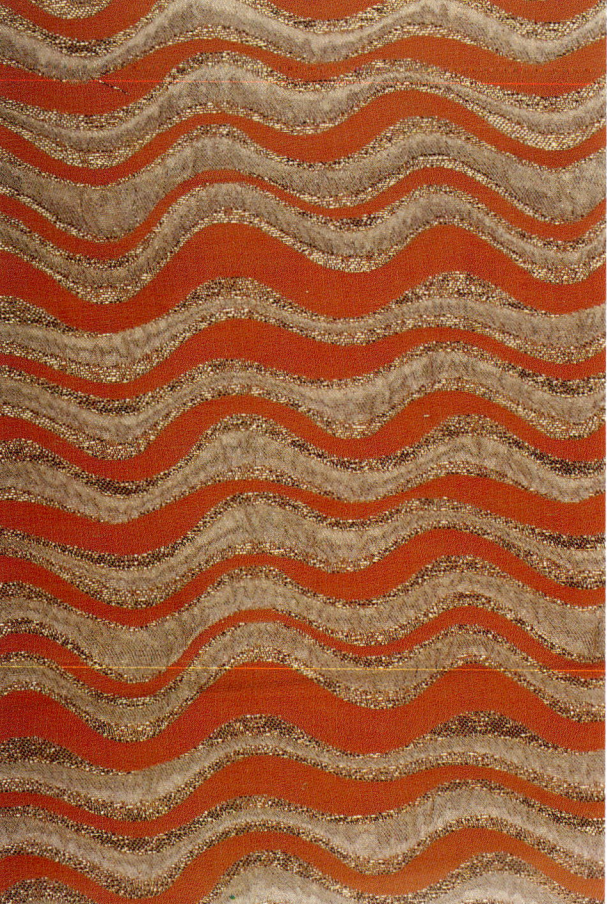

Mixed brocade of metallic-outlined stripes. Beige on orange. Yarn dyed acetate/nylon/polyester film/polyester, Japan, 1960s.

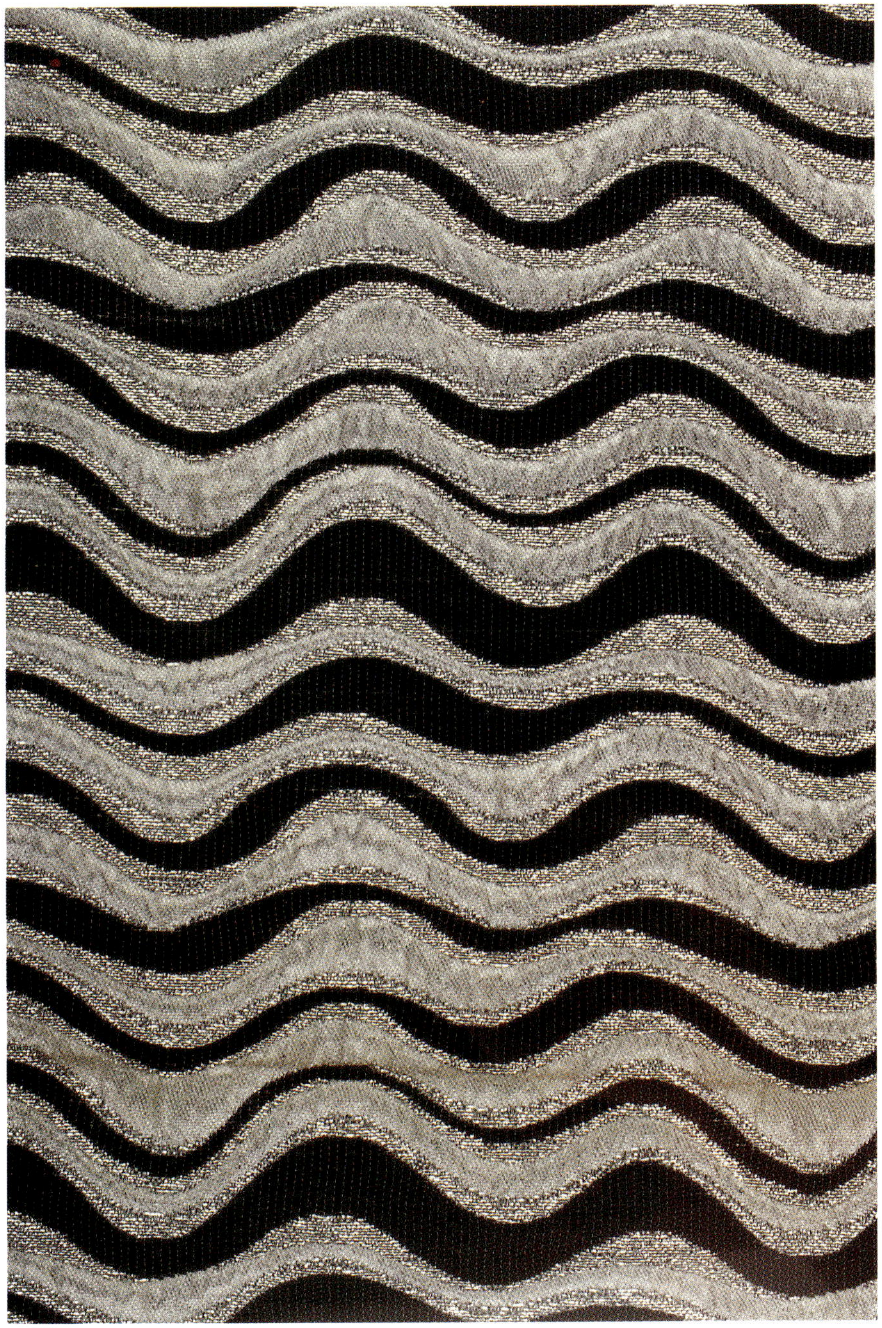

Mixed brocade of metallic-outlined stripes. White on black. Yarn dyed acetate/nylon/polyester film/polyester, Japan, 1960s.

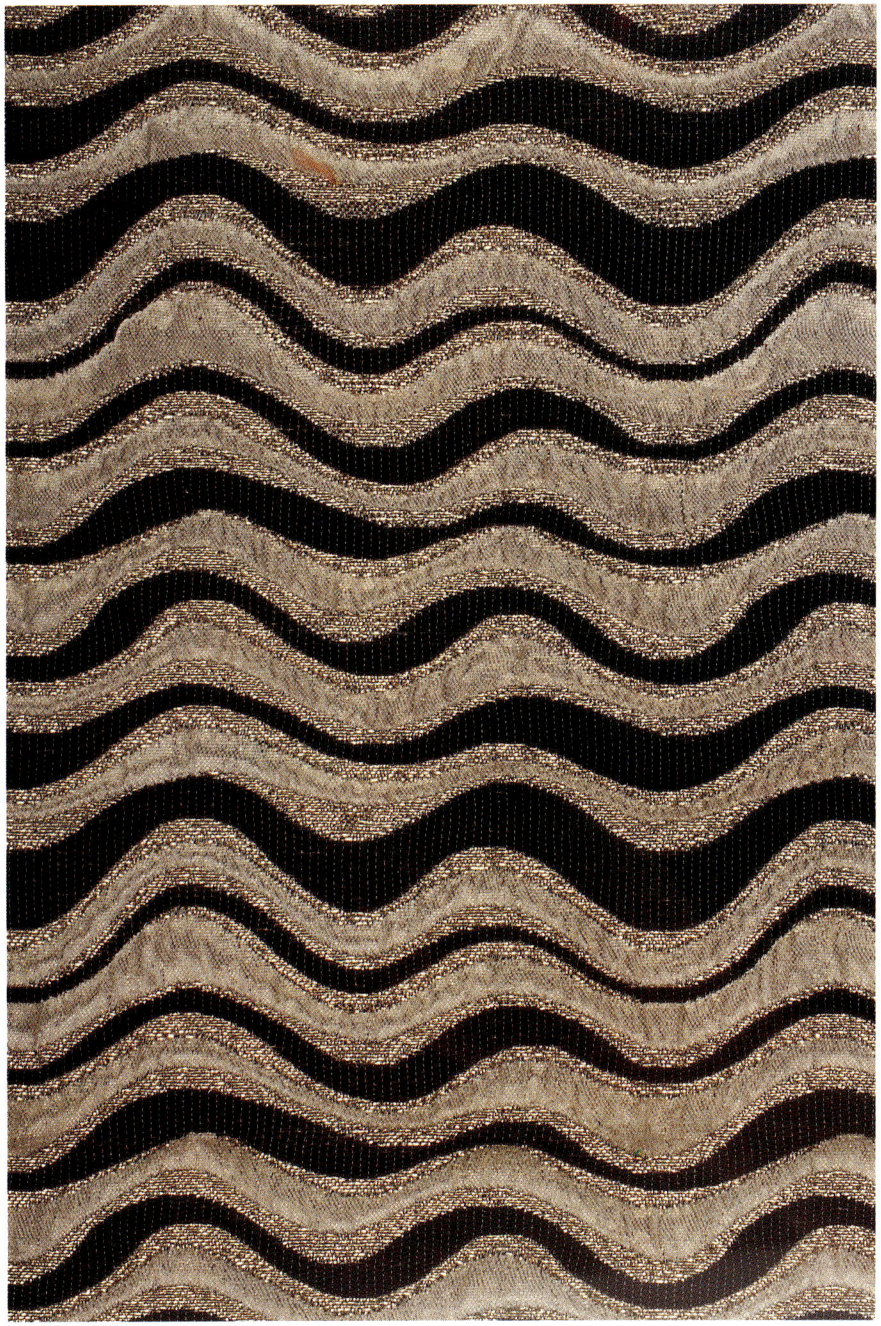

Mixed brocade of metallic-outlined stripes. Beige on black. Yarn dyed acetate/nylon/polyester film/polyester, Japan, 1960s.

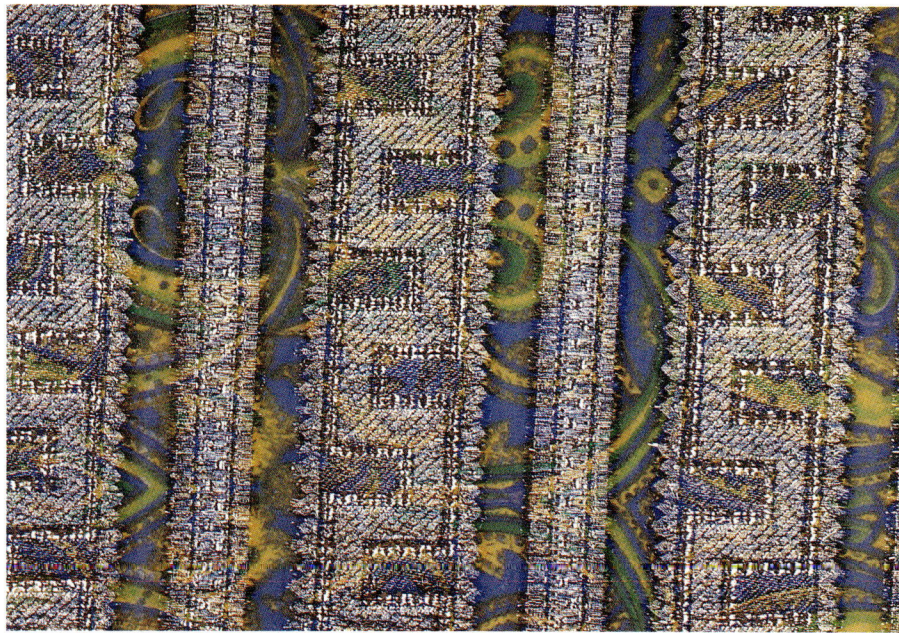

Vertical stripe pattern in silver over film printed with green, blue, and yellow paisley pattern. Nylon/polyester film, Japan, 1960s.

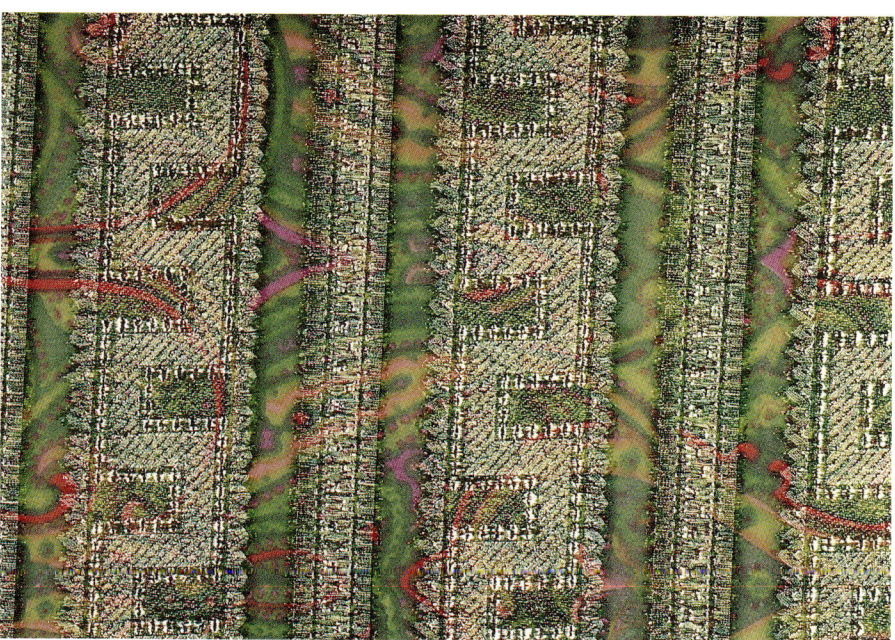

Vertical stripe pattern in silver over film printed green with pink accented paisley pattern. Nylon/polyester film, Japan, 1960s.

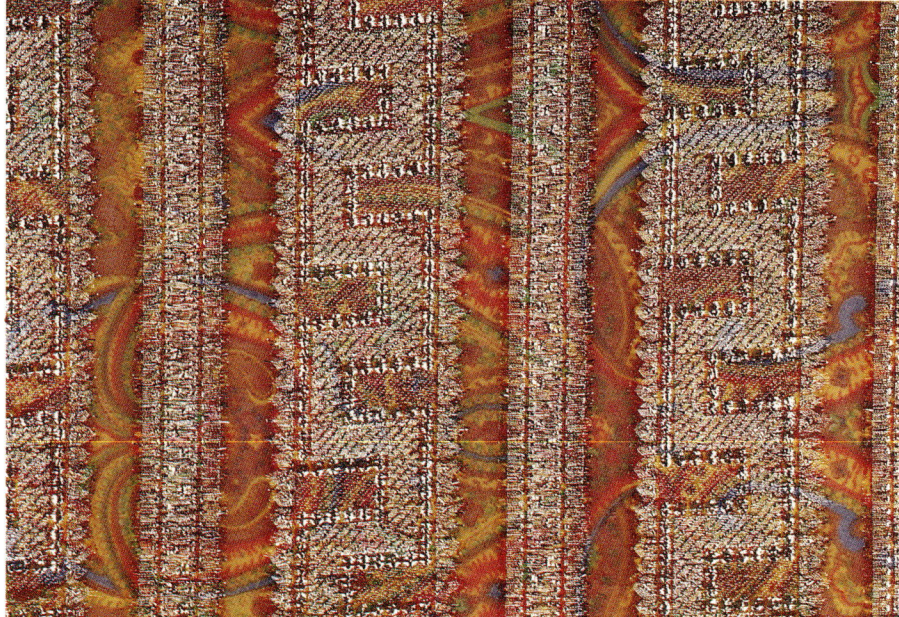

Vertical stripe pattern in silver over film printed blue with orange, yellow, and green paisley pattern. Nylon/polyester film, Japan, 1960s.

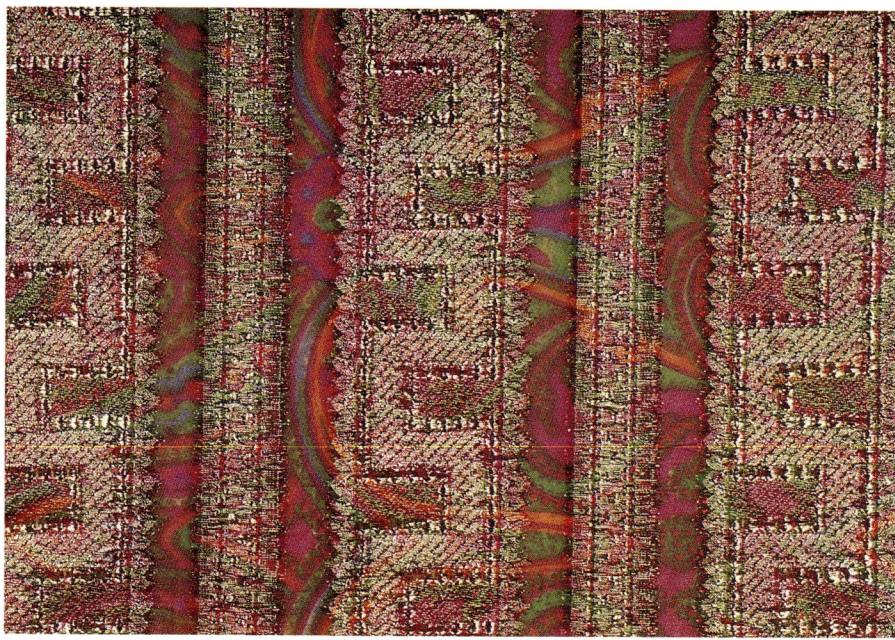

Vertical stripe pattern in silver over film printed with purple, green, and orange paisley pattern. Nylon/polyester film, Japan, 1960s.

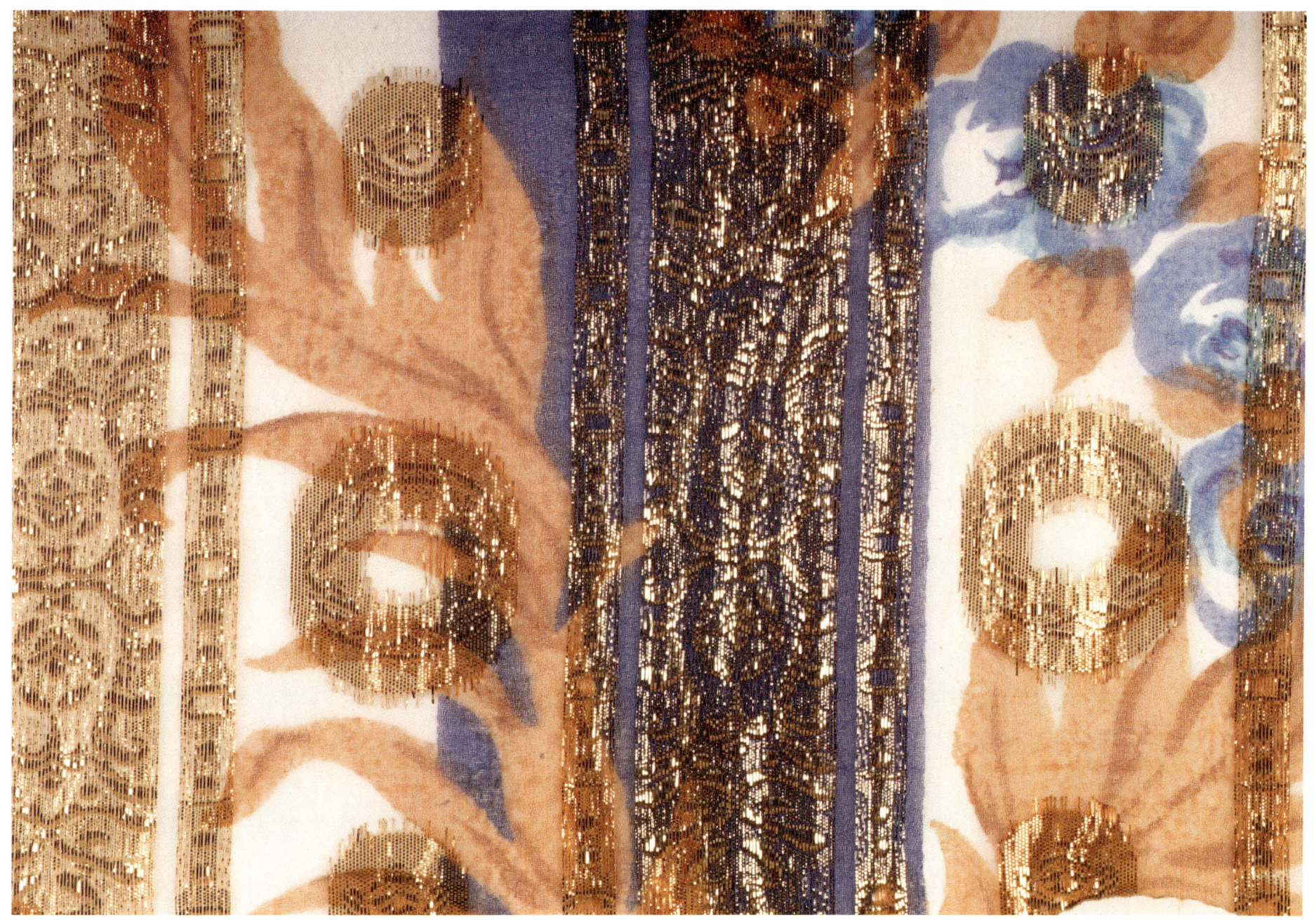
Elaborate gold stripes over floral print. Nylon/polyester, Japan, 1960s.

Chapter Three
PLAIDS

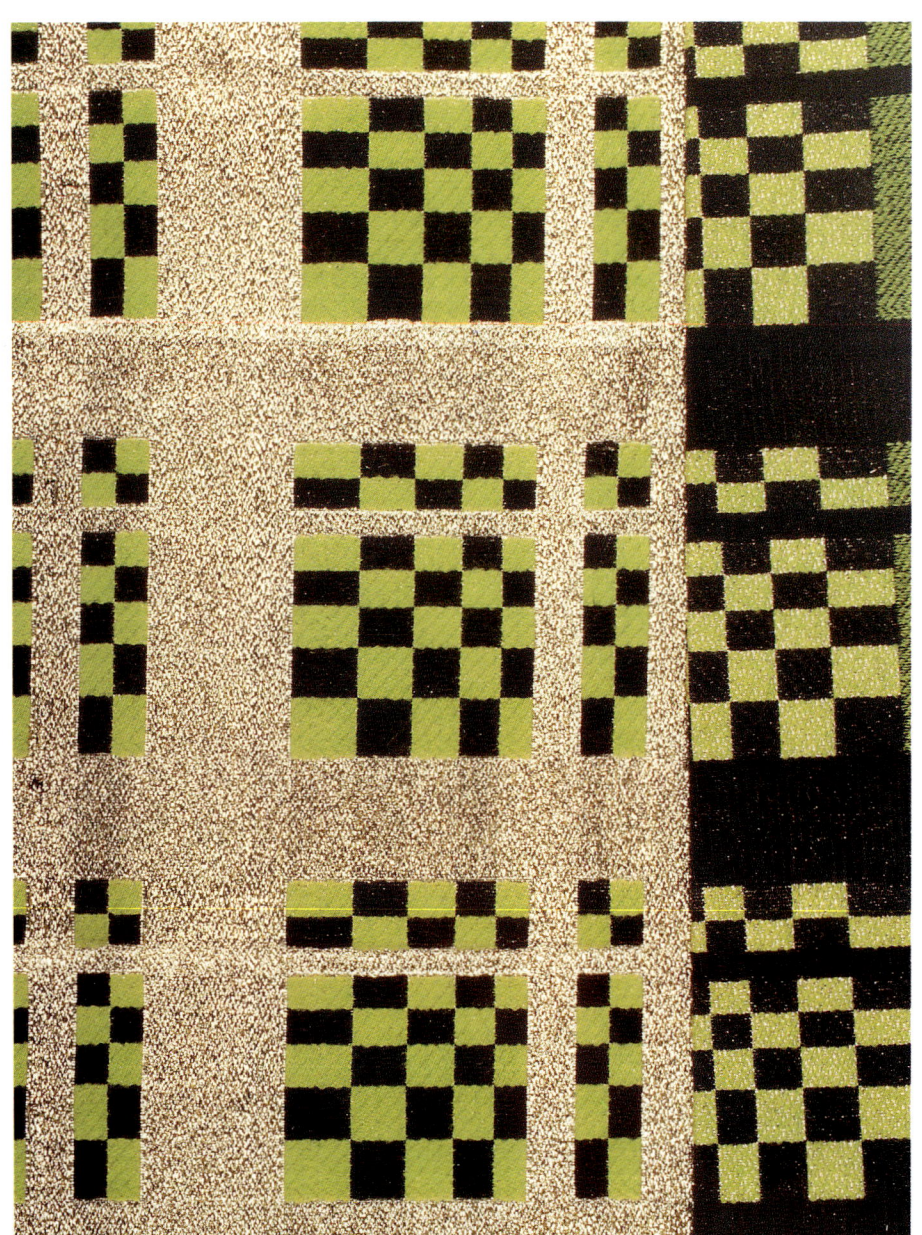

Racing check squares in large grid. Lime green. Fold back shows reverse. Acrylic, polyester/nylon, Japan, 1960s.

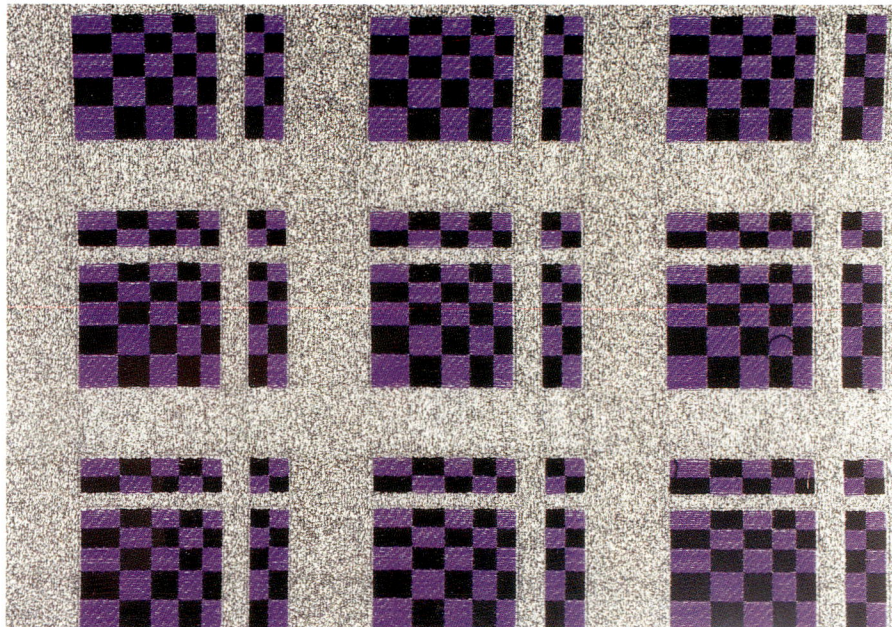

Racing check squares in large grid. Purple. Acrylic, polyester/nylon, Japan, 1960s.

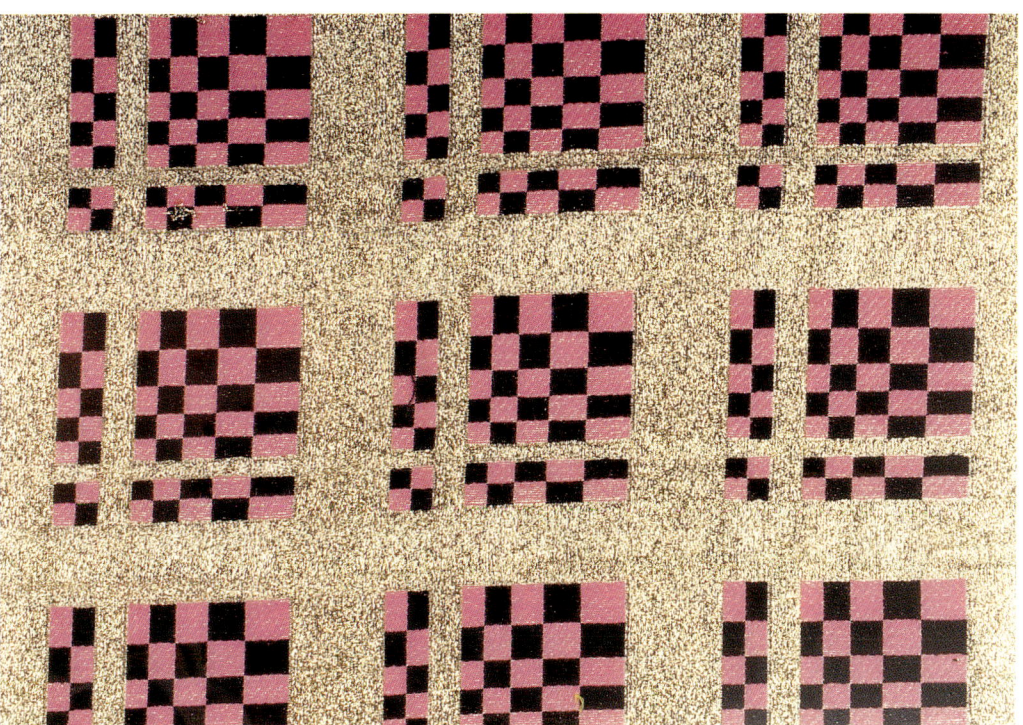

Racing check squares in large grid. Hot pink. Acrylic, polyester/nylon, Japan, 1960s.

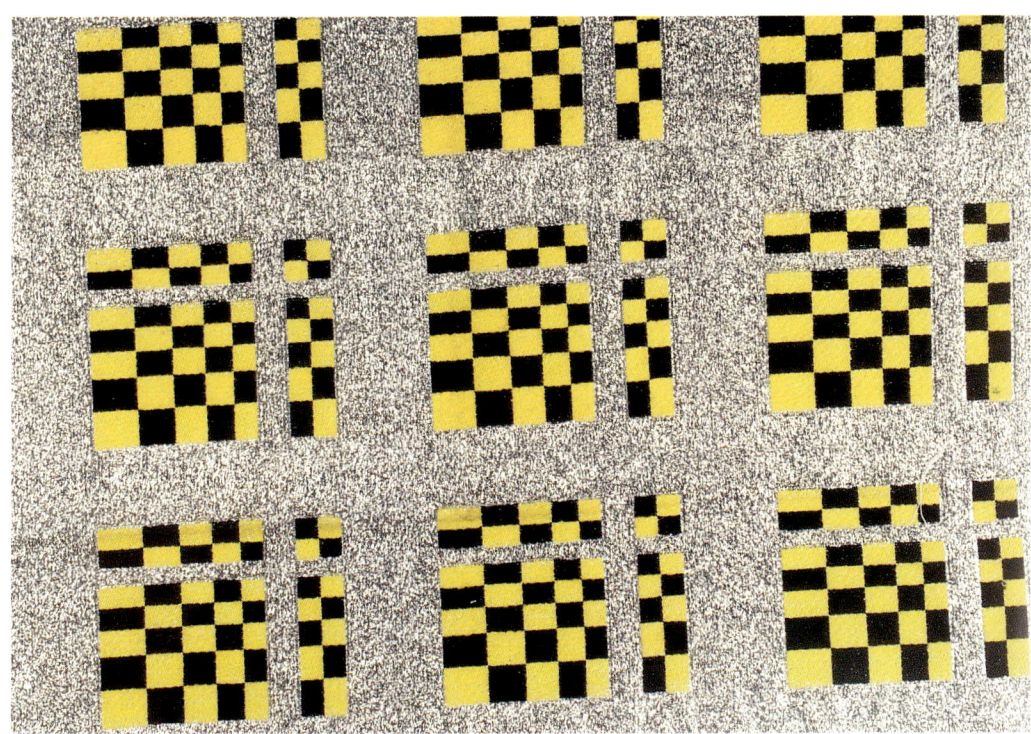

Racing check squares in large grid. Yellow. Acrylic, polyester/nylon, Japan, 1960s.

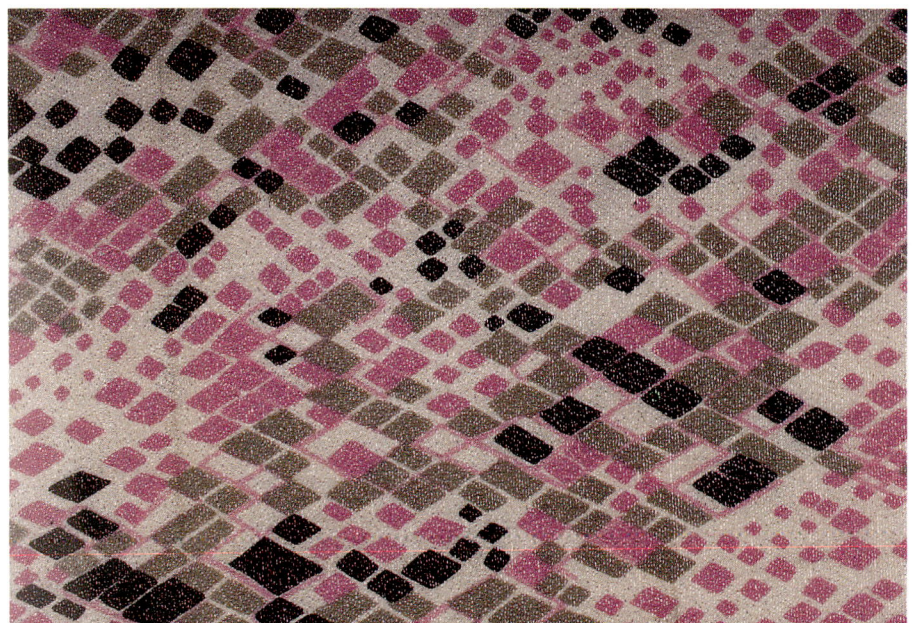
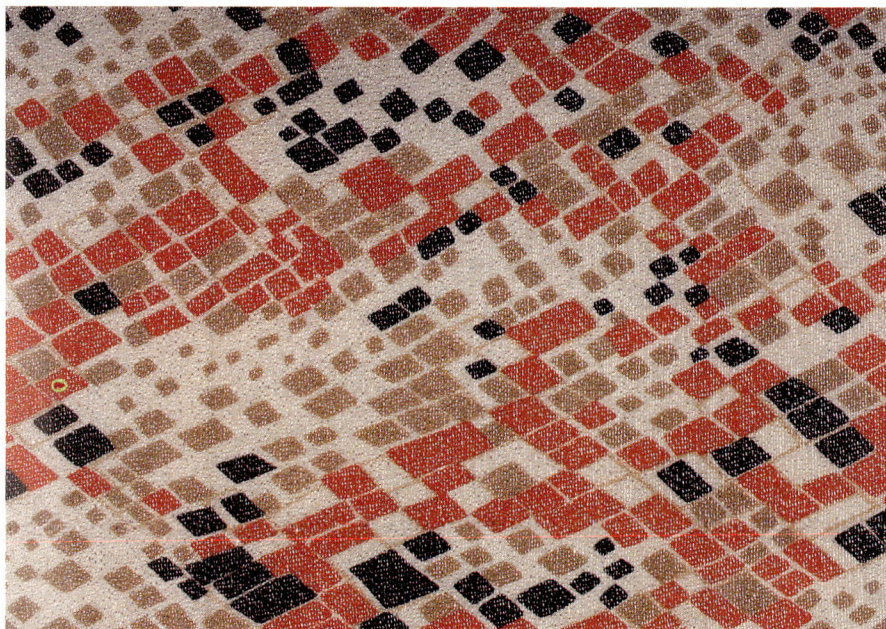
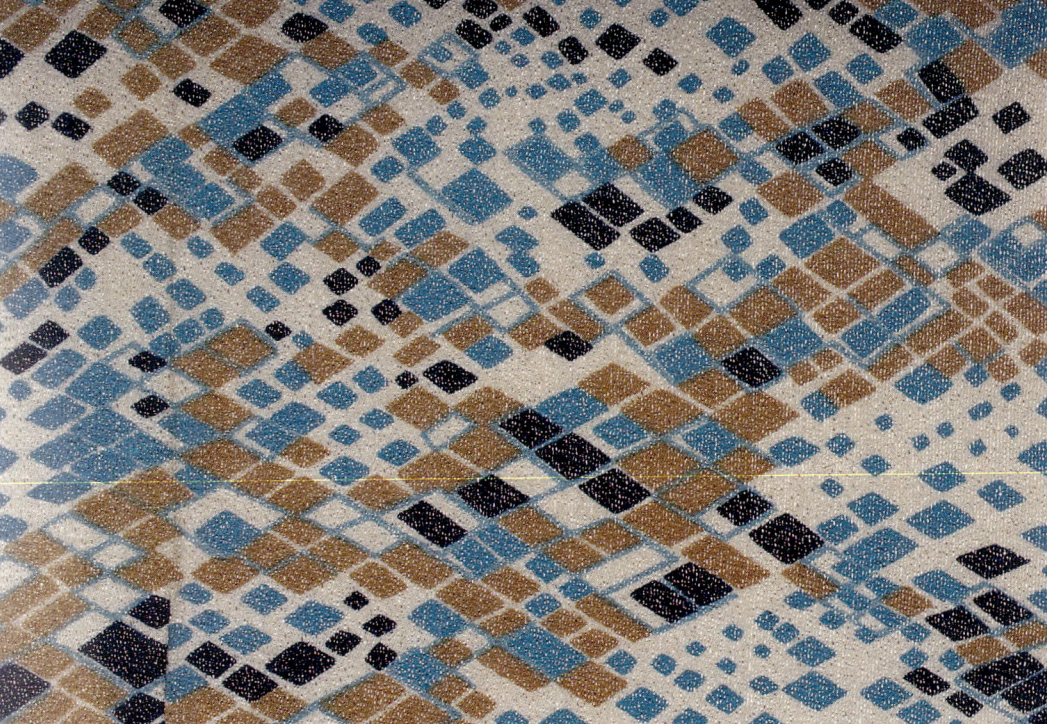

Top left: Erratic harlequin pattern, pink, olive, and black on bone ground with silver flecks. Rayon/spun rayon, Japan, 1960s.

Top right: Erratic harlequin pattern, red, black, and olive on bone ground with silver flecks. Rayon/spun rayon, Japan, 1960s.

Bottom left: Erratic harlequin pattern, light blue, black, and olive on bone ground with silver flecks. Rayon/spun rayon, Japan, 1960s.

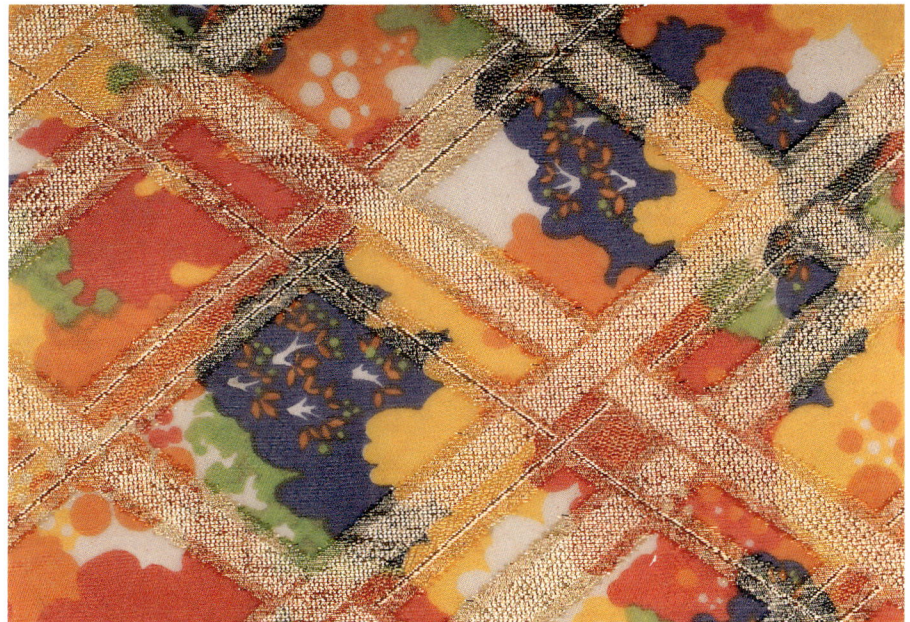

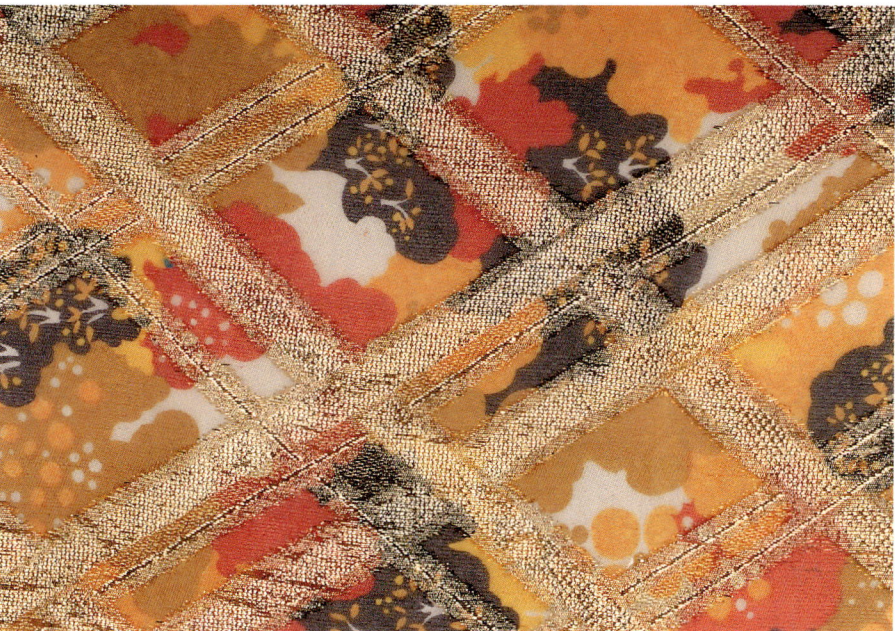

Top left: Gold check pattern over abstract print. Primary colors. Nylon/polyester film, Japan, 1960s.

Top right: Gold check pattern over abstract print. Orange, black, and yellow. Nylon/polyester film, Japan, 1960s.

Bottom left: Gold check pattern over abstract print. Pink, green, and yellow. Nylon/polyester film, Japan, 1960s.

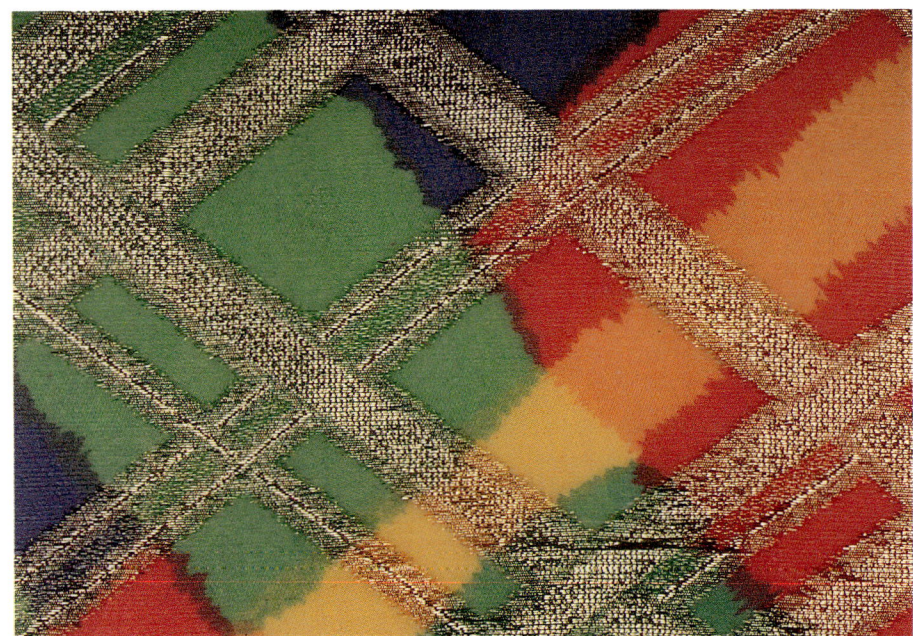

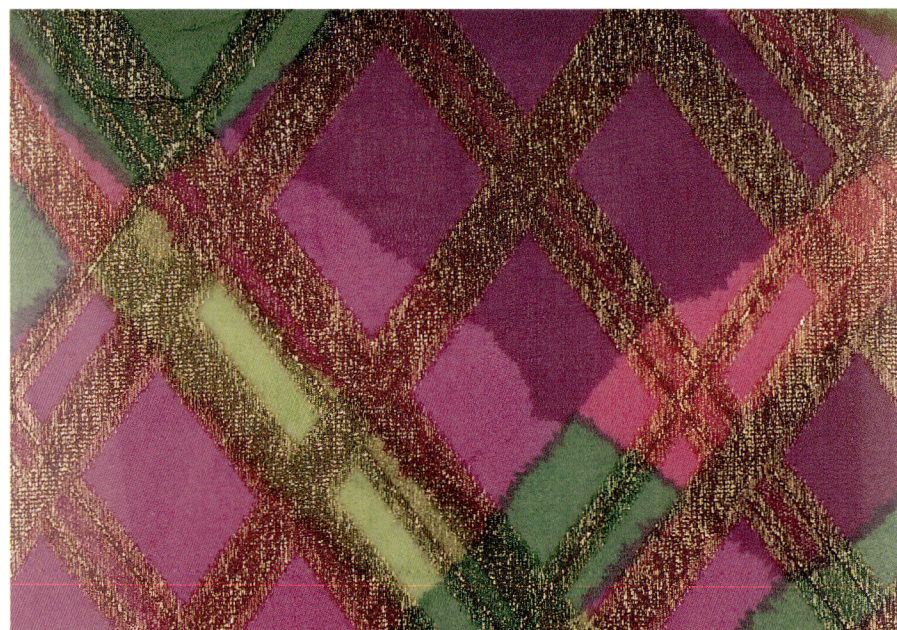

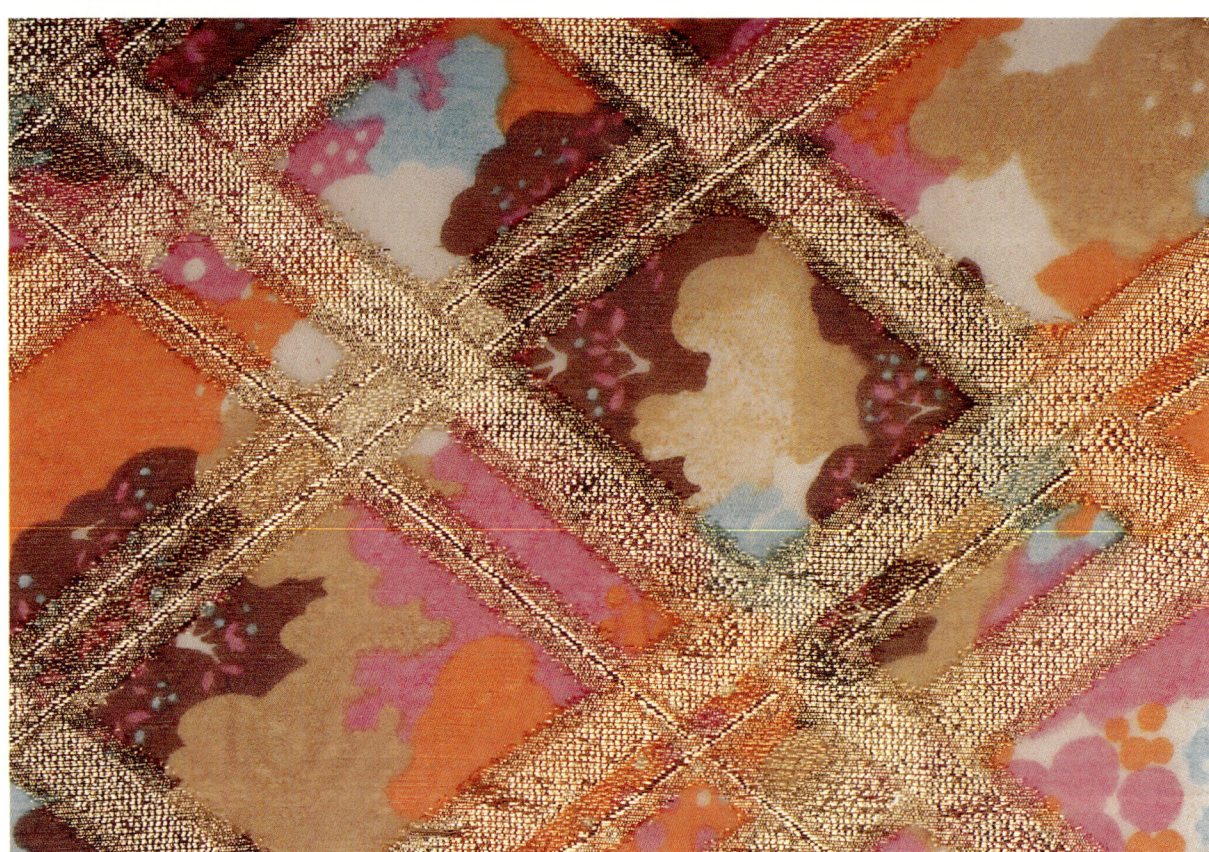

Top left: Oversize metallic gold plaid overlays filmy check pattern with watercolor effect dominated by red, green, and gold. Nylon/polyester film, Japan, 1960s.

Top right: Oversize metallic gold plaid overlays filmy check pattern with watercolor effect dominated by purple, green, and gold. Nylon/polyester film, Japan, 1960s.

Bottom right: Gold check pattern over abstract print. Orange, olive, and pink. Nylon/polyester film, Japan, 1960s.

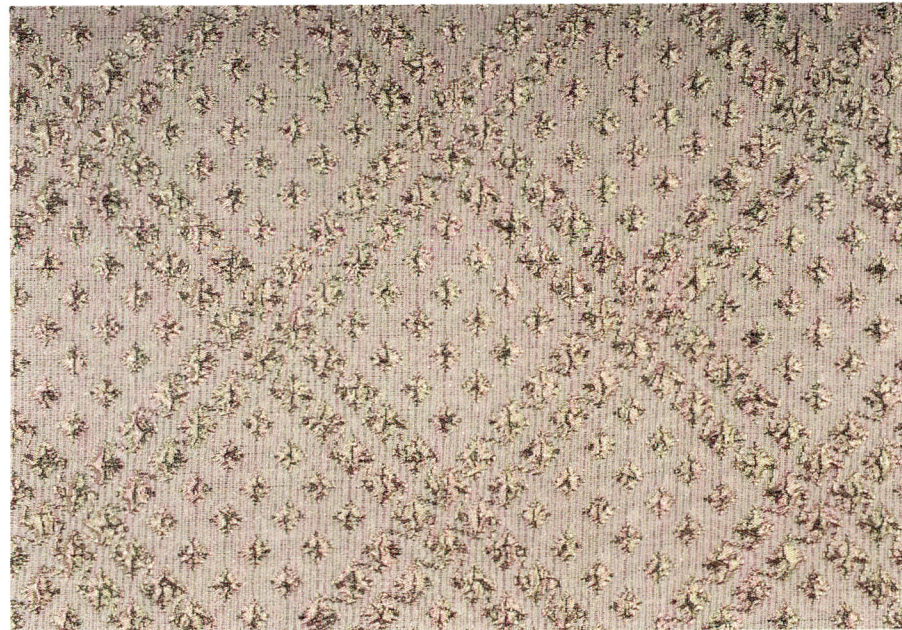

Raised pink and green lamé creates checked pattern on like-colored ground. Japan, 1970s.

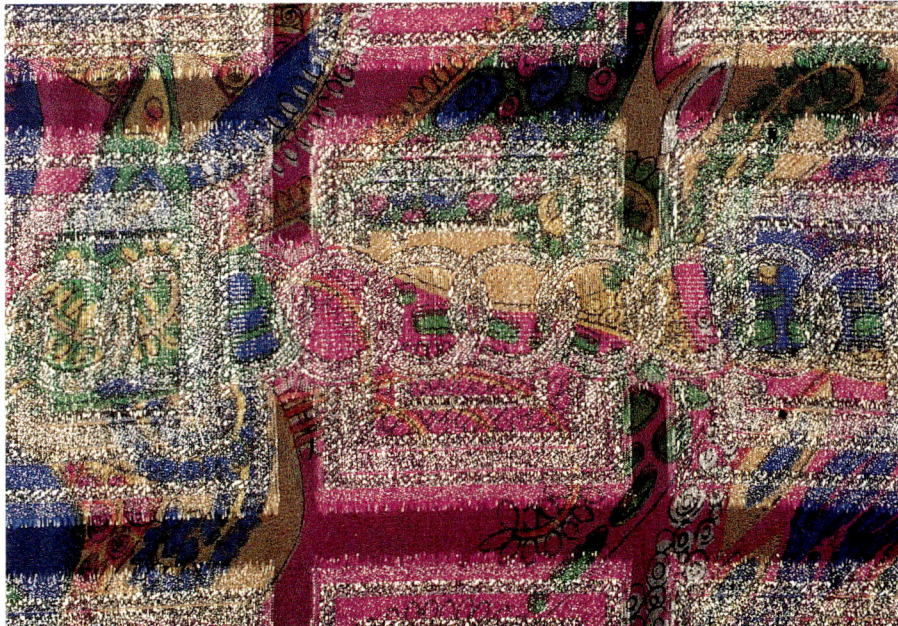

Silver highlights repeating square pattern connected by "linked-chain." Paisley underprint in hot colors. Nylon/polyester, Japan, 1960s.

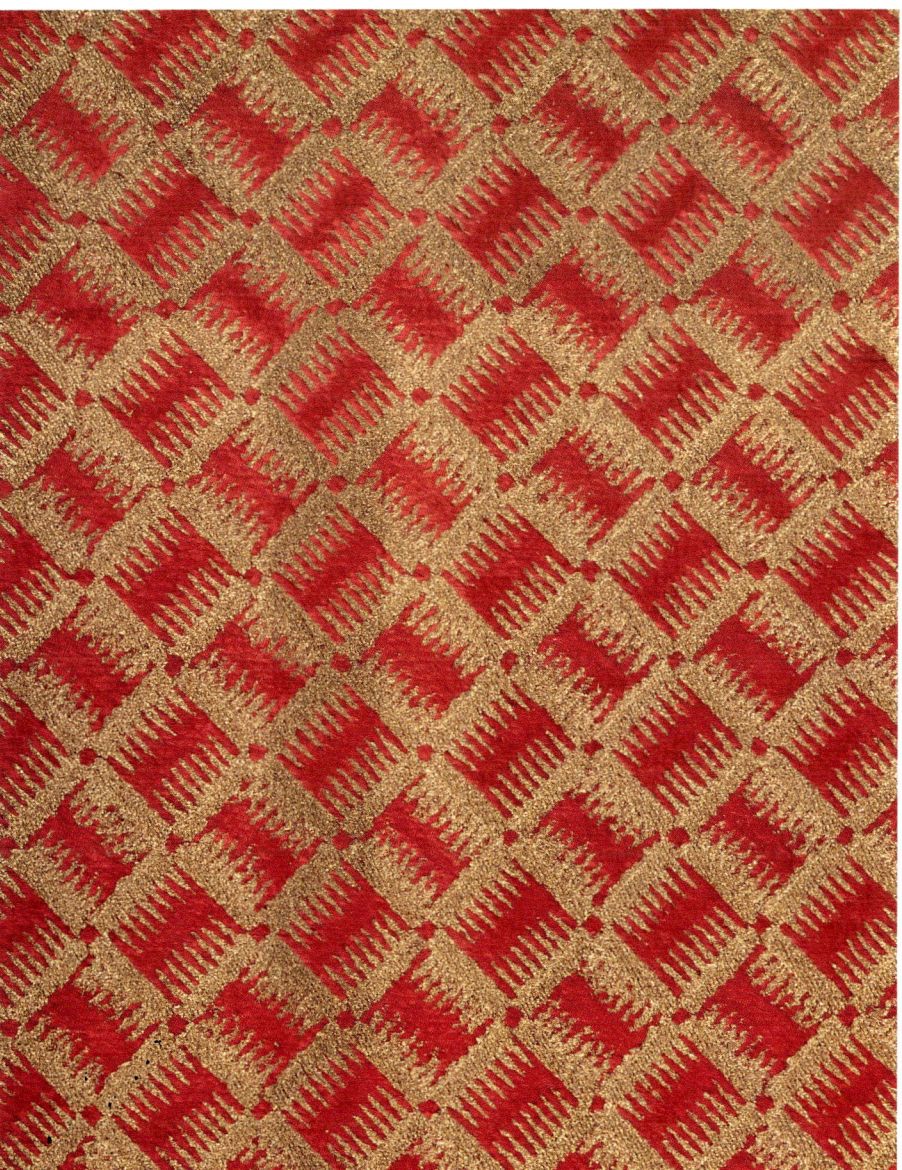

Metallic weave with raised magenta velour. France, 1959.

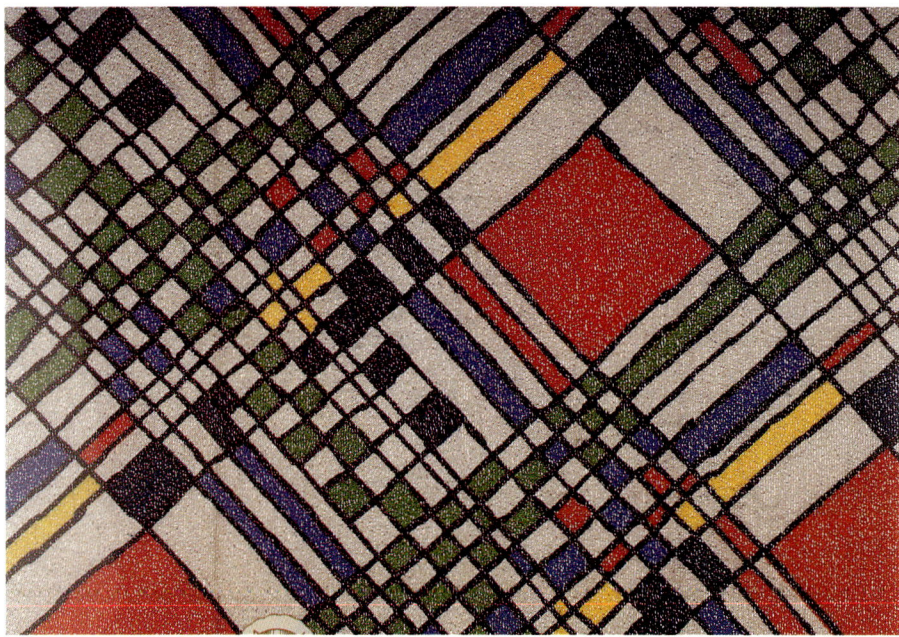

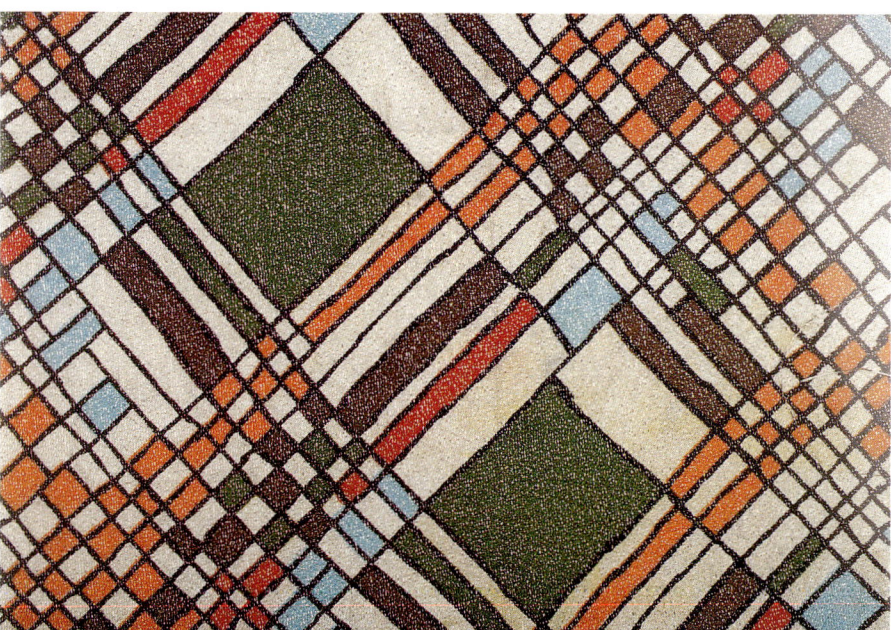

Erratic plaid with black outlines, red and other bold-colored centers, and silver flecks on white ground. Rayon/spun rayon, Japan, 1960s.

Erratic plaid with black outlines, green and other bold-colored centers, and silver flecks on bone ground. Rayon/spun rayon, Japan, 1960s.

Erratic plaid with black outlines, hot colored centers, and silver flecks on white ground. Rayon/spun rayon, Japan, 1960s.

Erratic plaid with black outlines, primary color centers, and silver flecks on white ground. Rayon/spun rayon, Japan, 1960s.

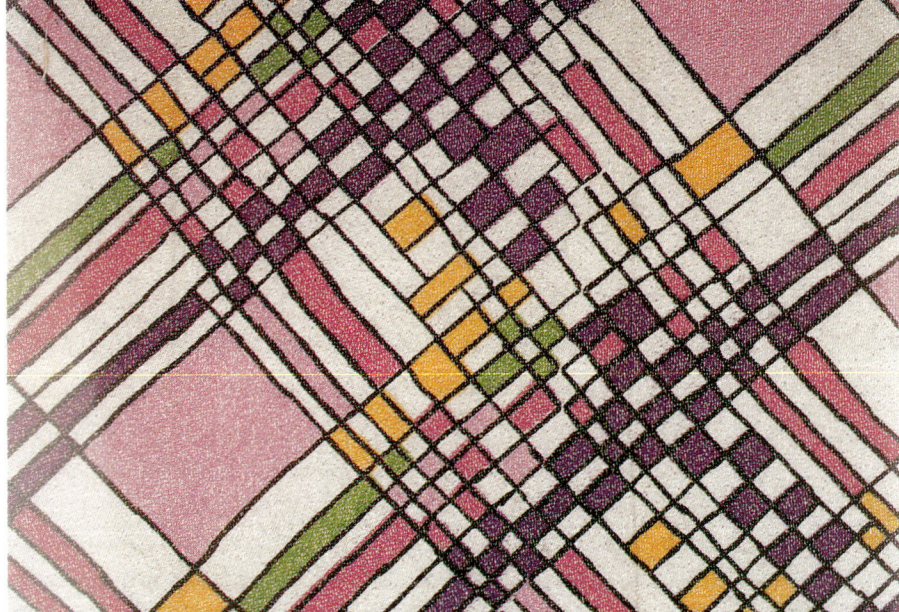

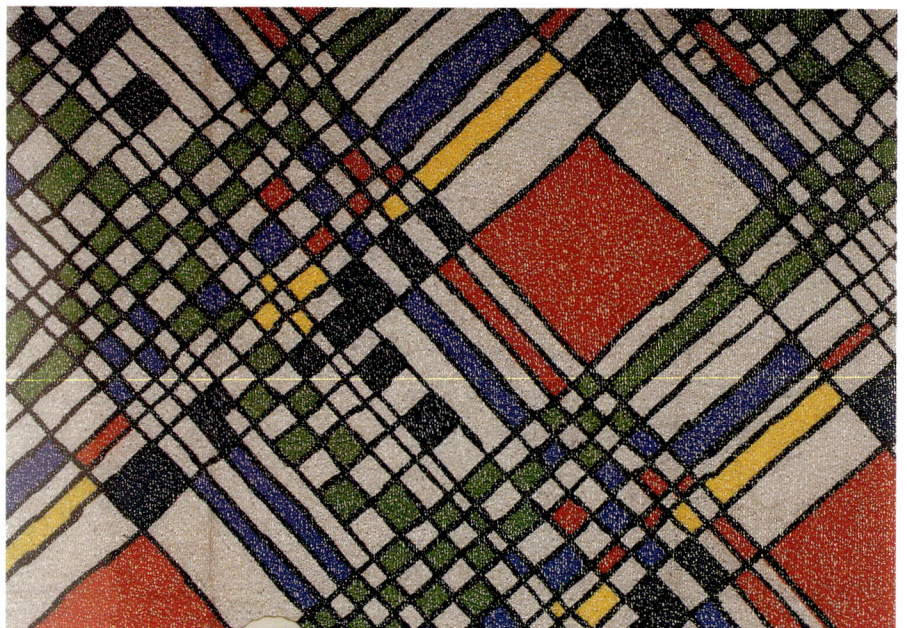

Chapter Four

FLORALS

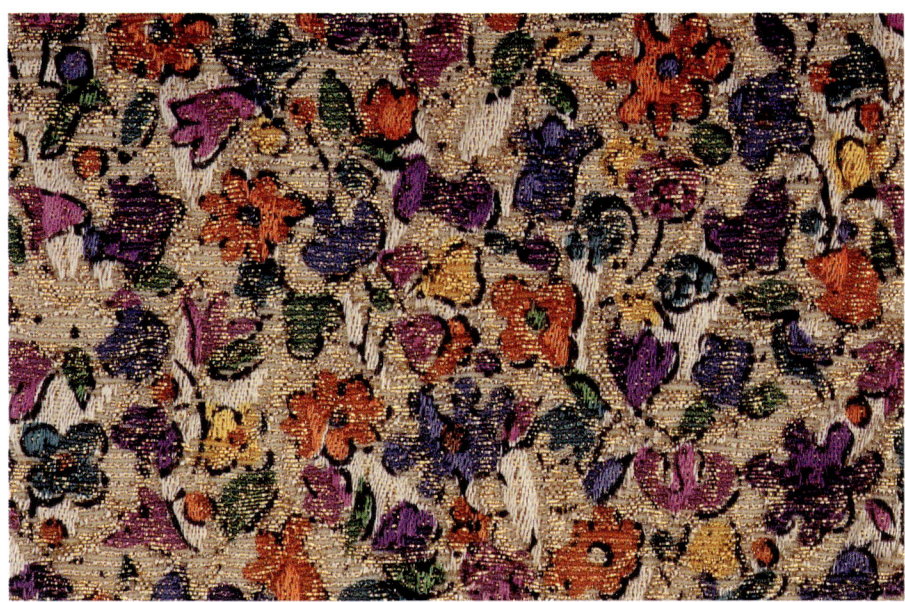

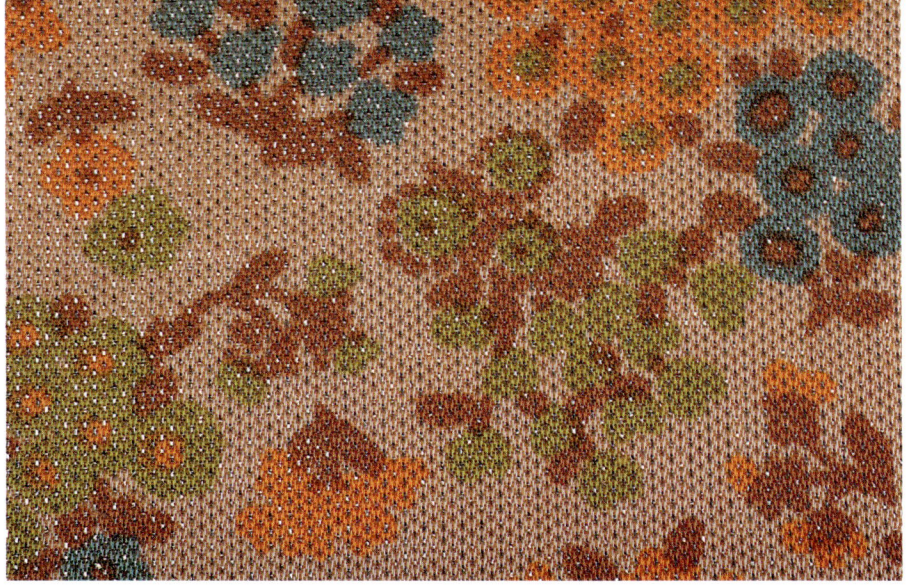

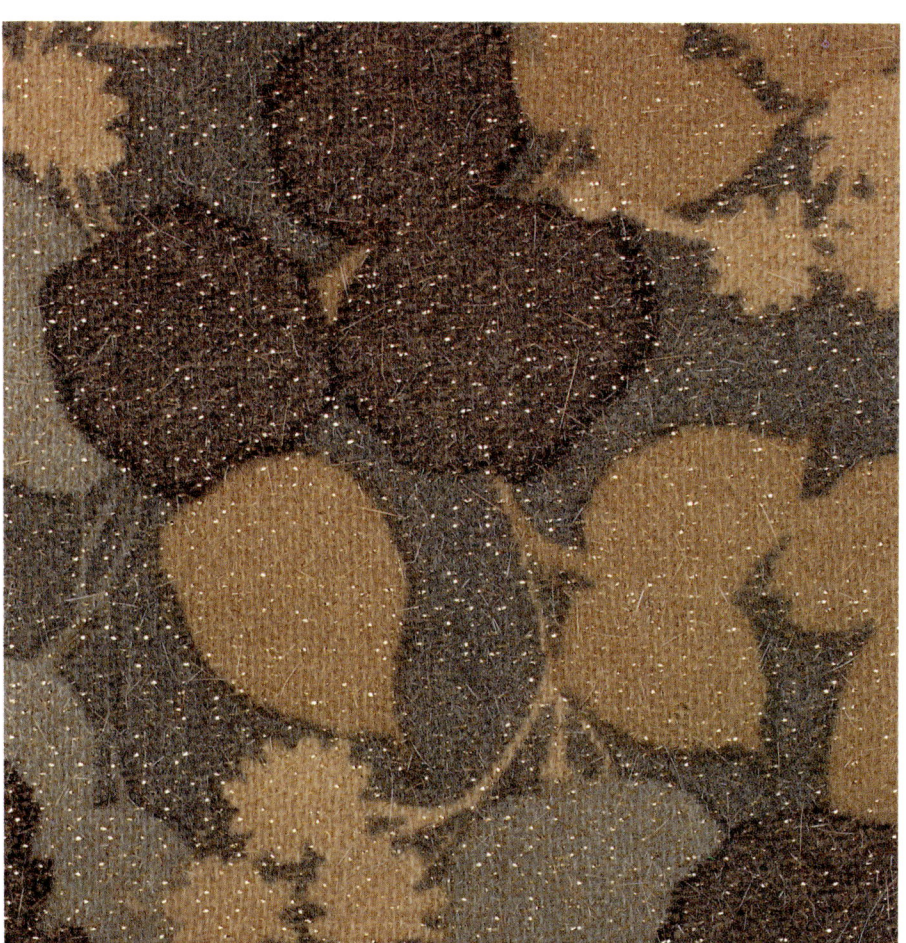

Top left: Horizontal gold threads in richly textured novelty weave with colorful floral print. Cotton blend, France, 1959.

Bottom left: Floral print on peach ground. Blue and copper vertical threads. Cotton and viscose and polyester, France, 1963.

Right: Floral design is flecked with gold. Wool blend, France, 1965.

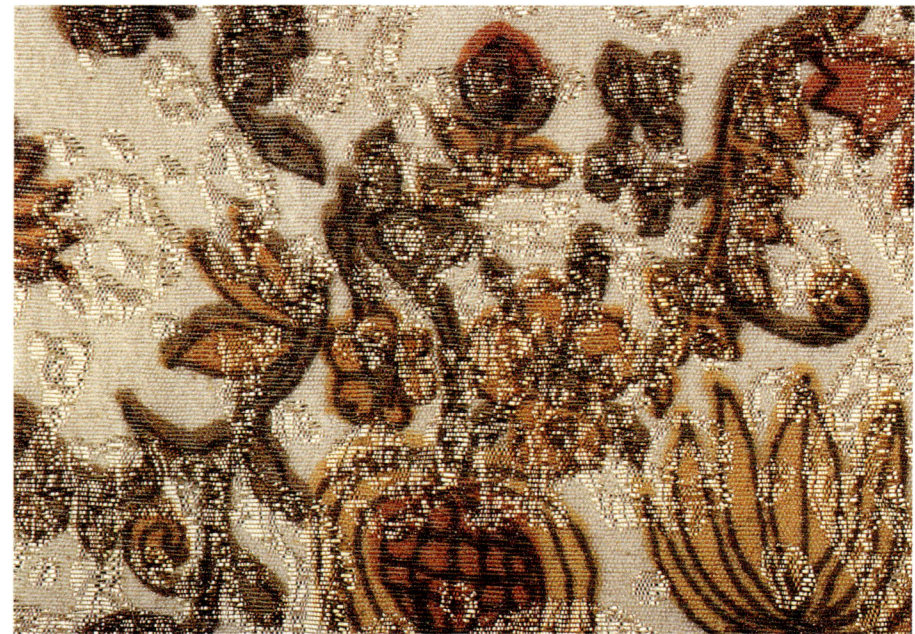

Floral design of gold threads overlays greens and golds on bone. France, 1965.

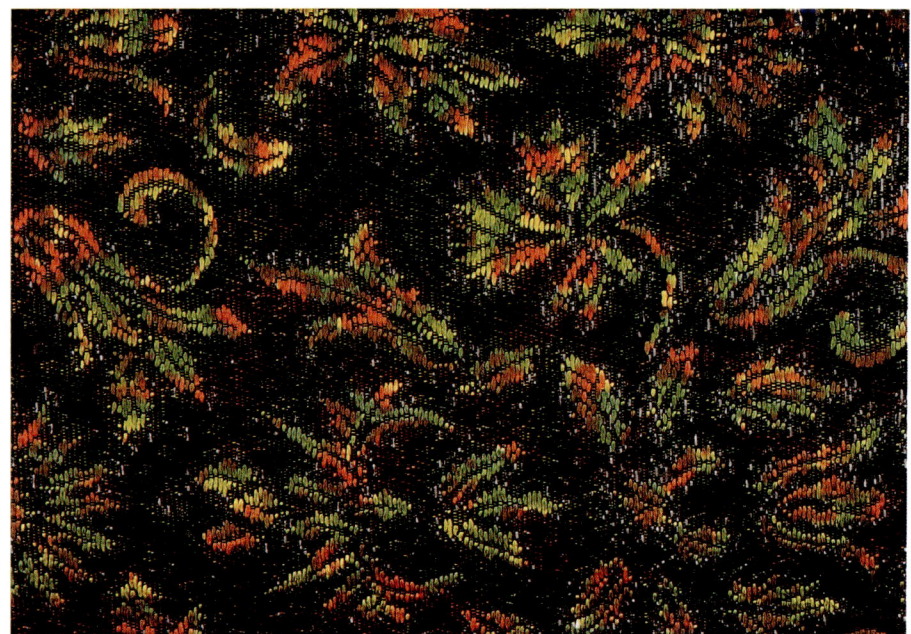

Black threads outline orange green and yellow floral motif on black ground. Cotton blend, France, 1962.

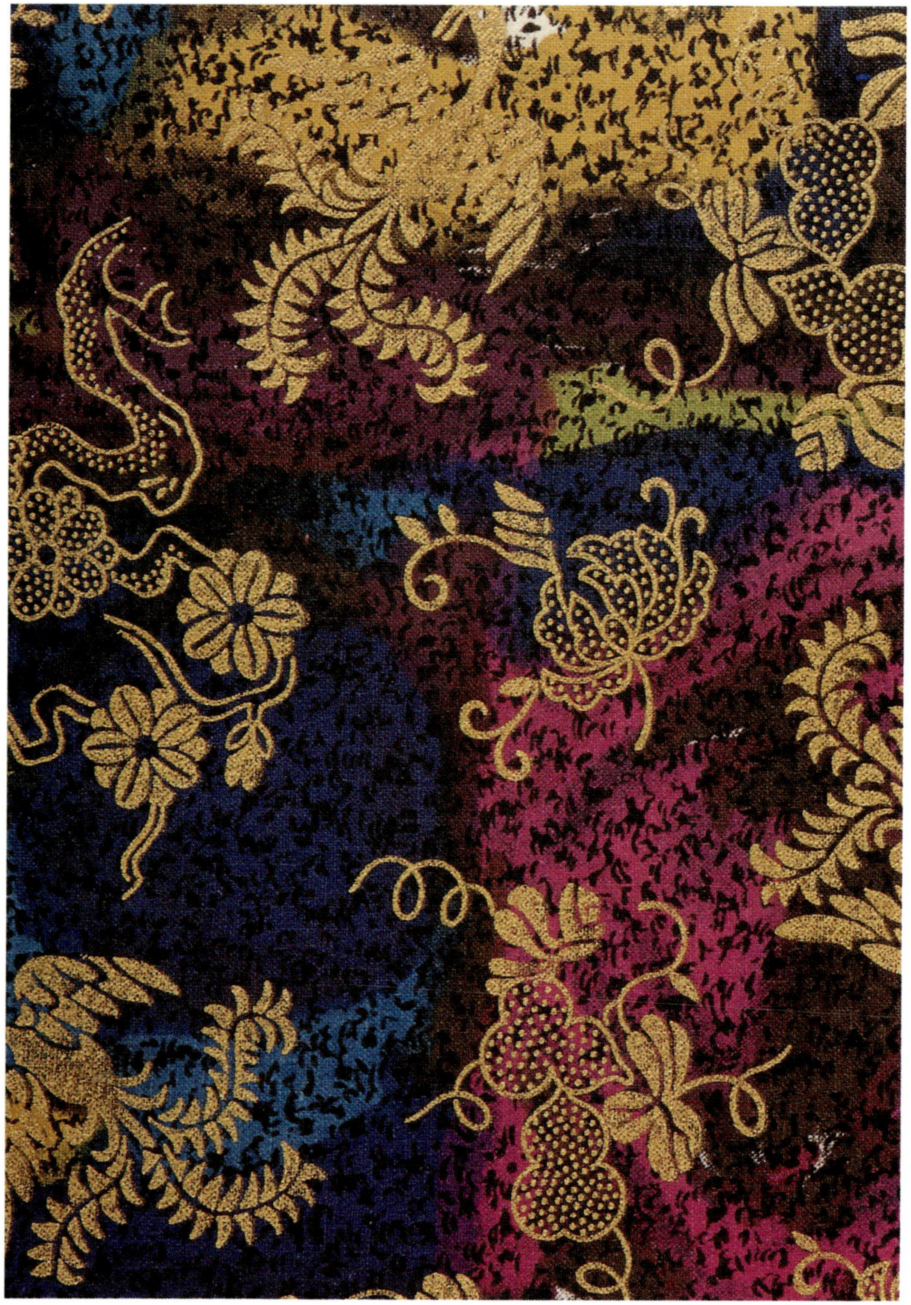

Metallic overprint adds Oriental flare to abstract ground. Polished cotton, France, 1961.

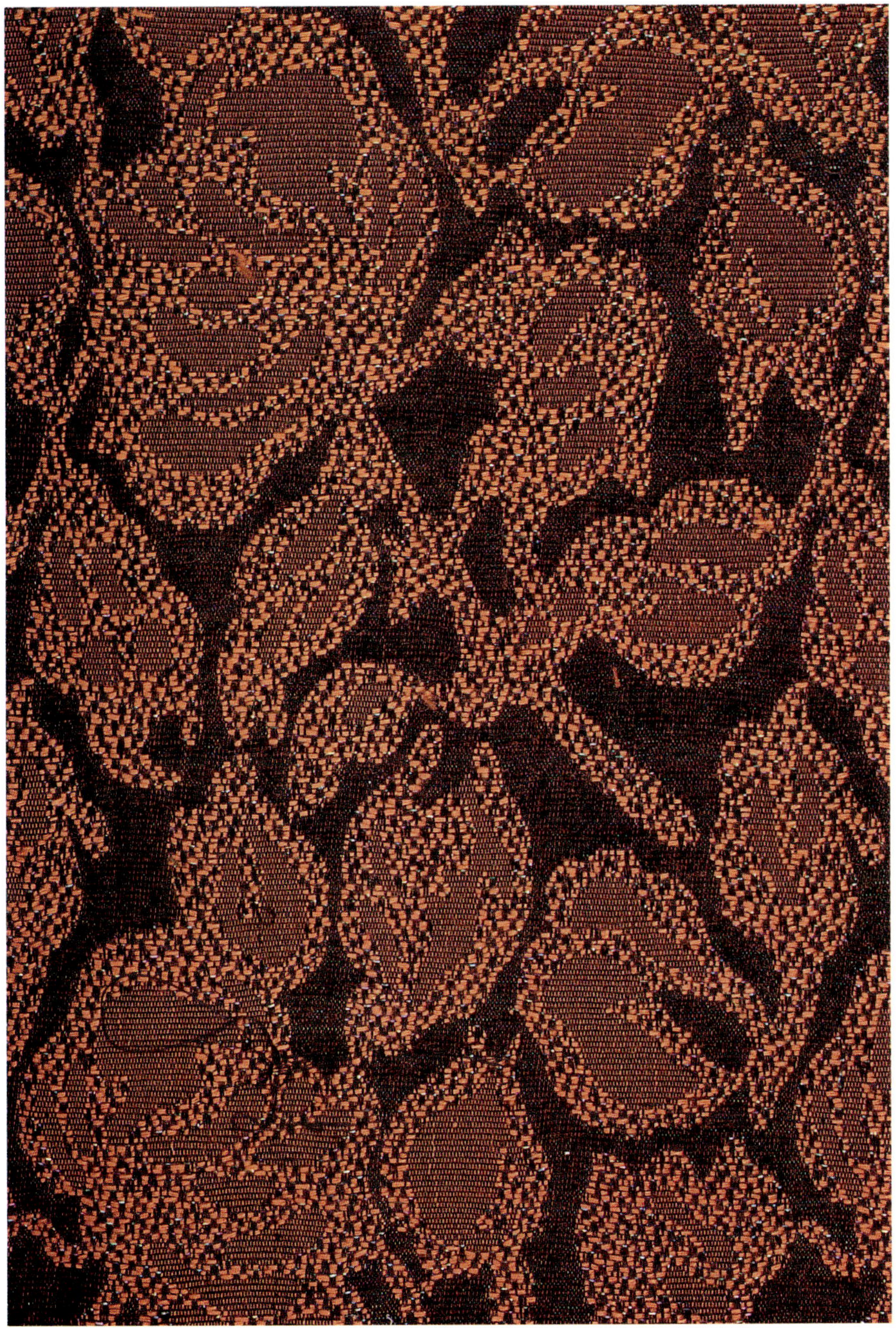

Upholstery weight fabric with gold flecks in brocade flowers. Japan, 1970s.

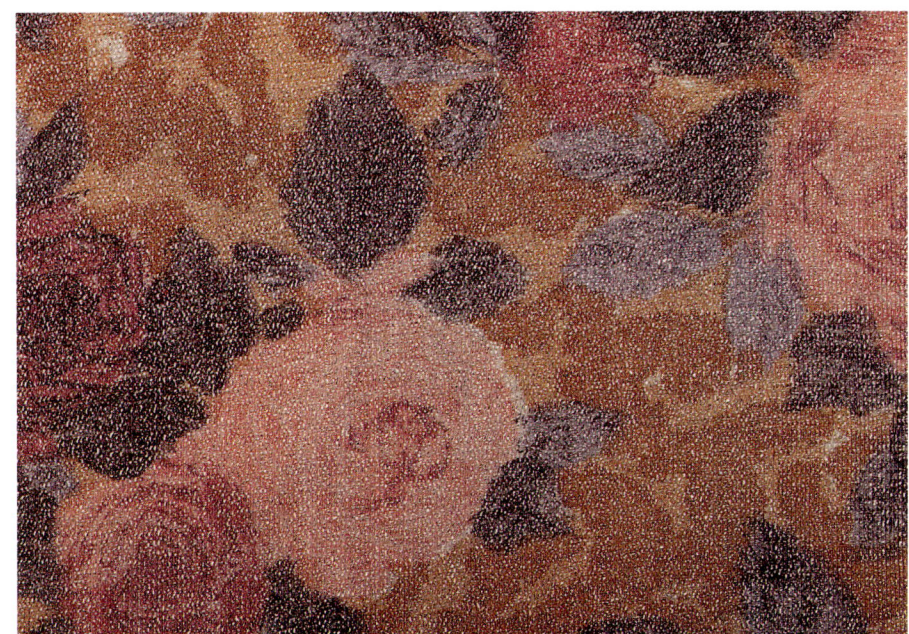

Peach-colored rose print with gray and brown accents, silver flecks. Japan, 1950s.

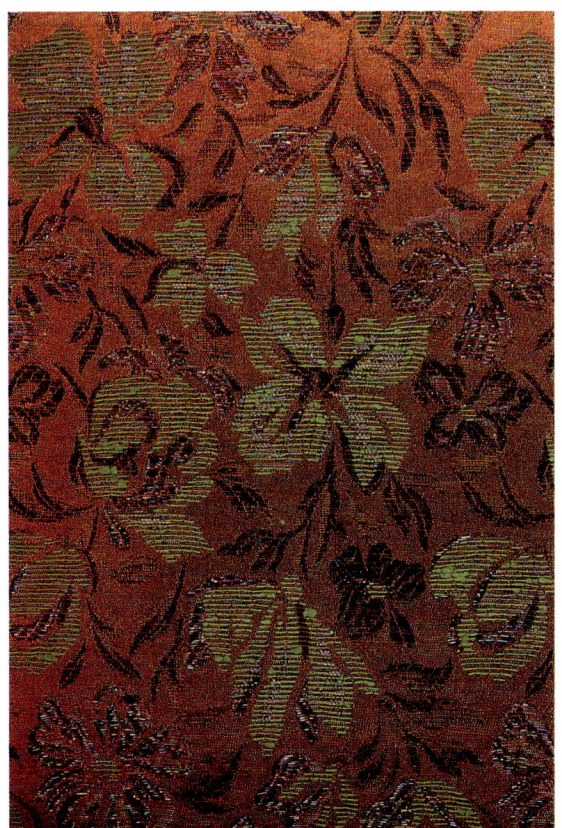

Multi-colored metallic threads add accent to green on rust pattern. Japan, 1970s.

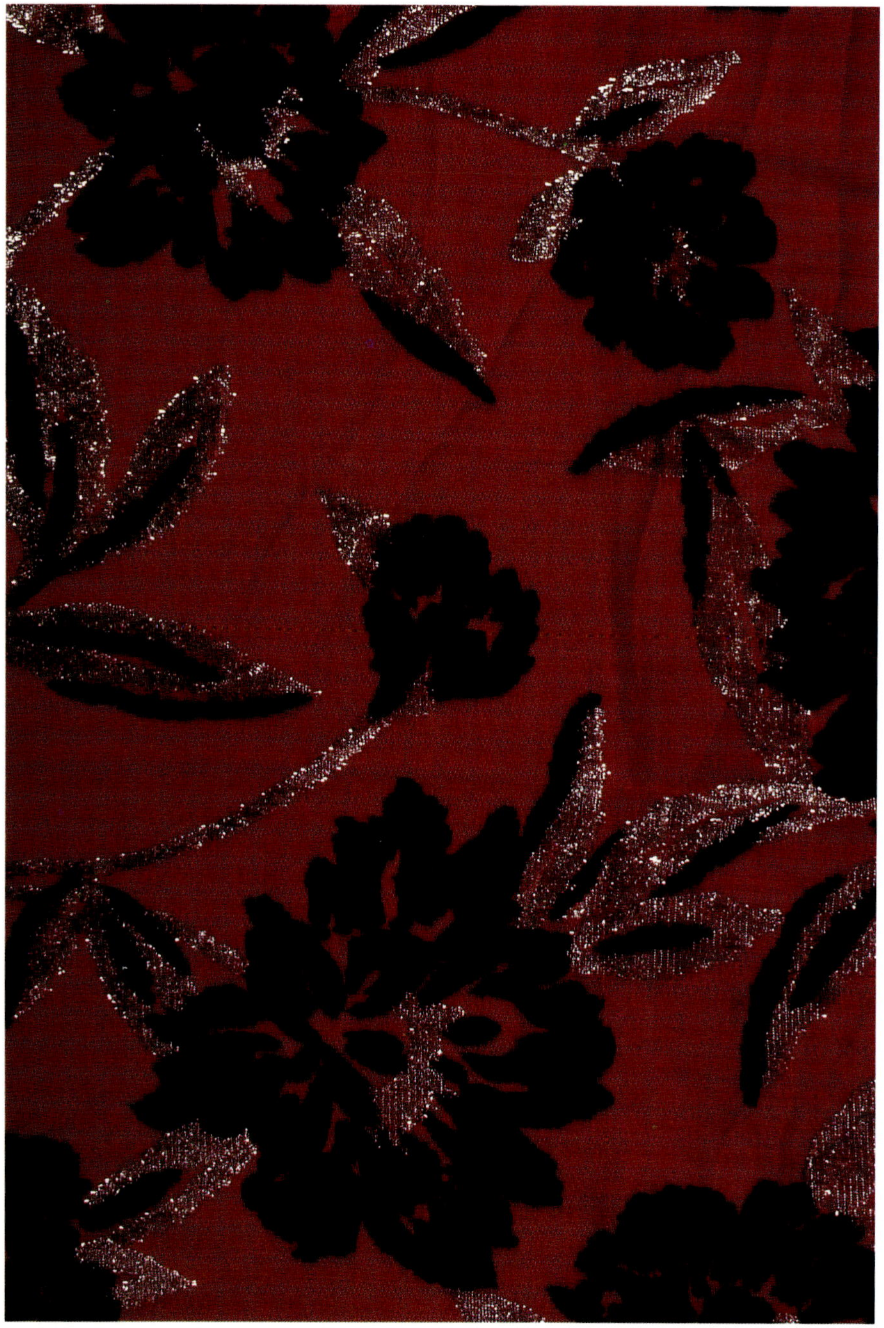

Rust colored film with black velour and silver. *Courtesy of Bouton-Renaud, Vaulx-En-Velin, France.*

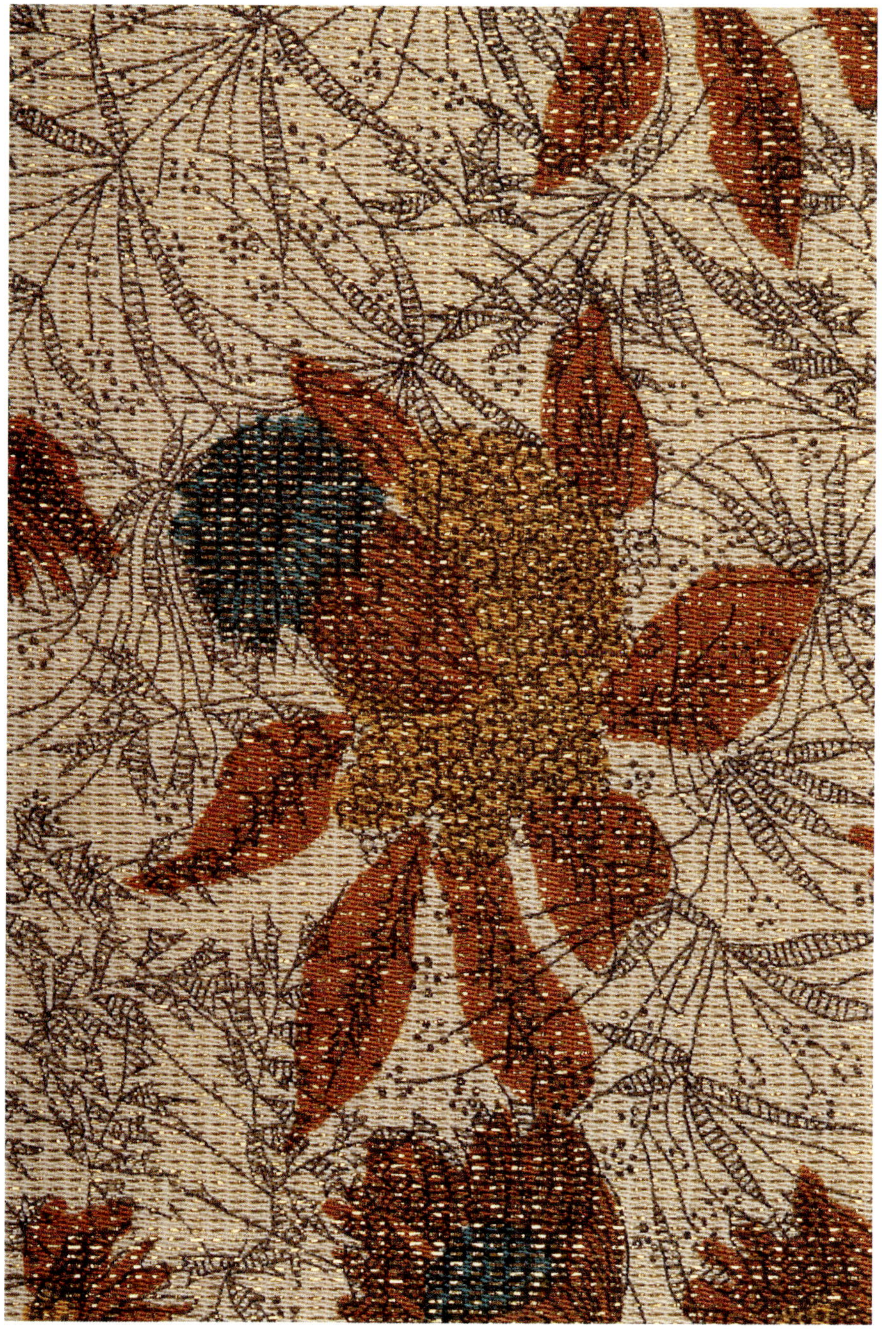

Horizontal gold filaments run through print of brown, blue, and pink petals over black and white foliage line print. Polyester blend, France, 1961.

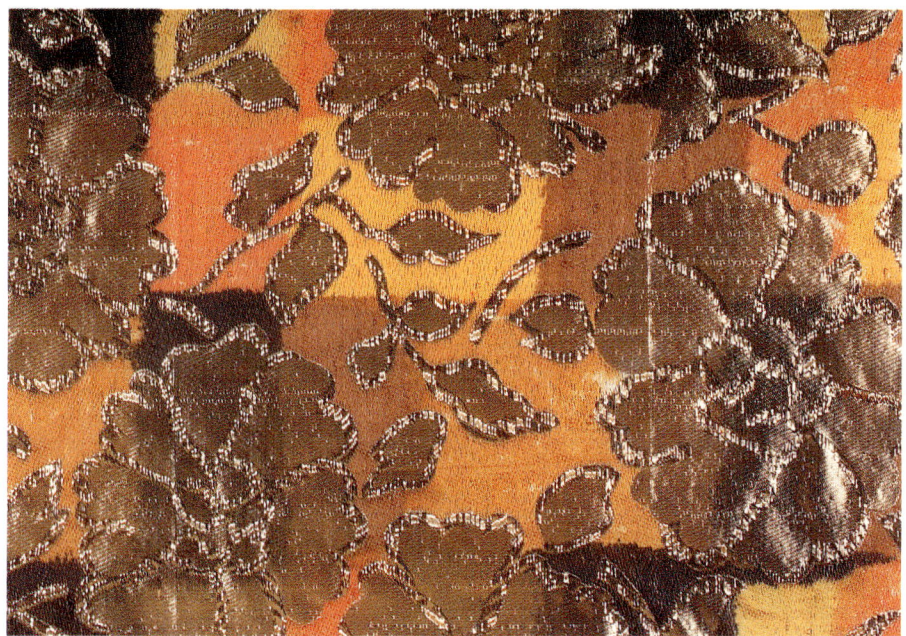

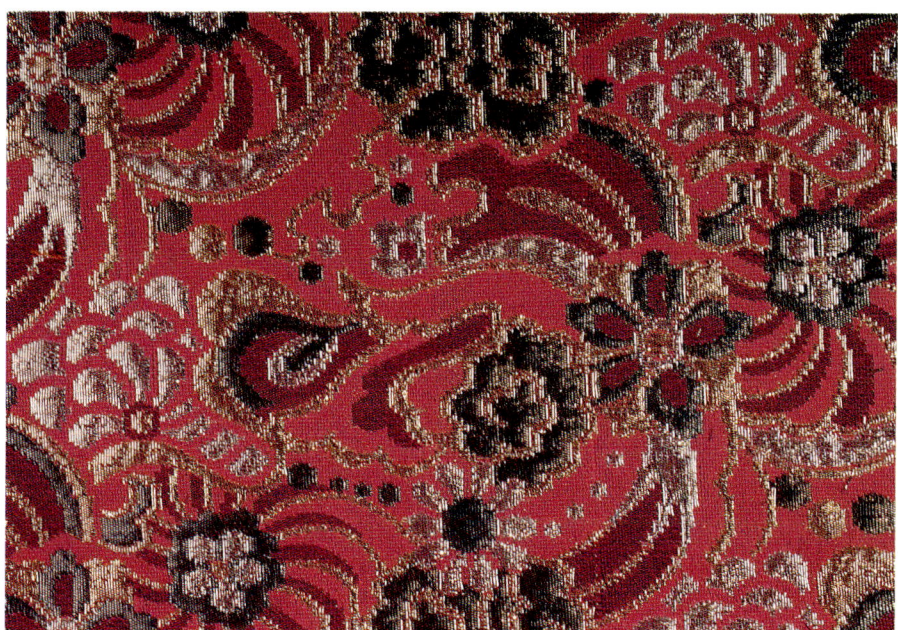

Gold flowers and foliage over abstract design of block colors—oranges, yellow, black, and browns. Rayon/polyester film/nylon, Japan, 1960s.

Gold, silver, and black metallic threads adorn brocade with two shades of pink. Japan, 1970s.

Impressionistic flower pattern on pink ground. Silk/polyester, France, 1953.

Gold adds almost undetectable sparkle to floral print knit. Wool/nylon/angora, France, 1963.

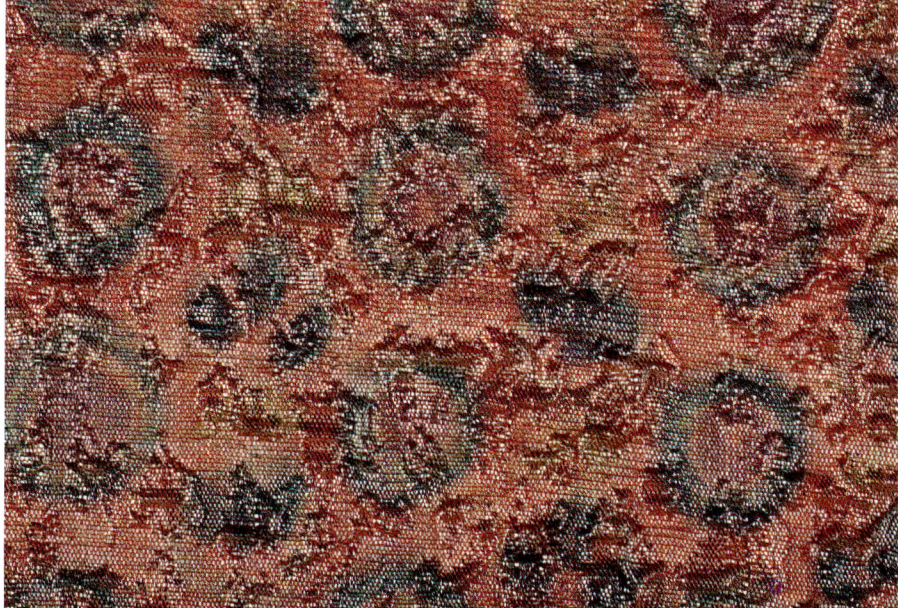

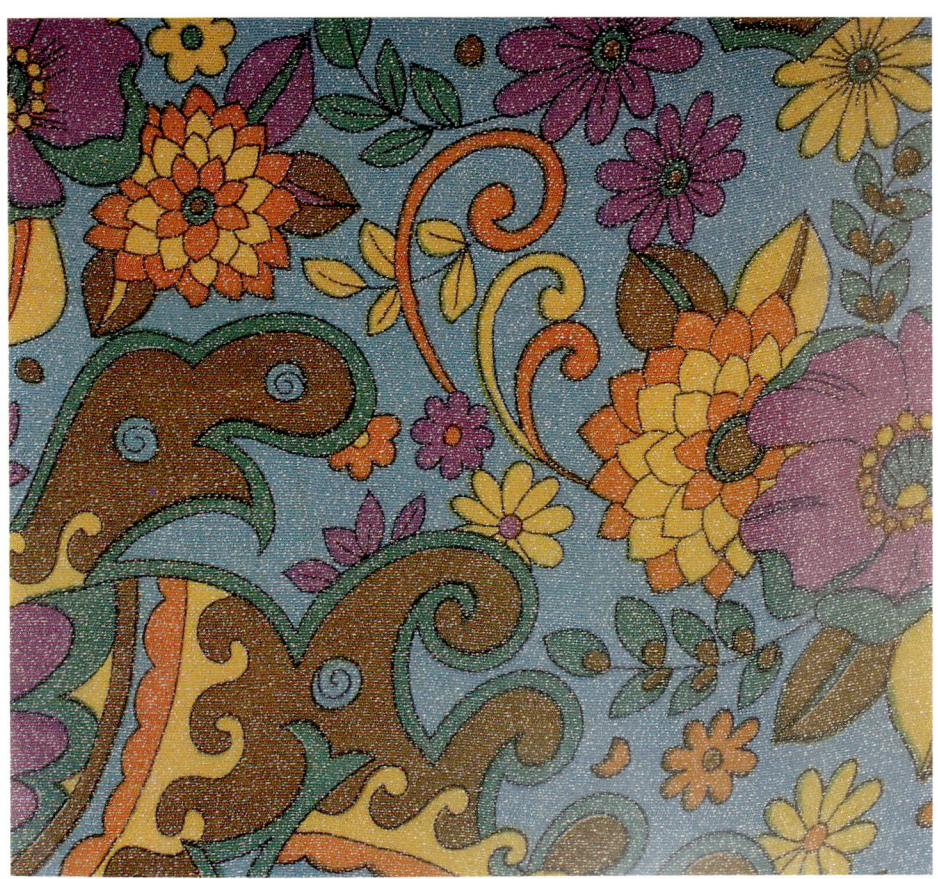

Psychedelic flower power print on baby blue ground with silver flecks. Printed rayon/spun rayon, Japan 1960s.

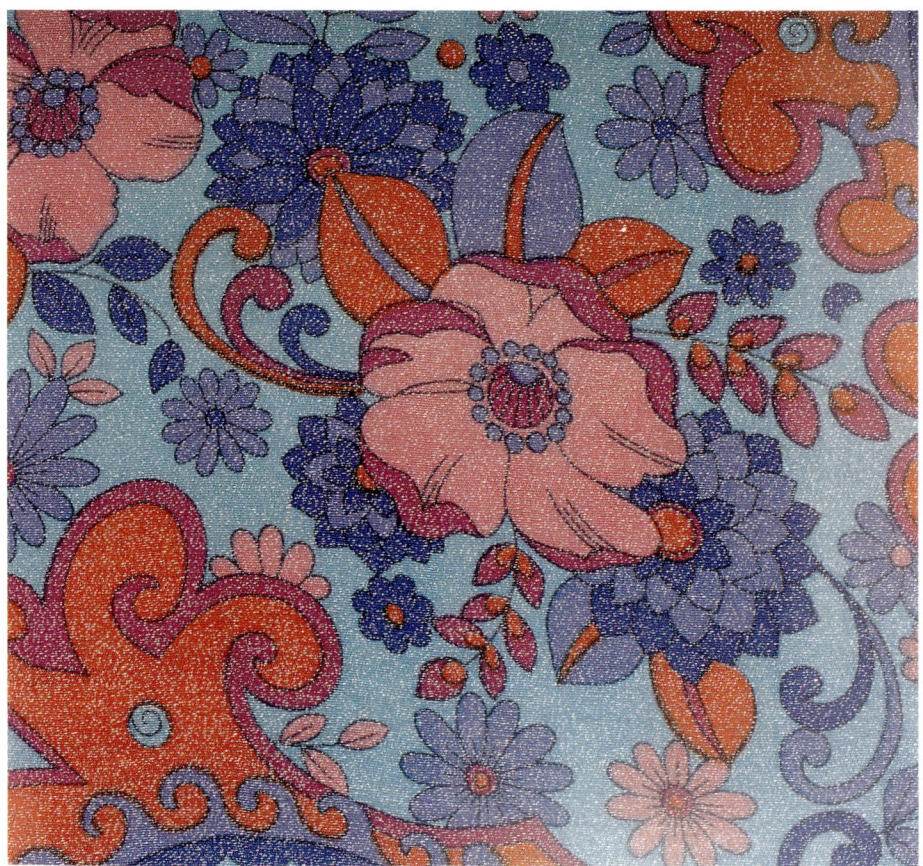

Psychedelic flower power print on baby blue ground with silver flecks. Printed rayon/spun rayon, Japan 1960s.

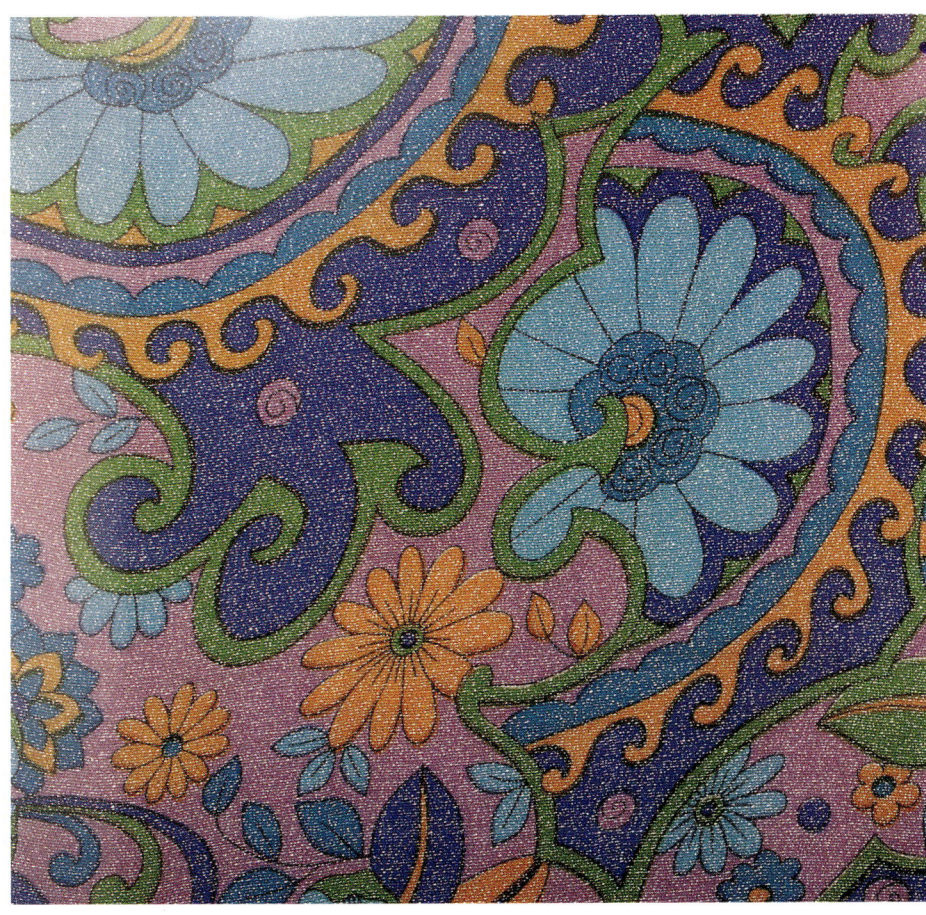

Psychedelic flower power print on pink ground with silver flecks. Printed rayon/spun rayon, Japan 1960s.

Psychedelic flower power print on yellow ground with silver flecks. Printed rayon/spun rayon, Japan 1960s.

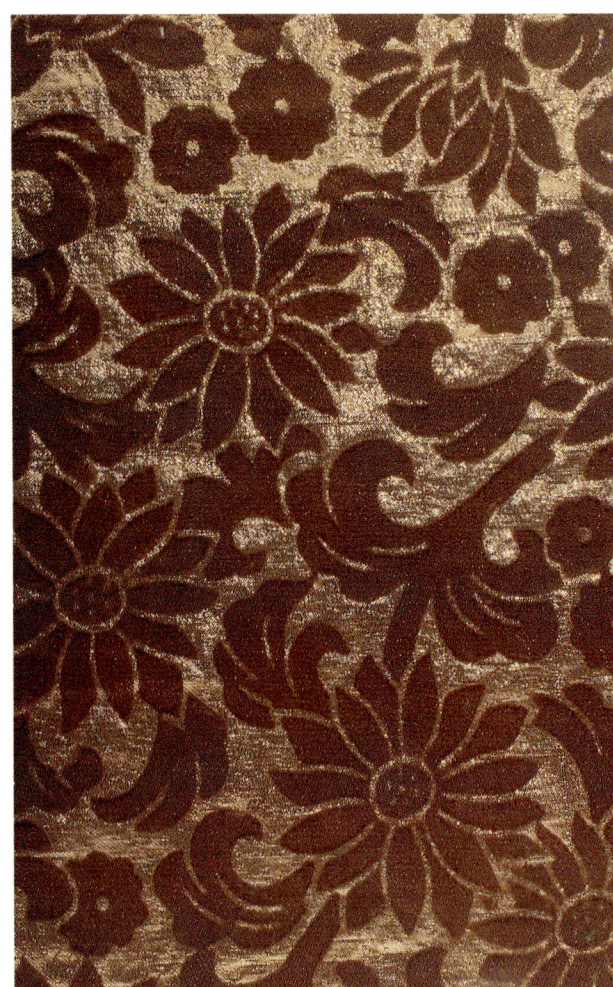

Brown flowers on gold lamé.
Japan, 1970s.

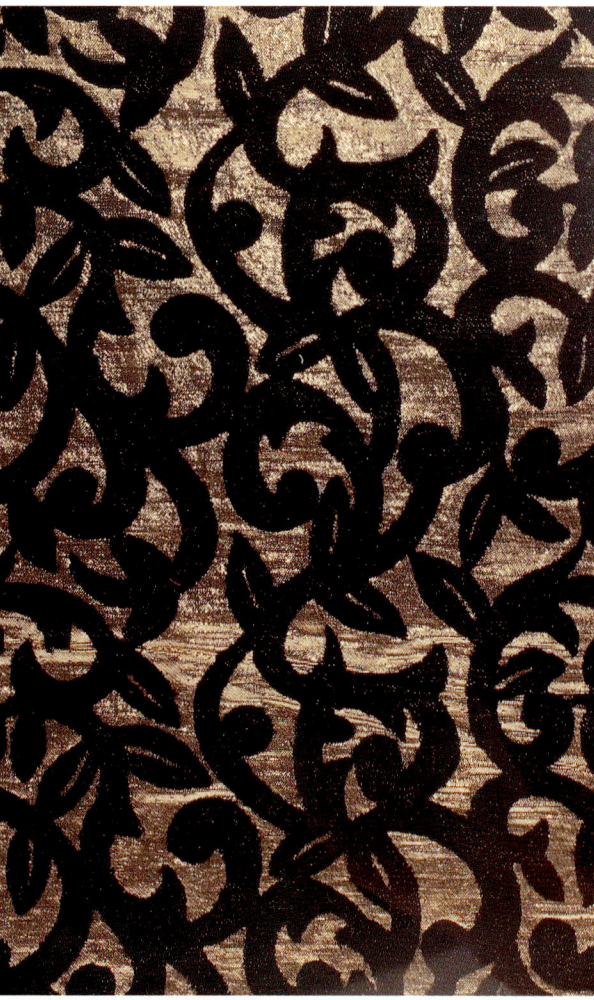

Black foliage on gold lamé.
Japan, 1970s.

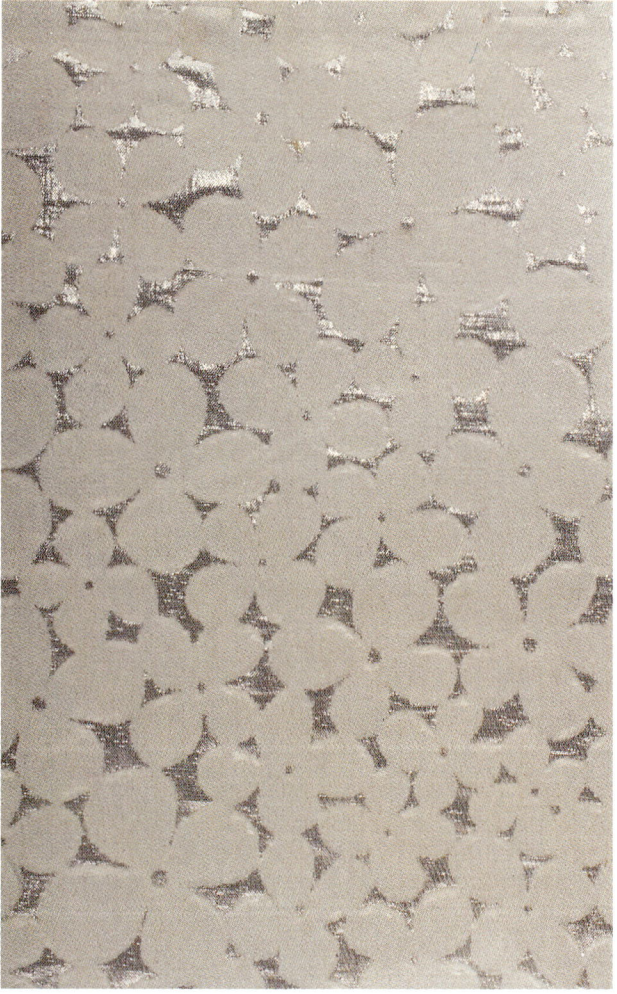

White flowers on silver lamé.
Japan, 1970s.

Purple floral motif on gold lamé. Japan, 1970s.

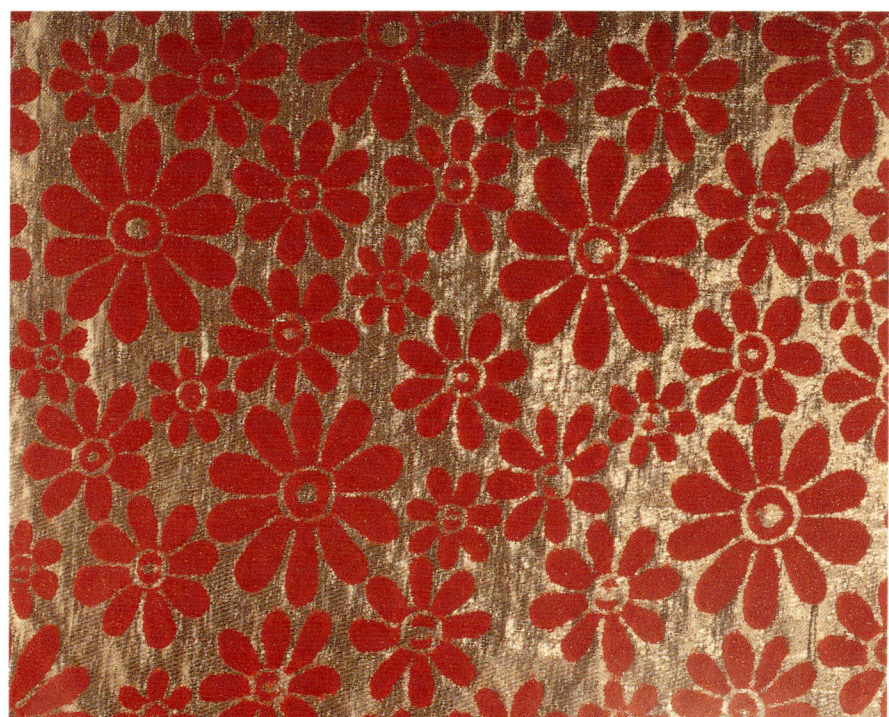

Red flower power on gold lamé. Japan, 1970s.

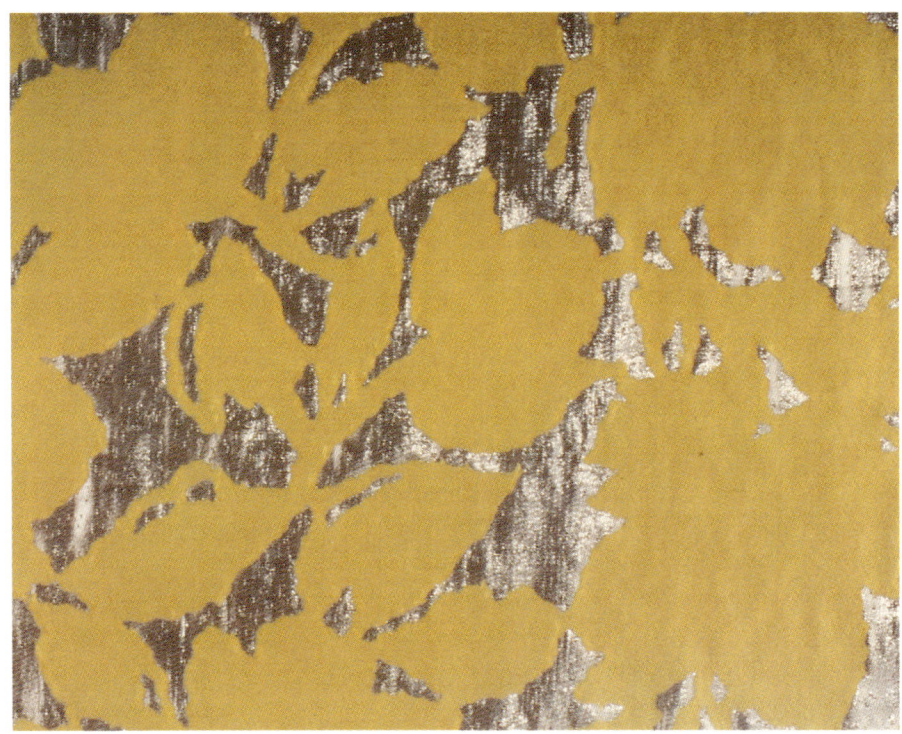

Yellow flowers on silver lamé. Japan, 1970s.

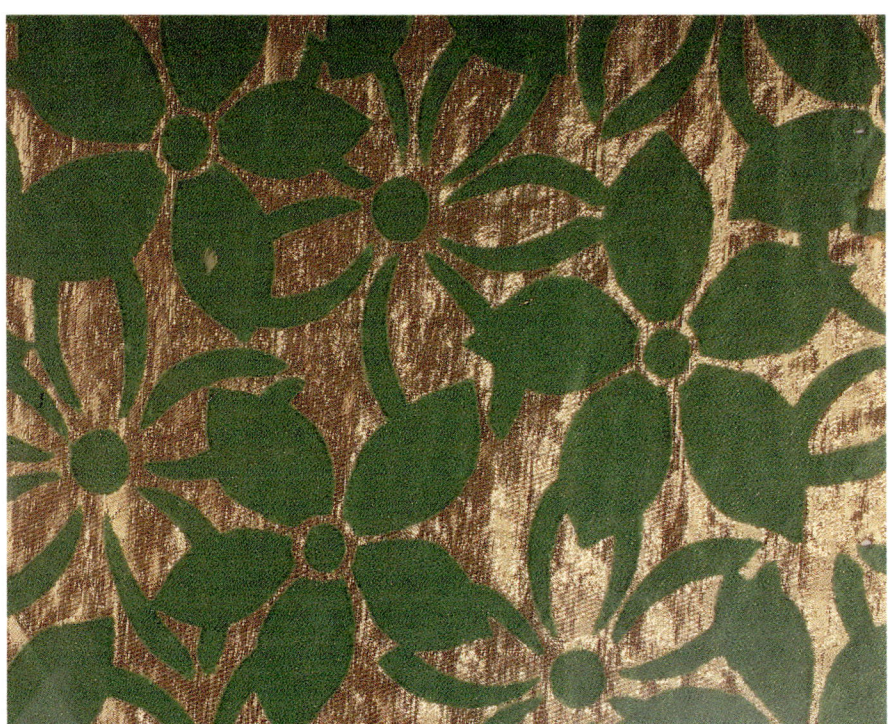

Negative and positive green flowers on gold lamé. Japan, 1970s.

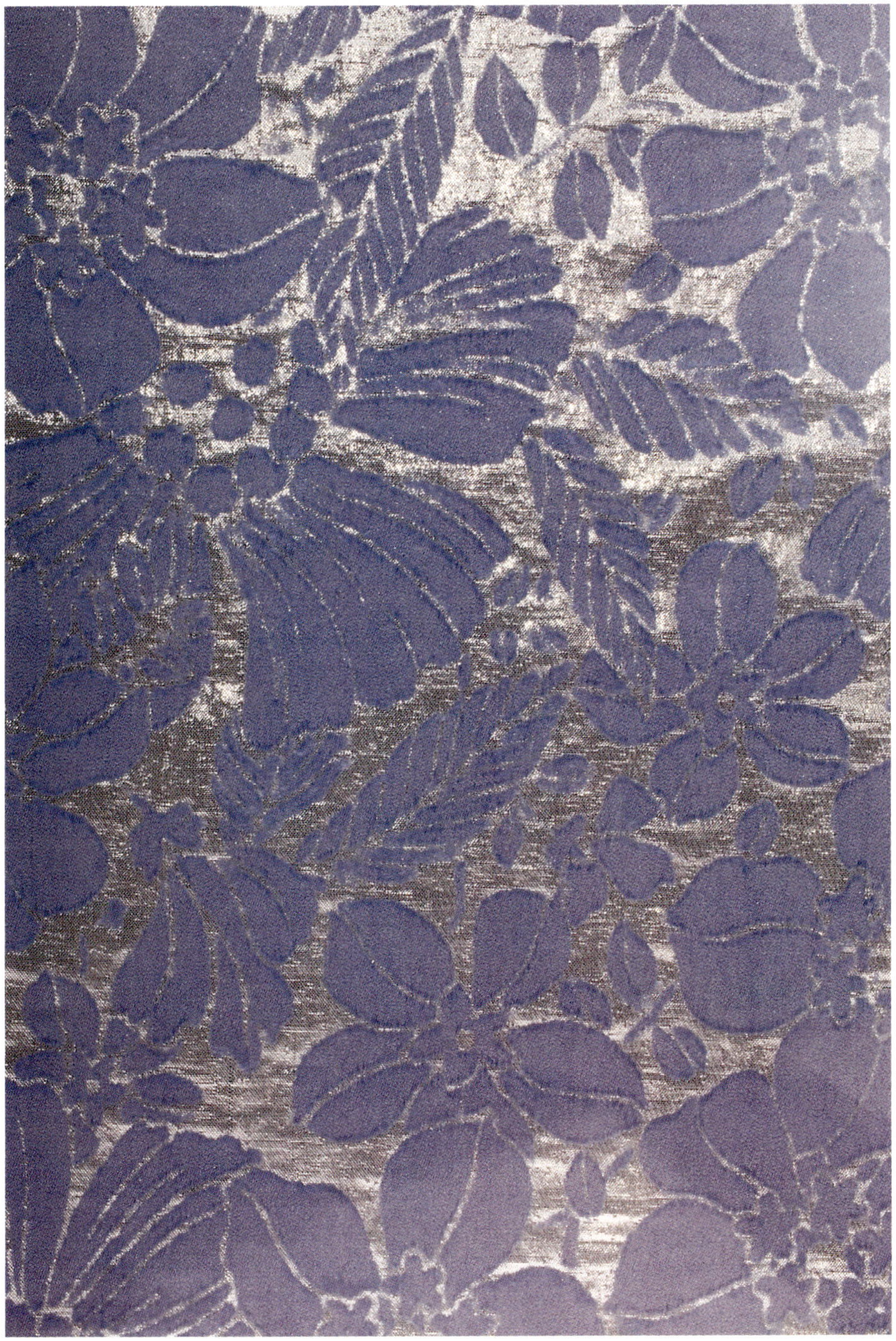

Lavendar flowers on silver lamé. Japan, 1970s.

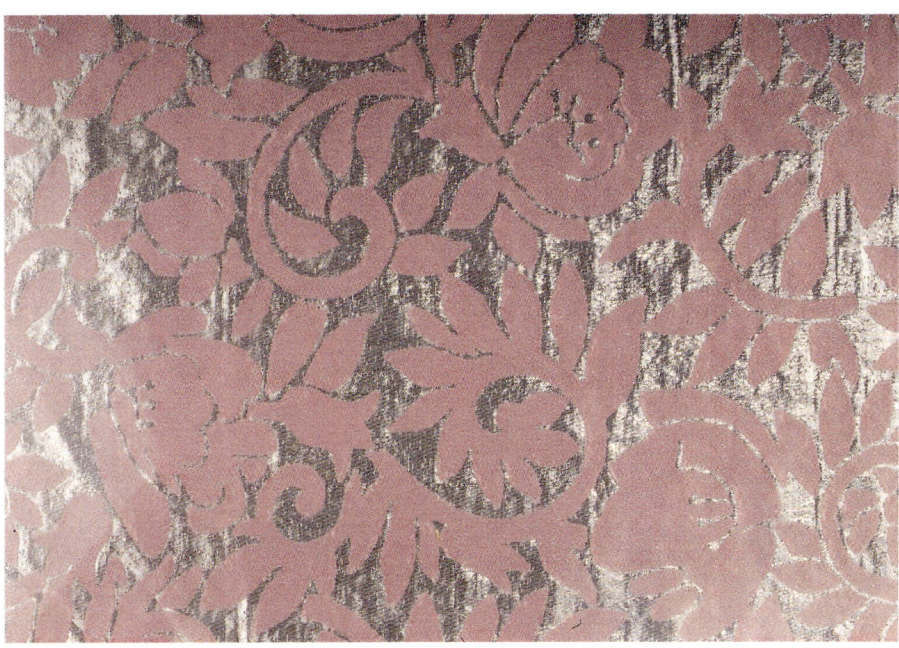

Pink flowers on silver lamé. Japan, 1970s.

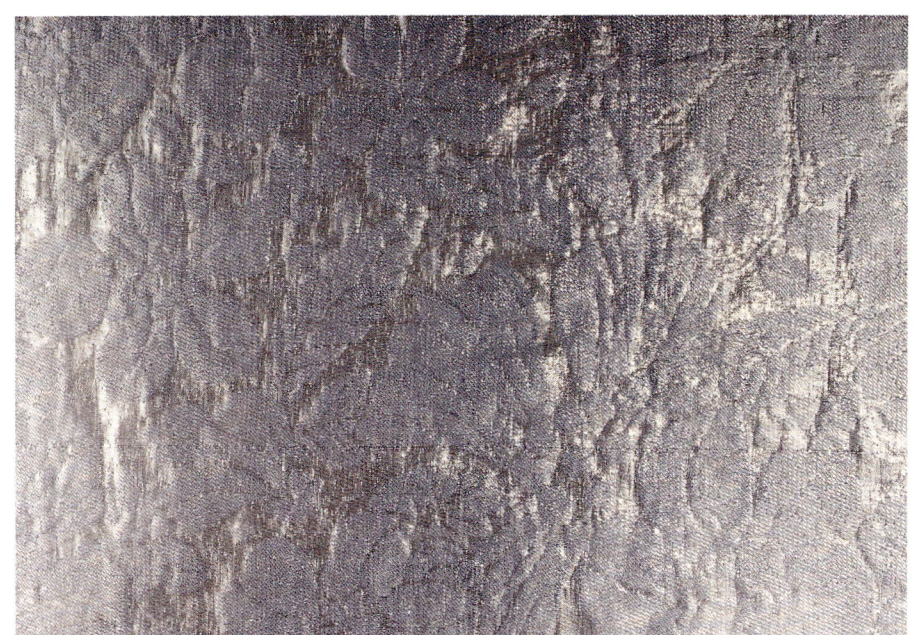

White and silver lamé. Japan, 1970s.

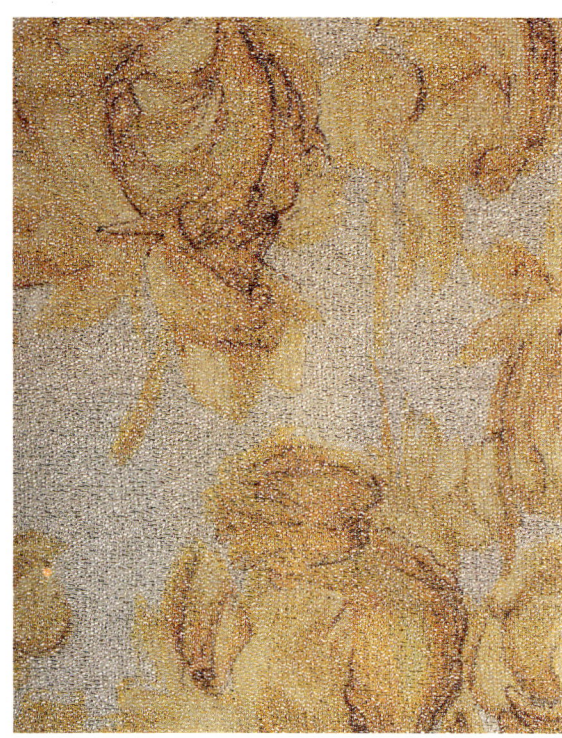

Yellow roses on white with silver. Japan, 1960.

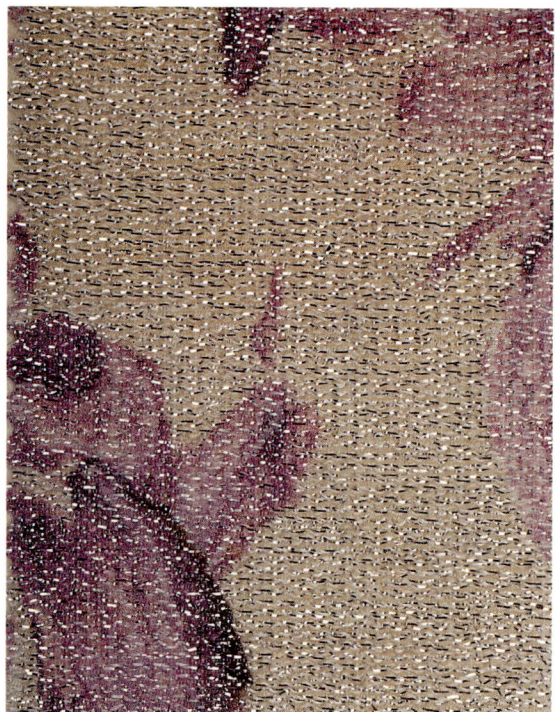

Lavender on white with silver. Japan, 1960.

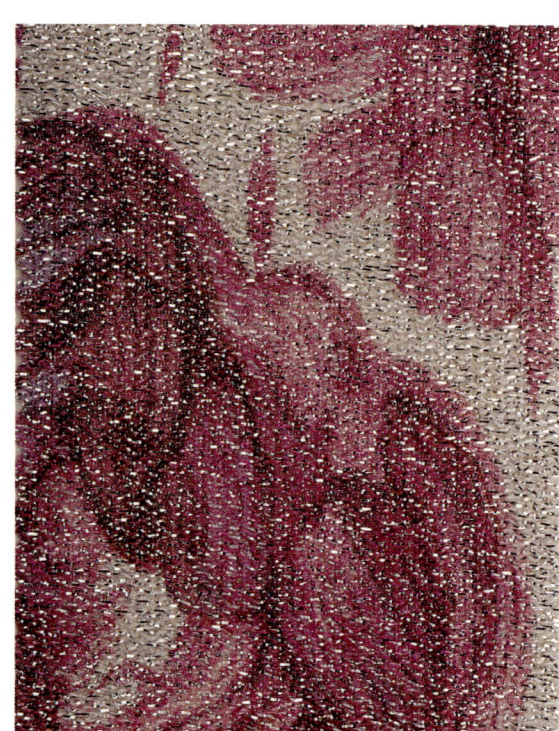

Pink roses on white with silver. Japan, 1960.

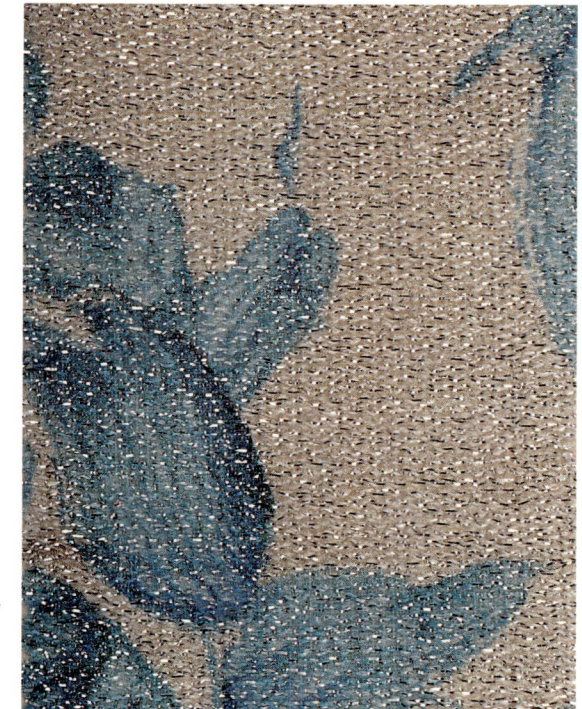

Blue with white on silver. Japan, 1960.

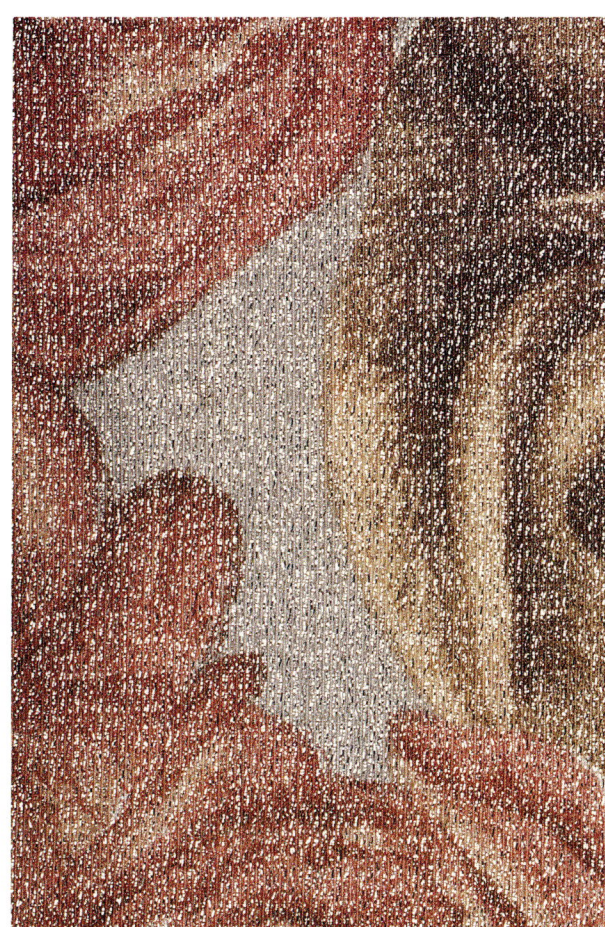

Pink and gold roses on gray with silver. Japan, 1960.

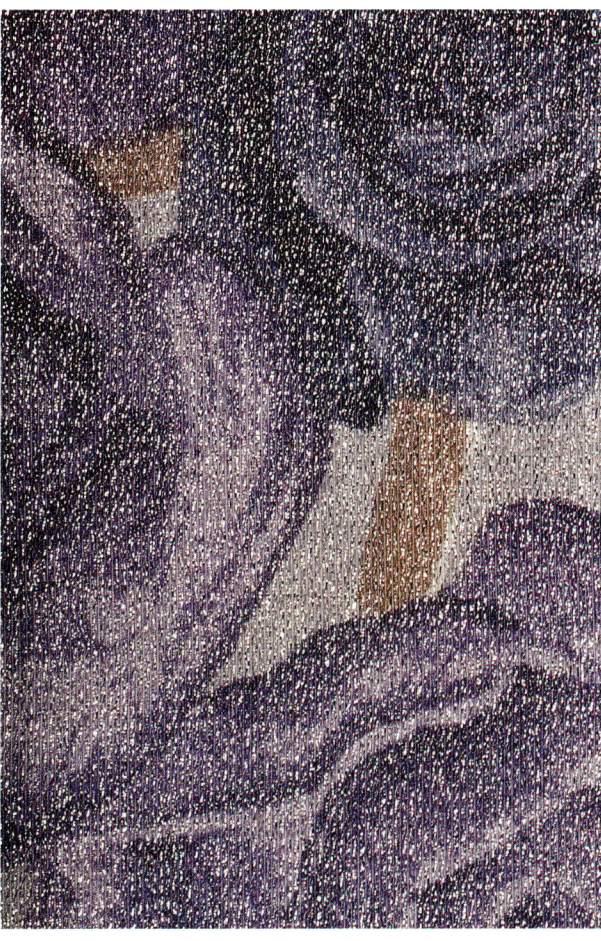

Lavender and blue roses on gray with silver. Japan, 1960.

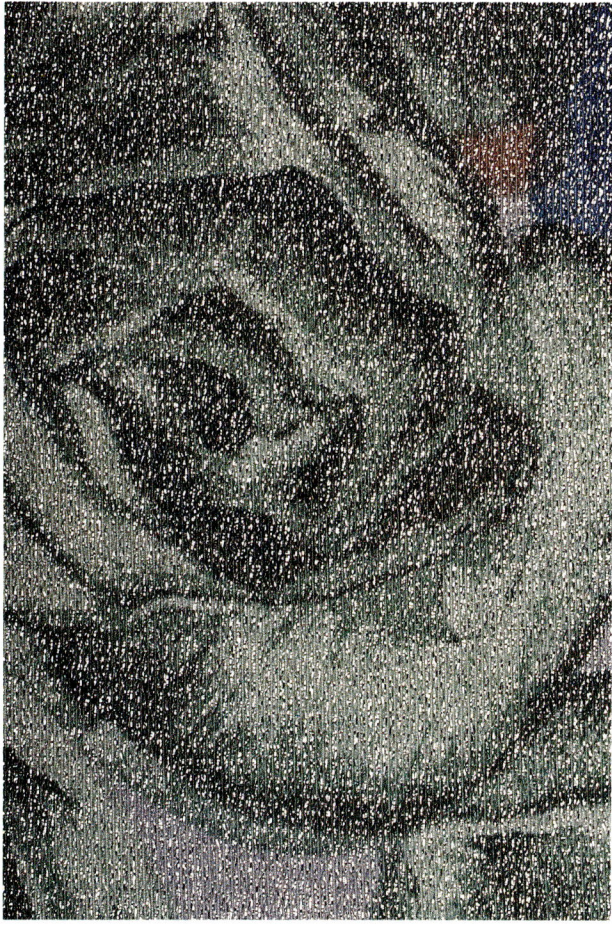

Greens with silver. Japan, 1960.

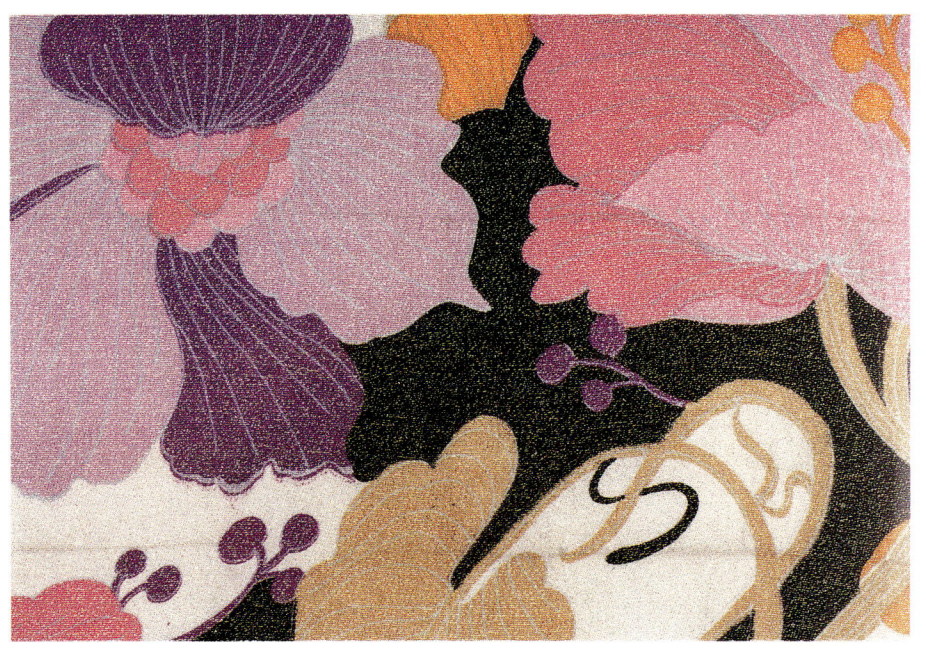

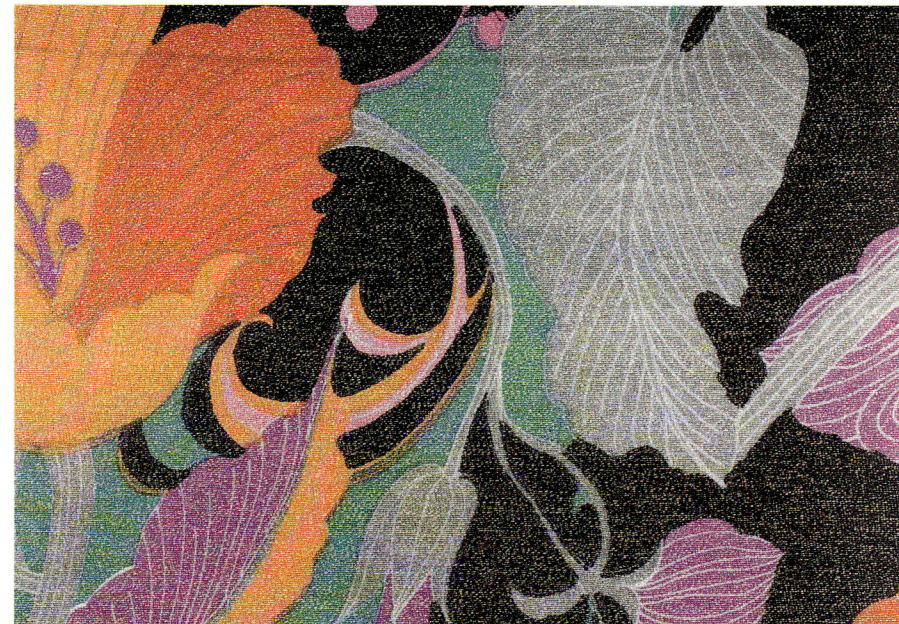

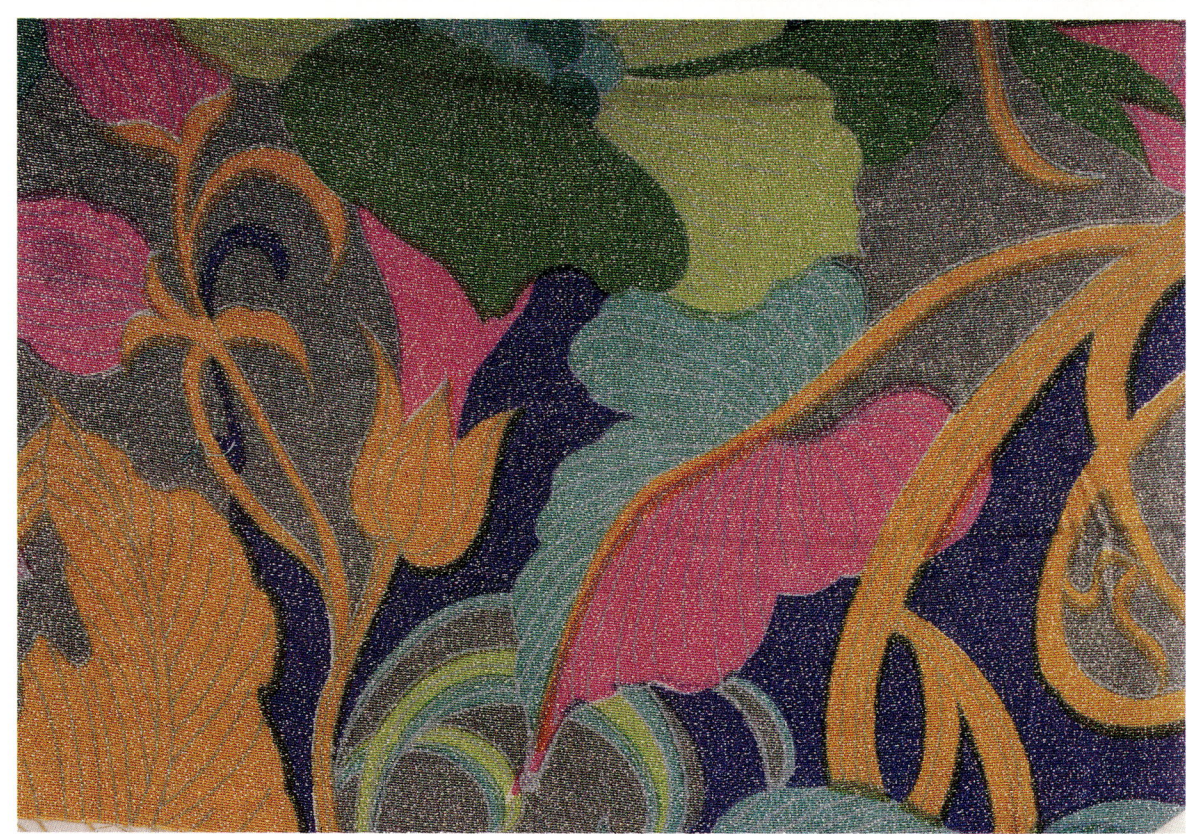

Top left: Oversize flowers on black ground sparked by silver. Pinks, purples, taupe, and black. Rayon/spun rayon, Japan, 1960s.

Top right: Oversize flowers on black ground sparked by silver. Oranges, purple, pink, gray, and black. Rayon/spun rayon, Japan, 1960s.

Bottom right: Oversize flowers on black ground sparked by silver. Hot pink, greens, taupe, and turquoise on blue ground. Rayon/spun rayon, Japan, 1960s.

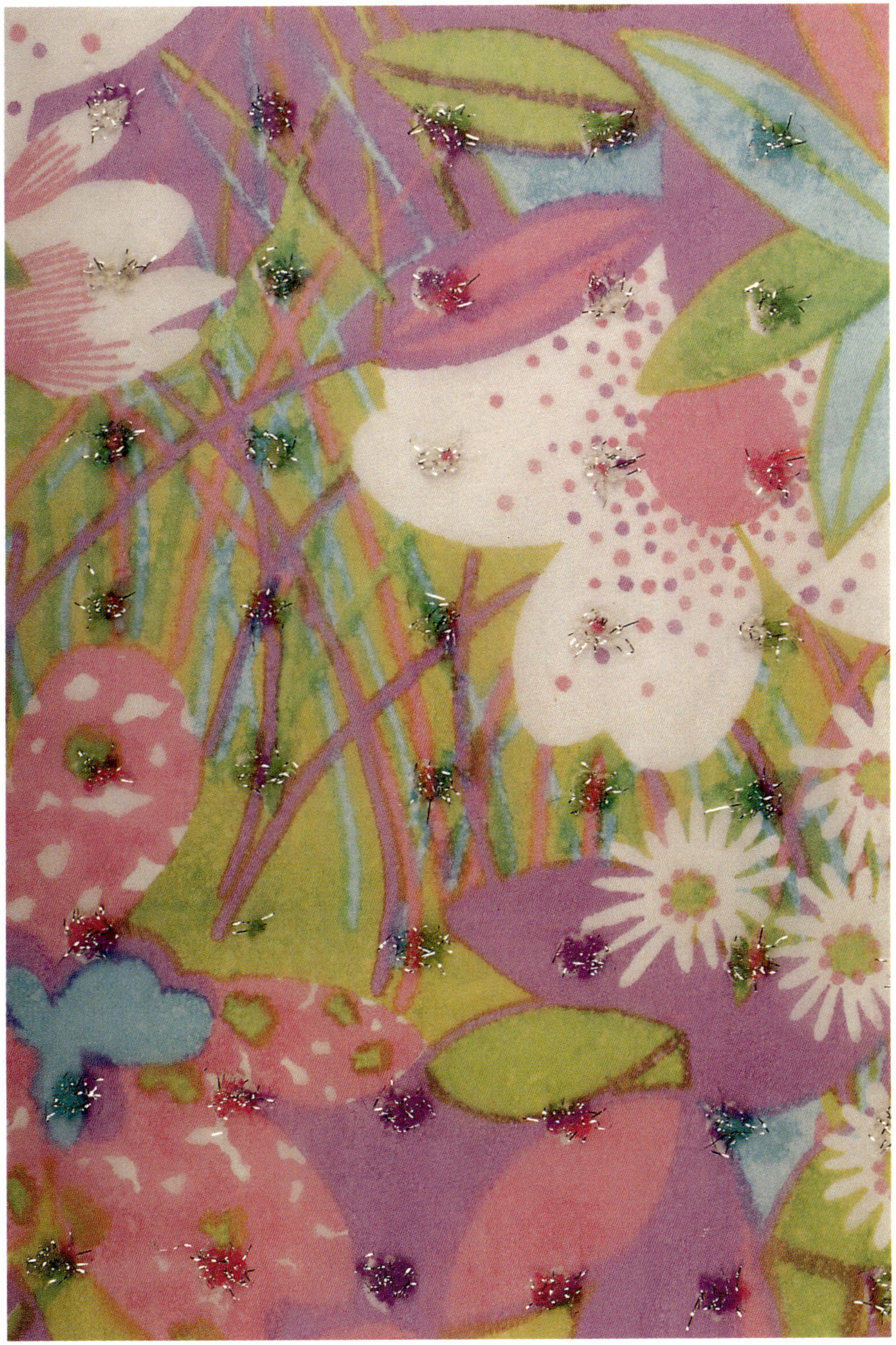

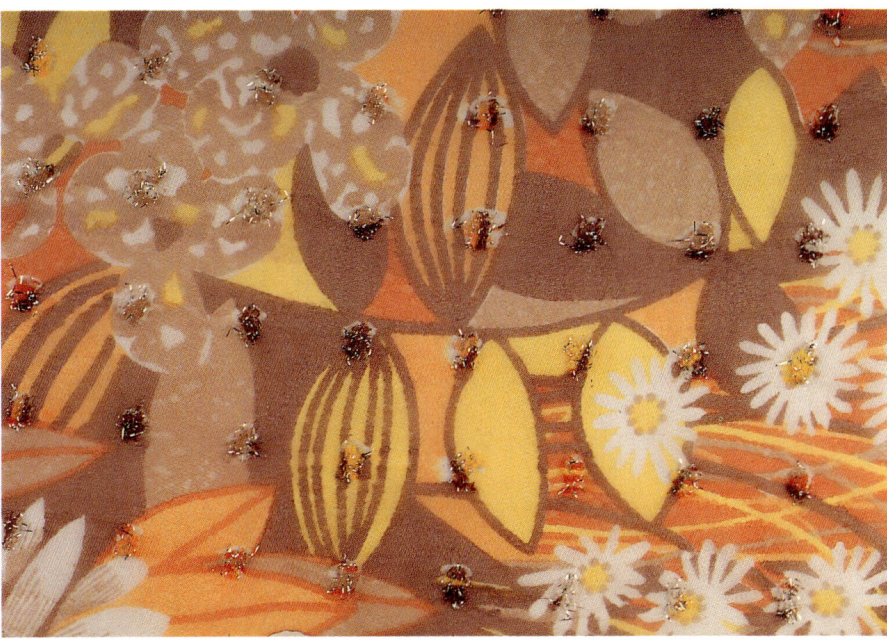

Daisy and foliage motif on polyester film with metallic and velour dots. Printed orange, yellow, and brown. Nylon/polyester, Japan, 1960s.

Daisy and foliage motif on polyester film with metallic and velour dots. Printed pink and grays. Nylon/polyester, Japan, 1960s.

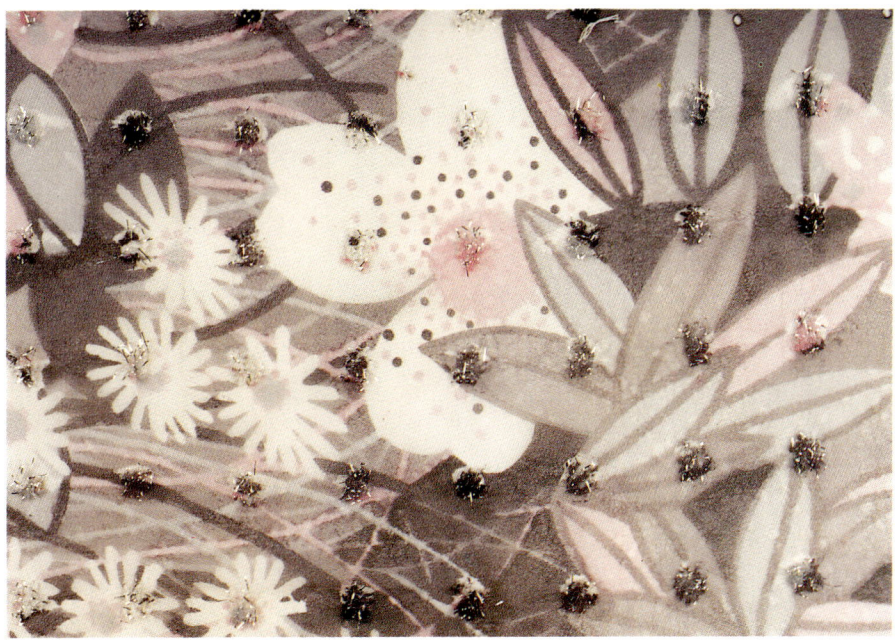

Daisy and foliage motif on polyester film with metallic and velour dots. Printed purple, pink, and green. Nylon/polyester, Japan, 1960s.

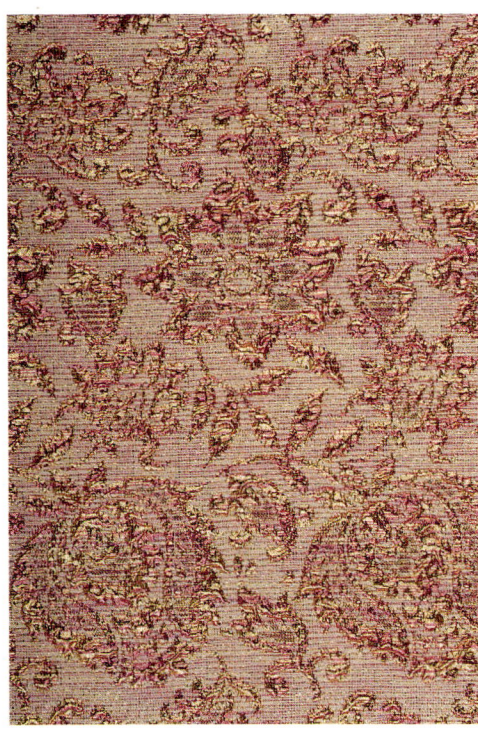

Raised rose and gold lamé creates floral relief against like-colored ground. Japan, 1970s.

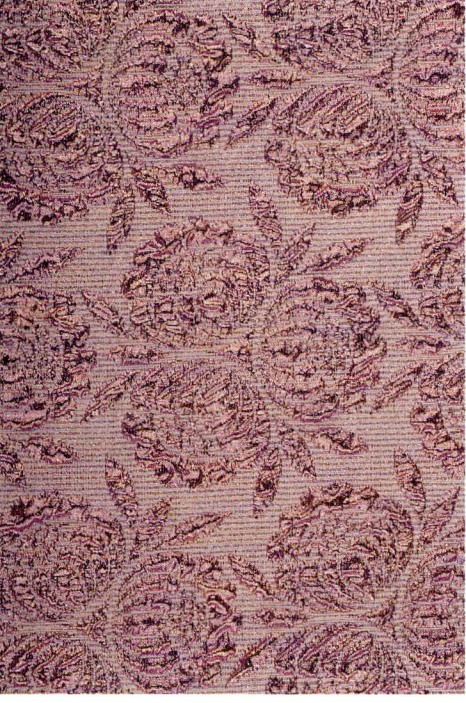

Raised lavender lamé creates floral relief against like-colored ground. Japan, 1970s.

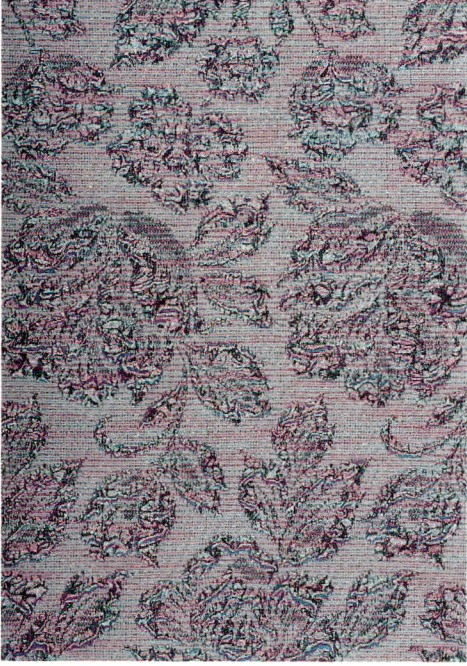

Raised mint-green and pink lamé creates floral relief against like-colored ground. Japan, 1970s.

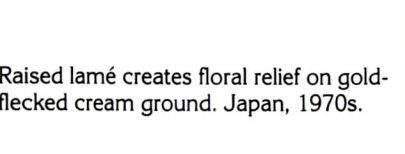

Raised lamé creates floral relief on gold-flecked cream ground. Japan, 1970s.

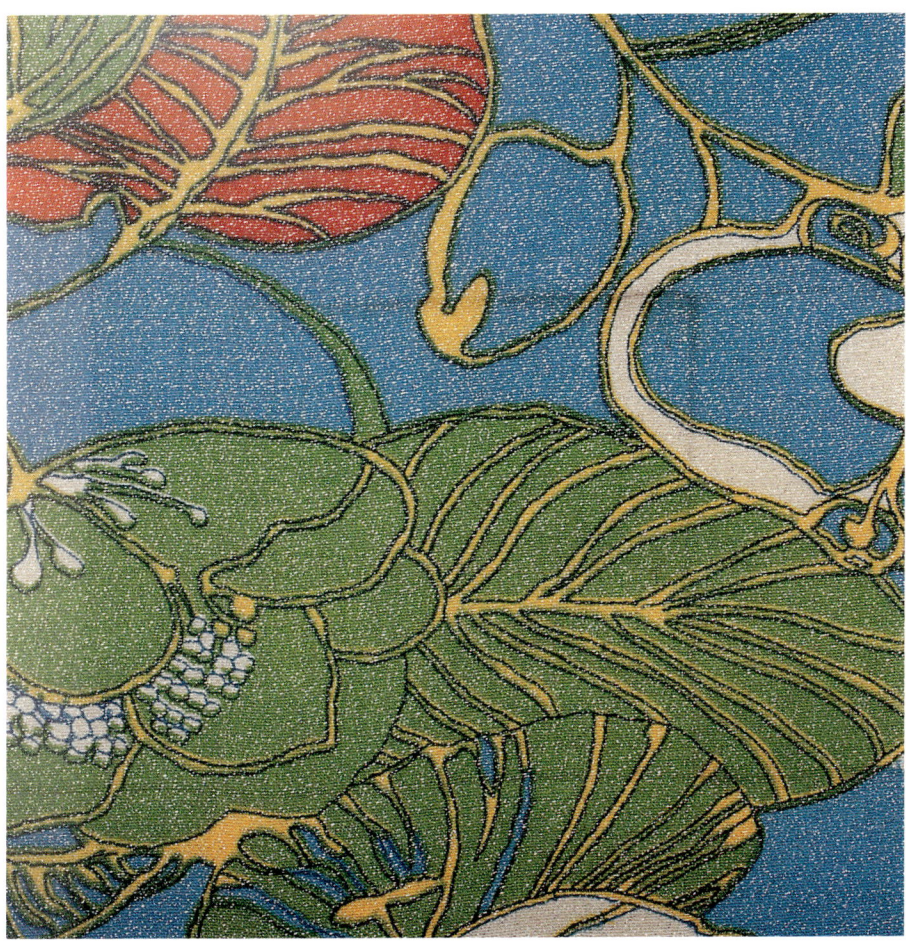

Oversize floral design on blue ground with silver flecks. Printed rayon/spun rayon, Japan, 1960s.

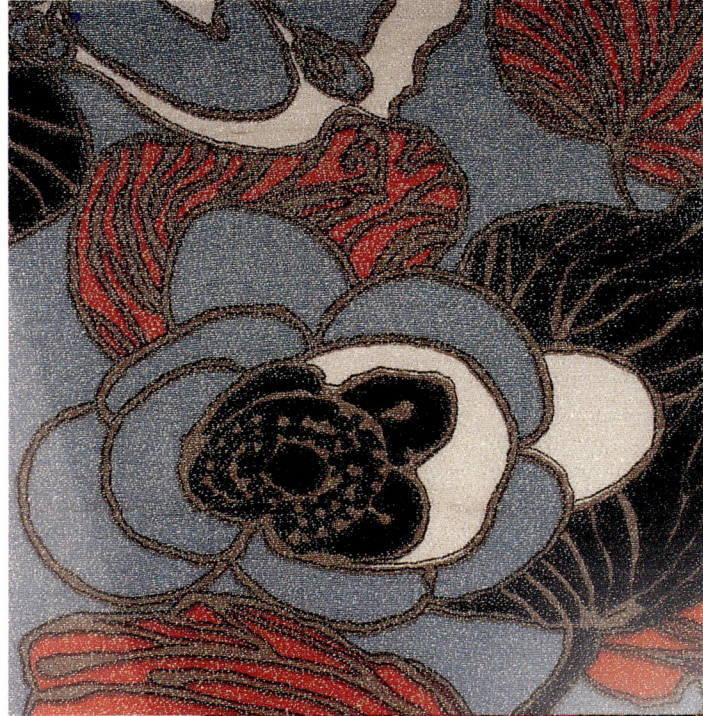

Oversize floral design on gray ground with silver flecks. Printed rayon/spun rayon, Japan, 1960s.

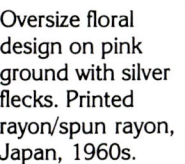

Oversize floral design on pink ground with silver flecks. Printed rayon/spun rayon, Japan, 1960s.

Mixed brocade with floral/paisley pattern on black ground. Rayon/spun rayon, Japan, 1960s.

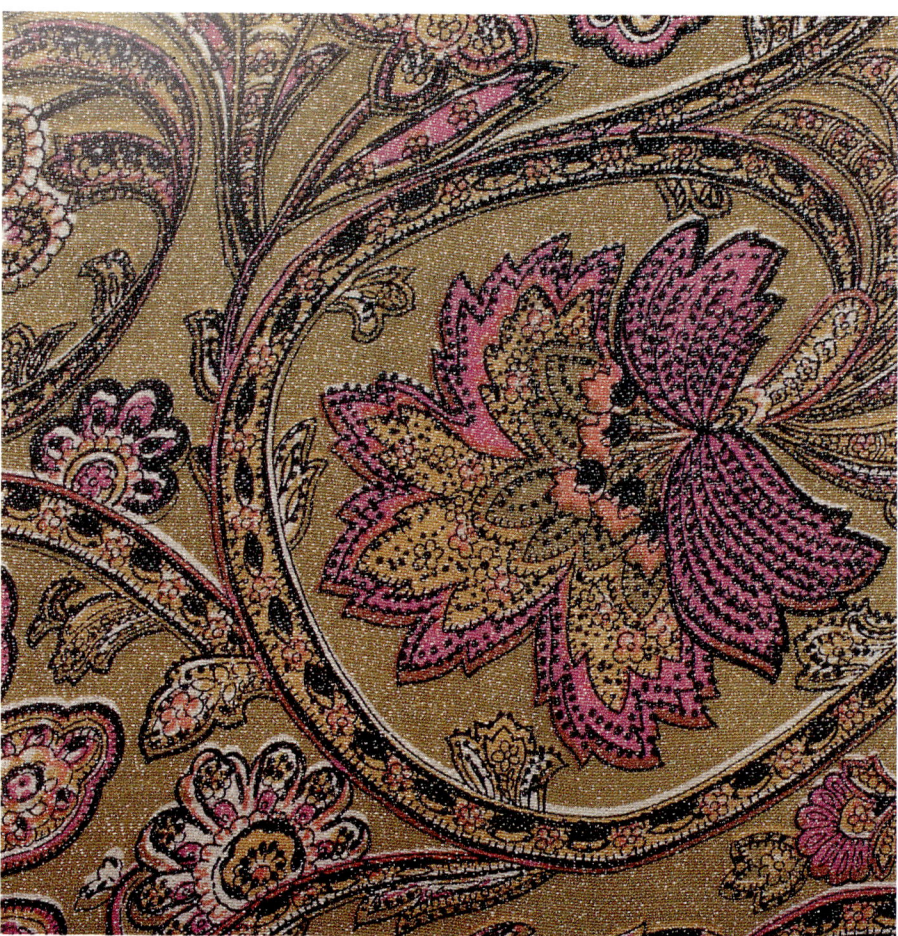

Mixed brocade with floral/paisley pattern on olive green ground. Rayon/spun rayon, Japan, 1960s.

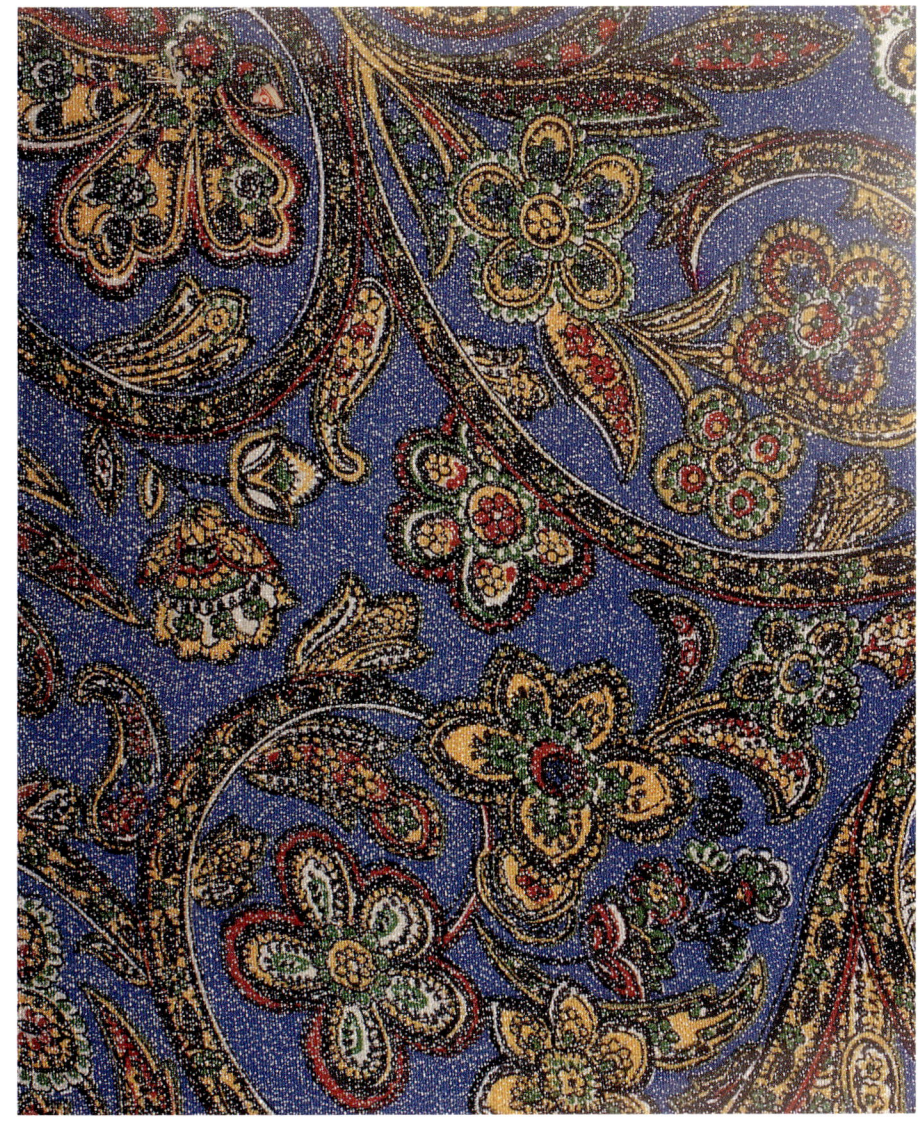
Mixed brocade with floral/paisley pattern on dark blue. Rayon/spun rayon, Japan, 1960s.

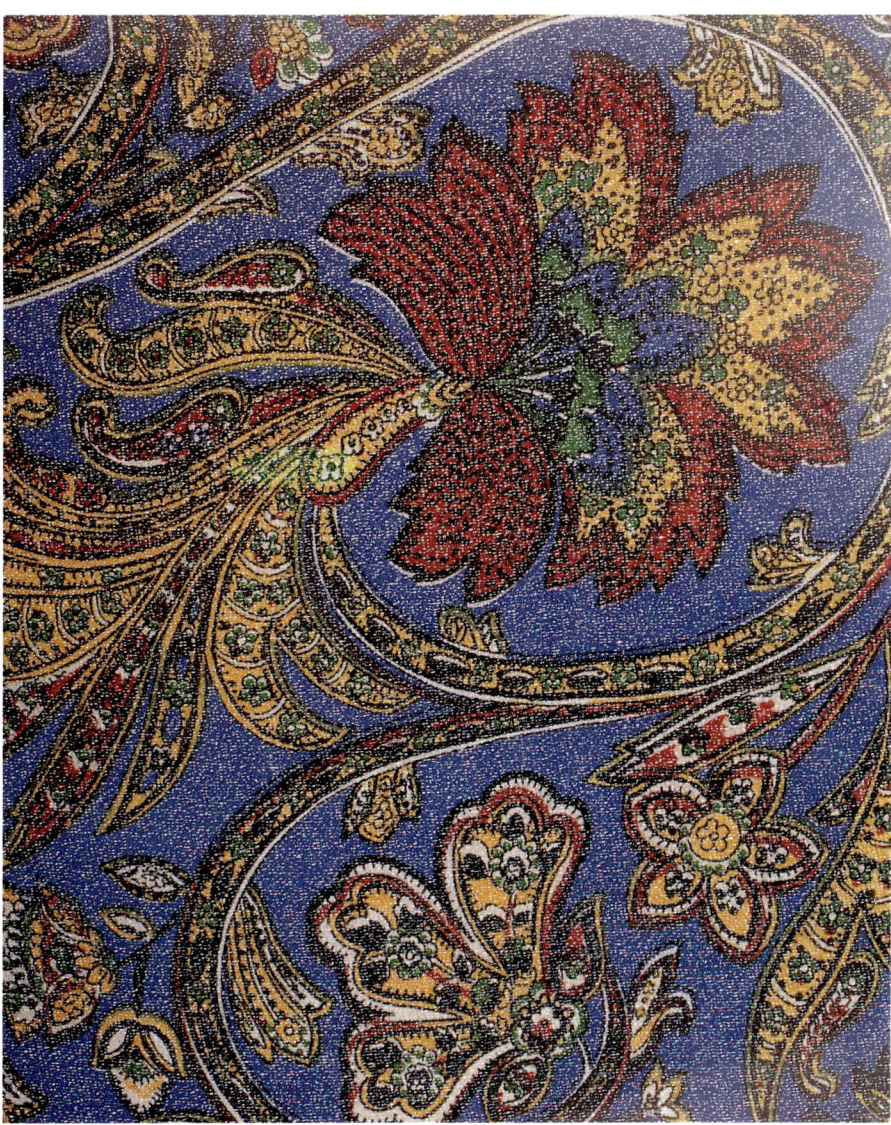
Mixed brocade with floral/paisley pattern on dark blue. Rayon/spun rayon, Japan, 1960s.

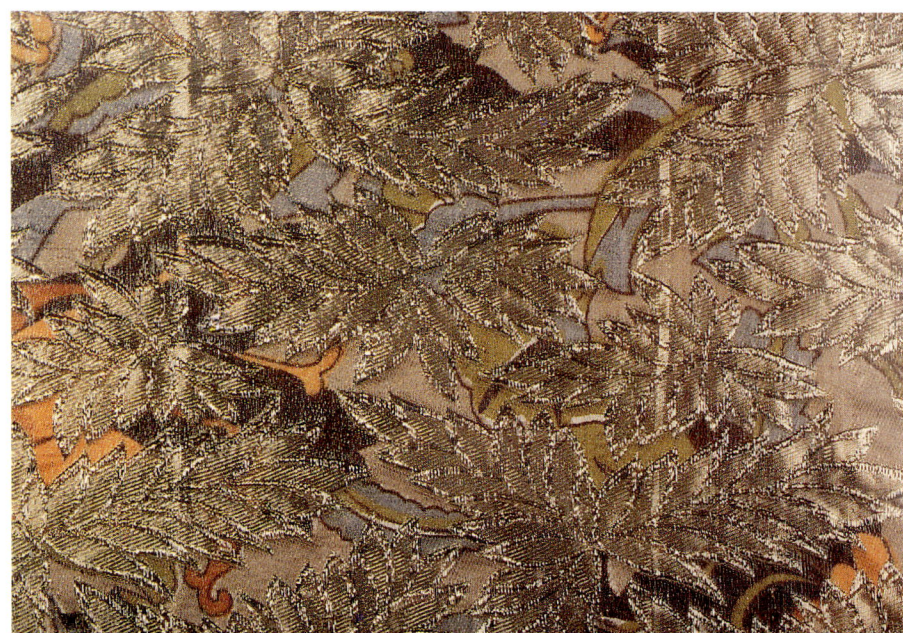
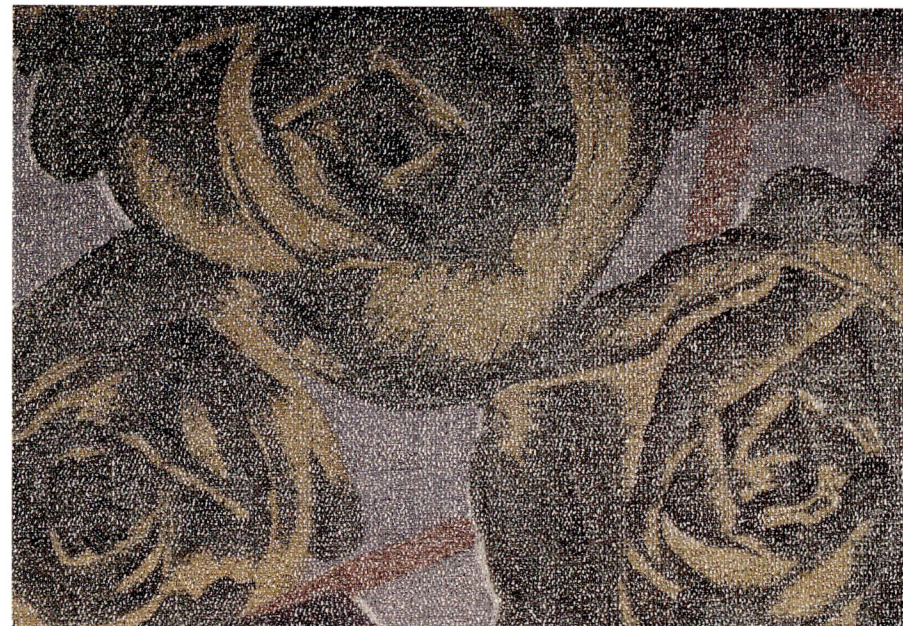
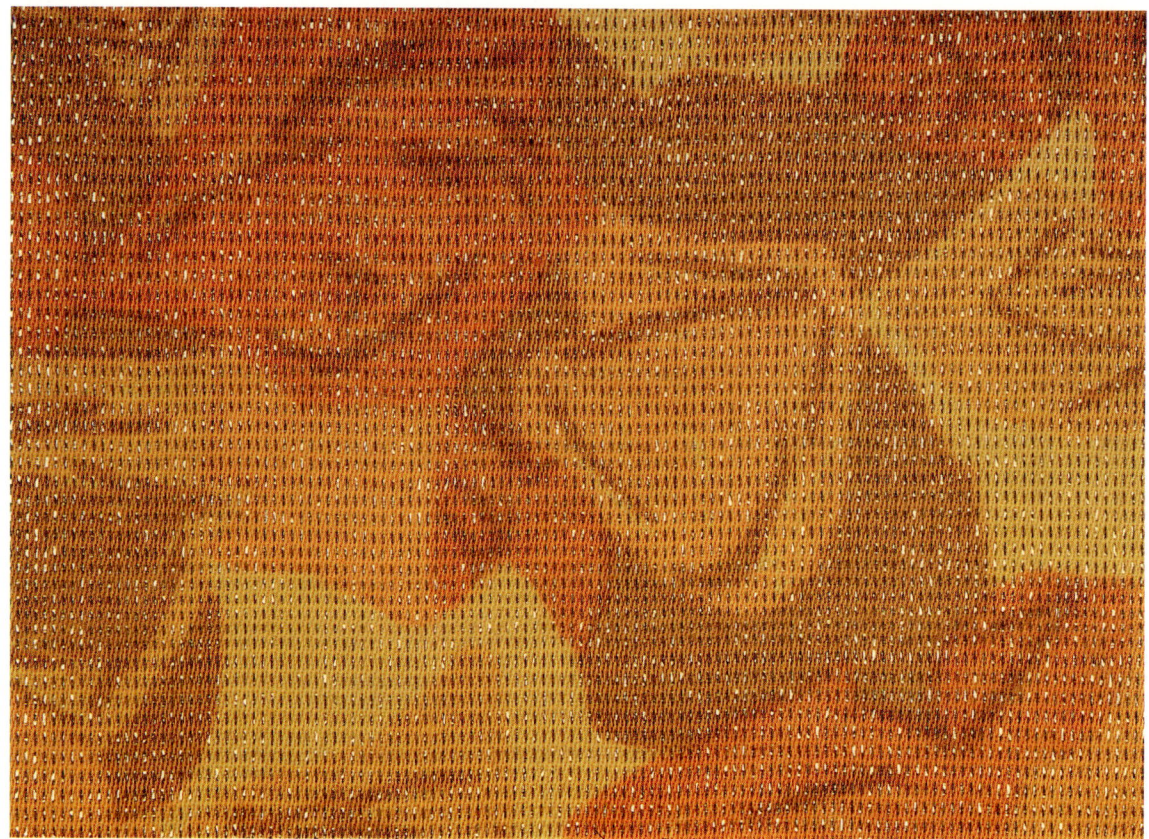

Top left: "Gilded" leaf design brocade with orange and green. Hand-printed rayon/polyester film, Japan, 1960s.

Top right: Floral print on gray ground. Japan, 1950s.

Bottom right: Rose design with vertical gold metallic threads. Cotton/polyester, France, 1963.

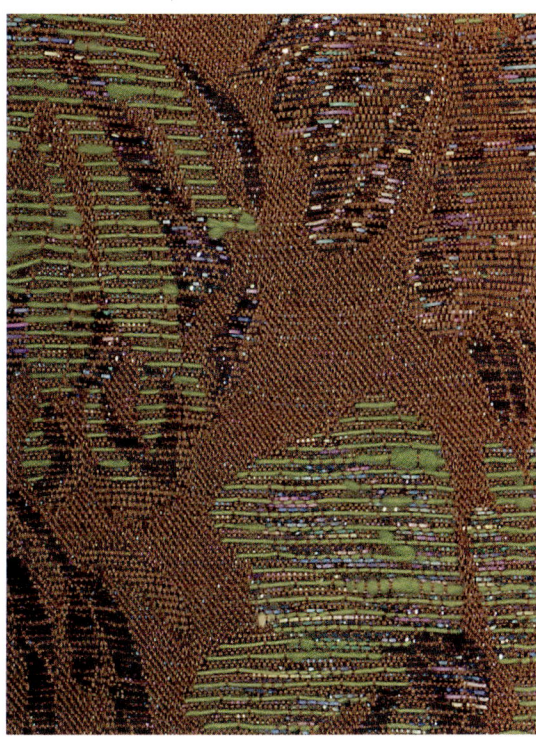
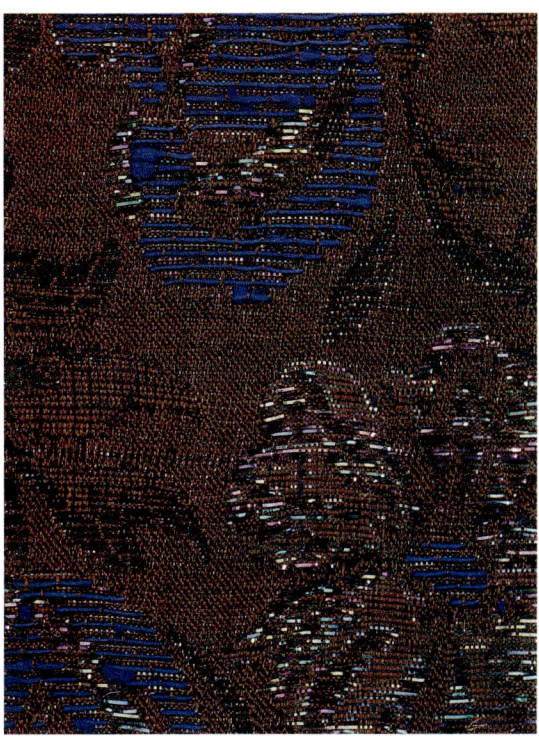
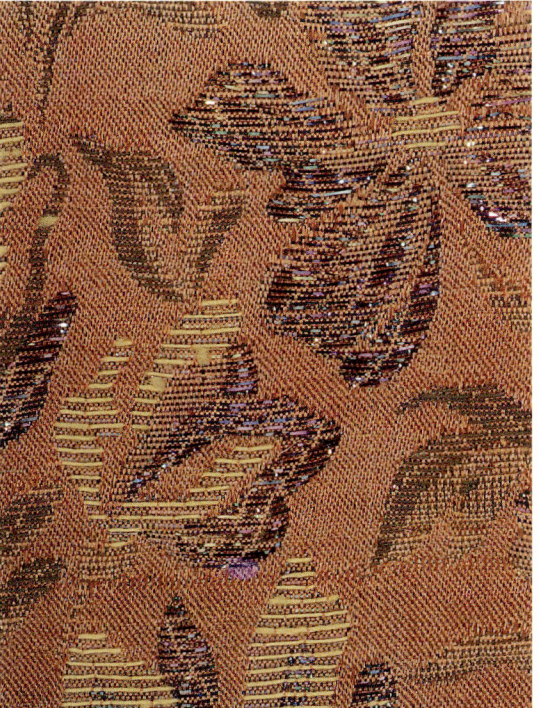

Thin, colored metallic threads add subtle interest to four color variations in a floral design. Japan, 1950s.

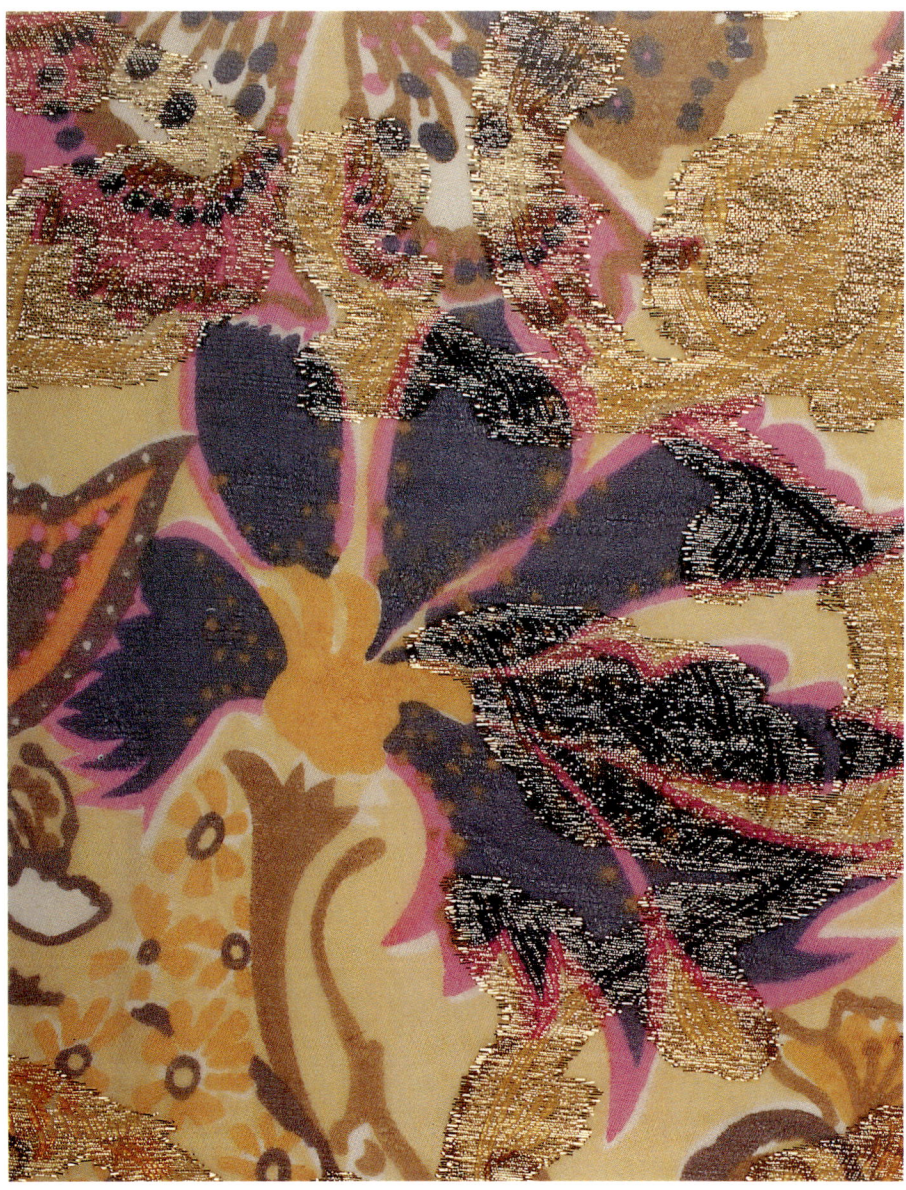

Gilded vine overlays print pattern of hot pink and neutrals on yellow ground. Nylon/polyester film mixed brocade, Japan, 1960s.

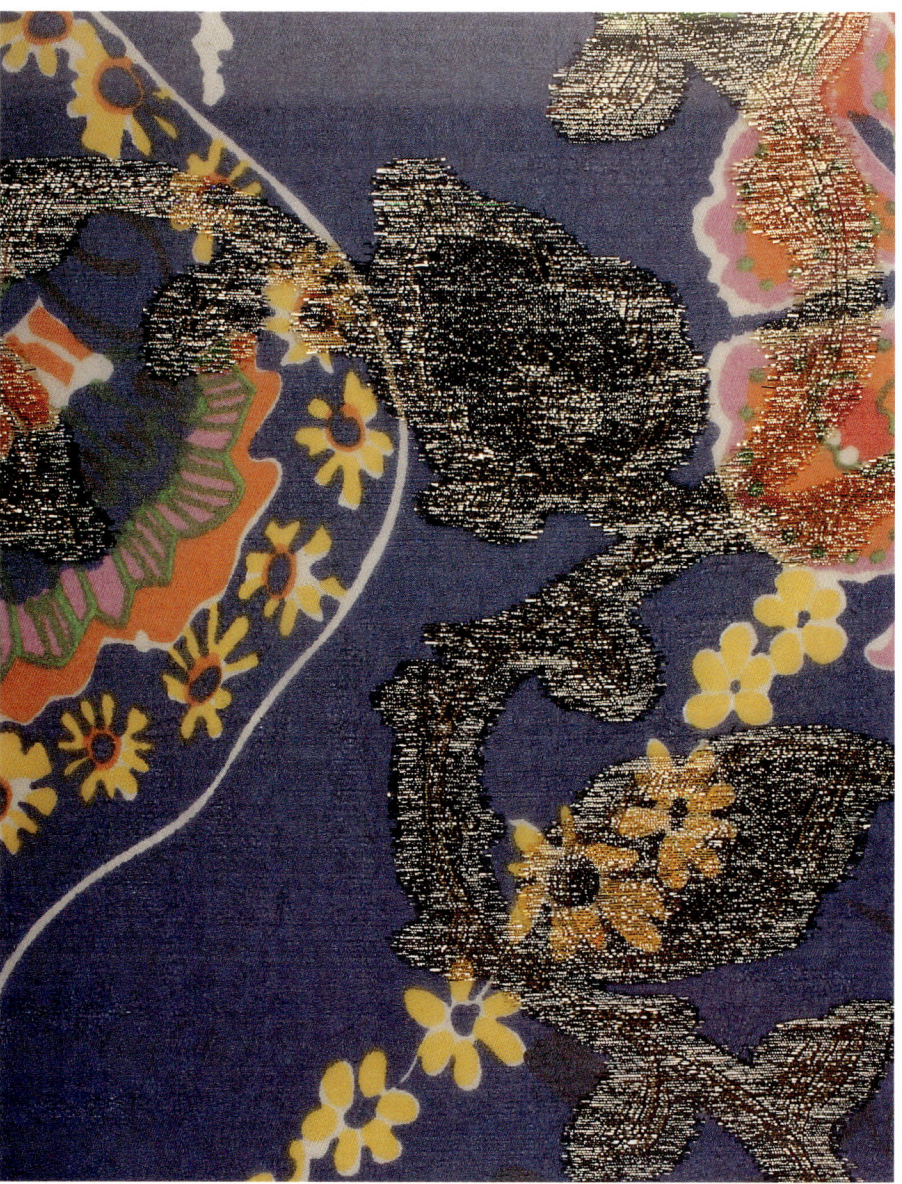

Gilded vine overlays print pattern on navy ground. Nylon/polyester film mixed brocade, Japan, 1960s.

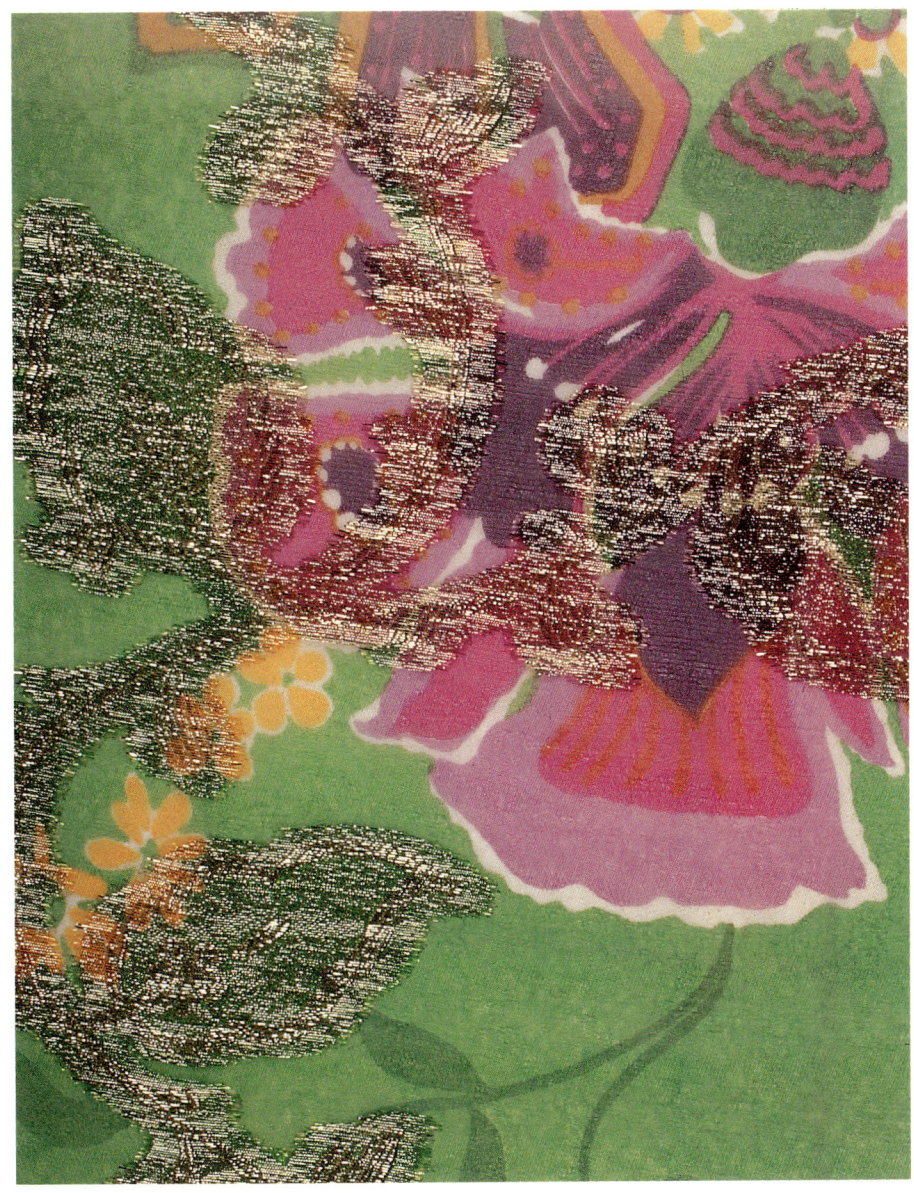

Gilded vine overlays print pattern on green ground. Nylon/polyester film mixed brocade, Japan, 1960s.

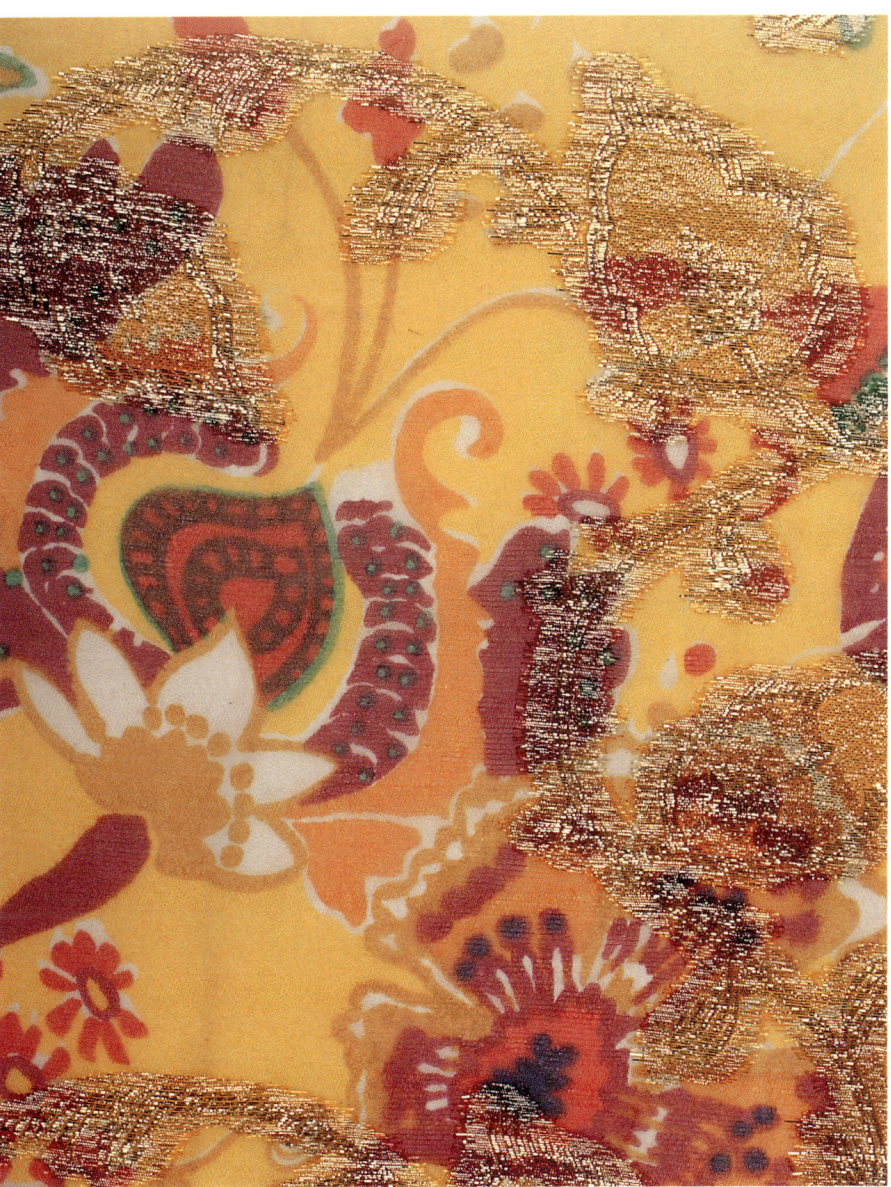

Gilded vine overlays print pattern on yellow ground. Nylon/polyester film mixed brocade, Japan, 1960s.

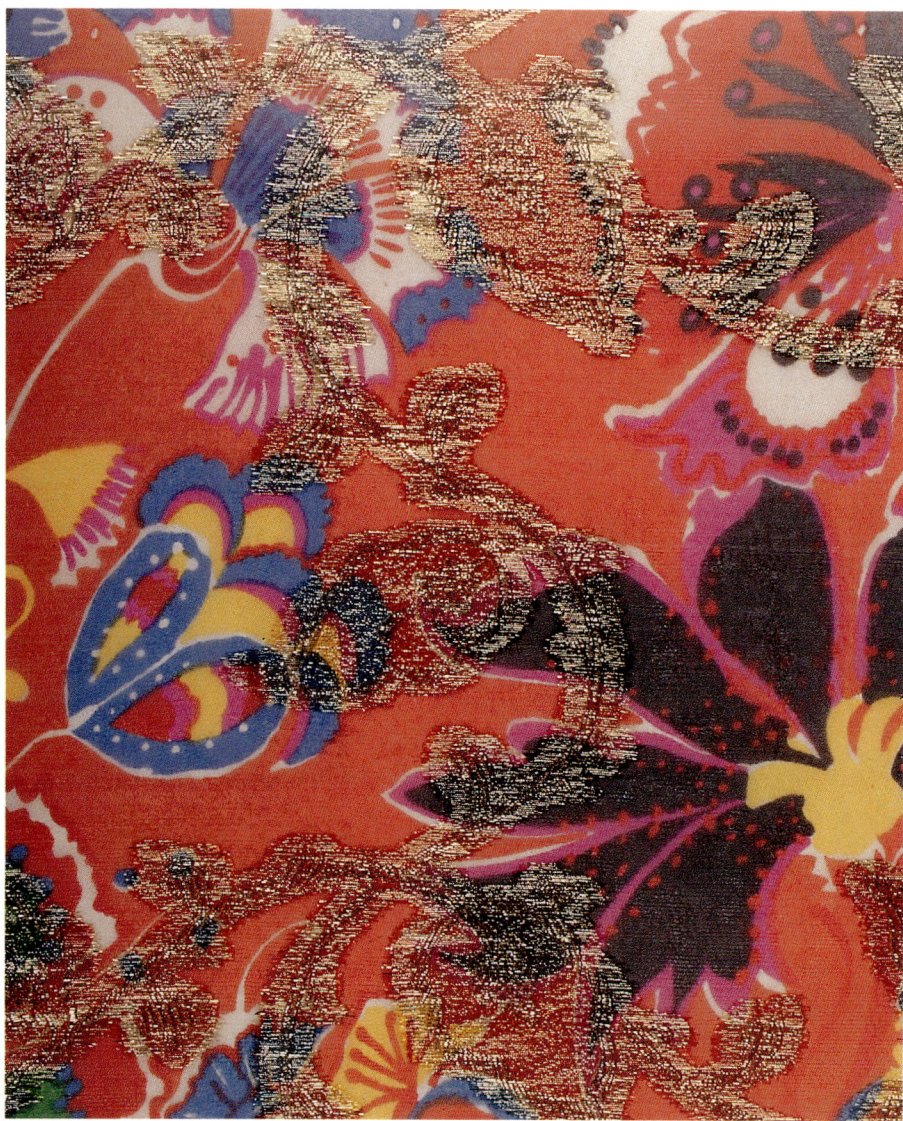

Gilded vine overlays print pattern on red ground. Nylon/polyester film mixed brocade, Japan, 1960s.

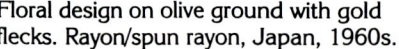

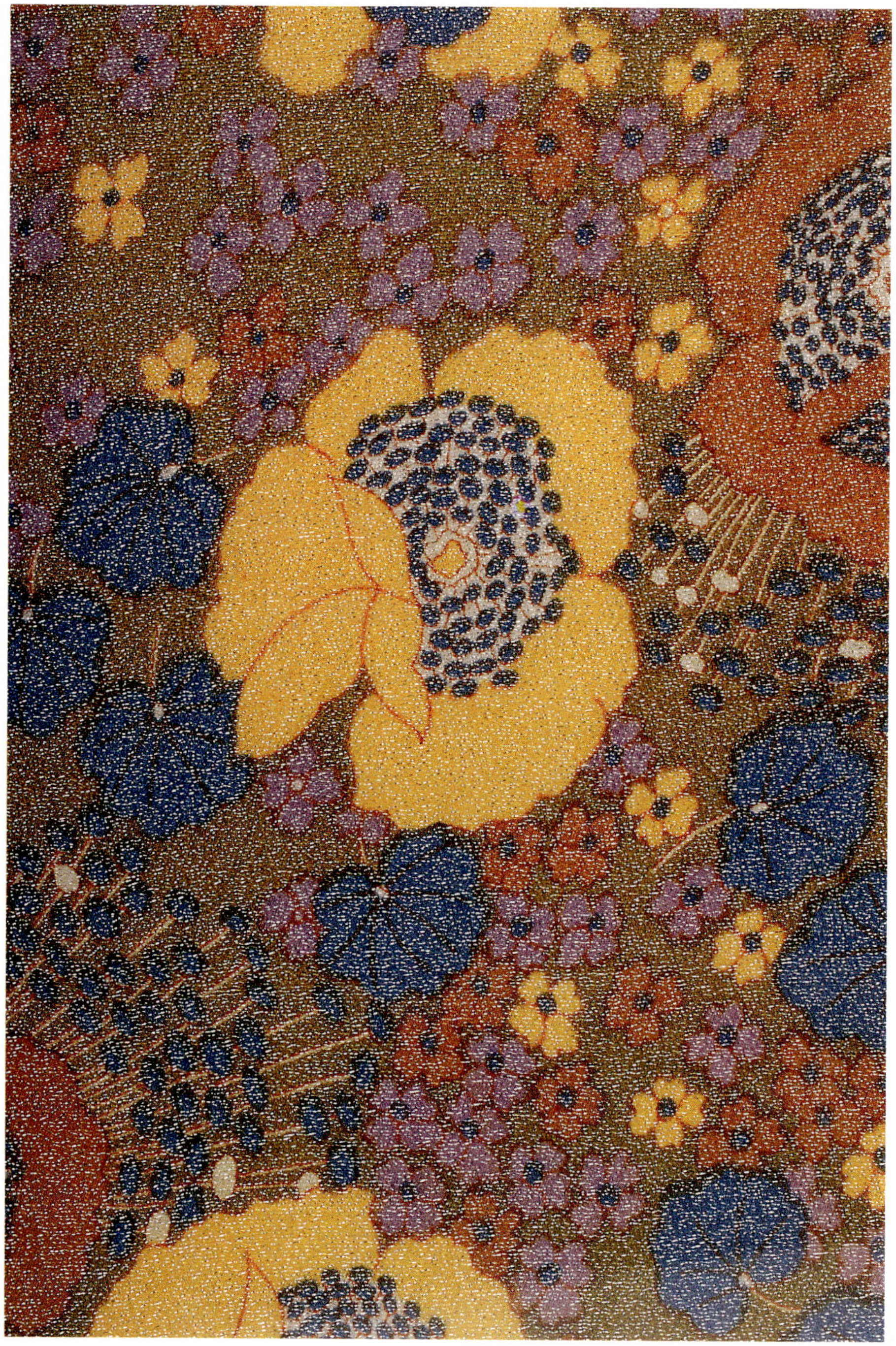

Floral design on olive ground with gold flecks. Rayon/spun rayon, Japan, 1960s.

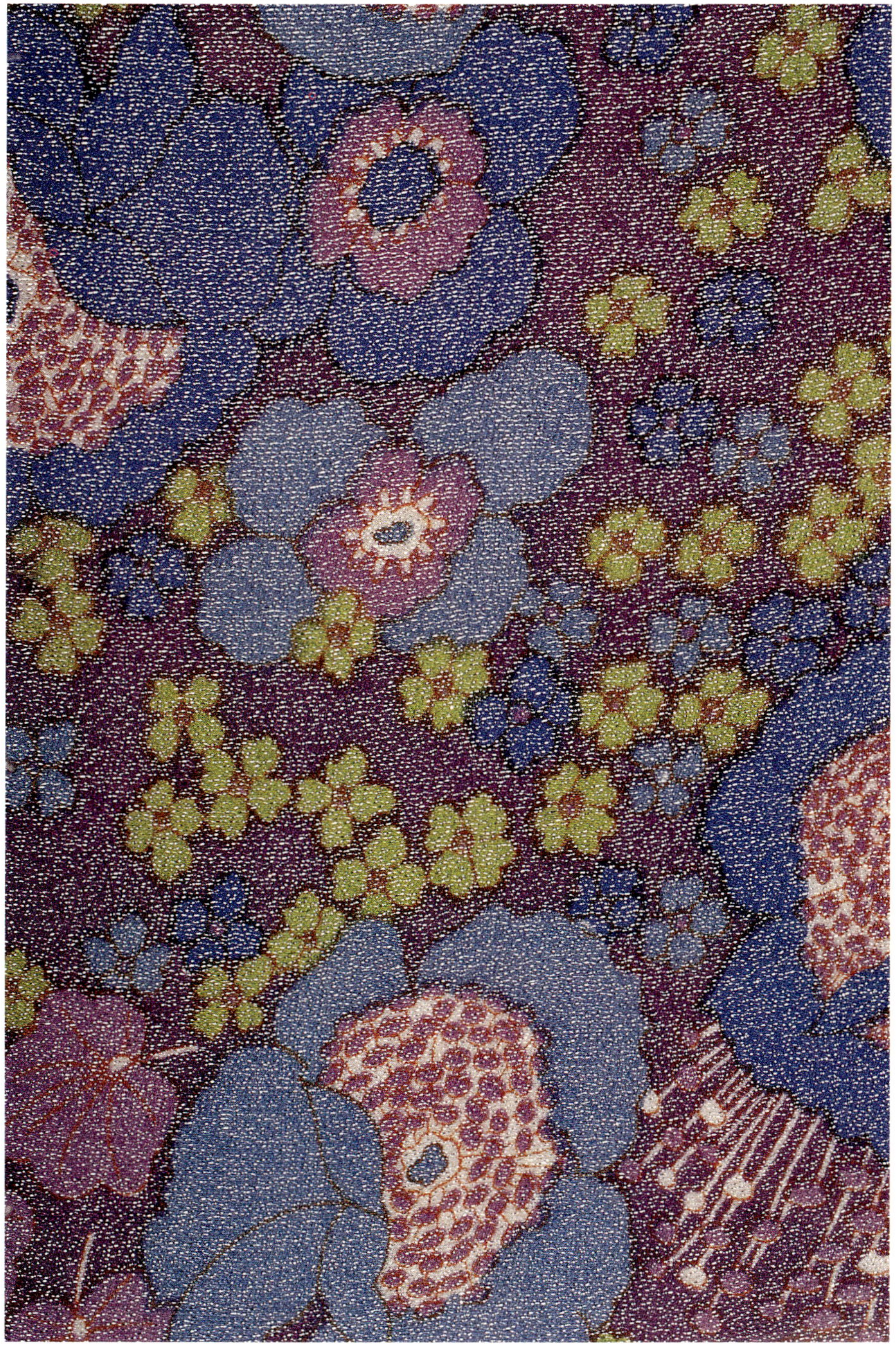

Floral design on purple ground with silver flecks. Rayon/spun rayon, Japan, 1960s.

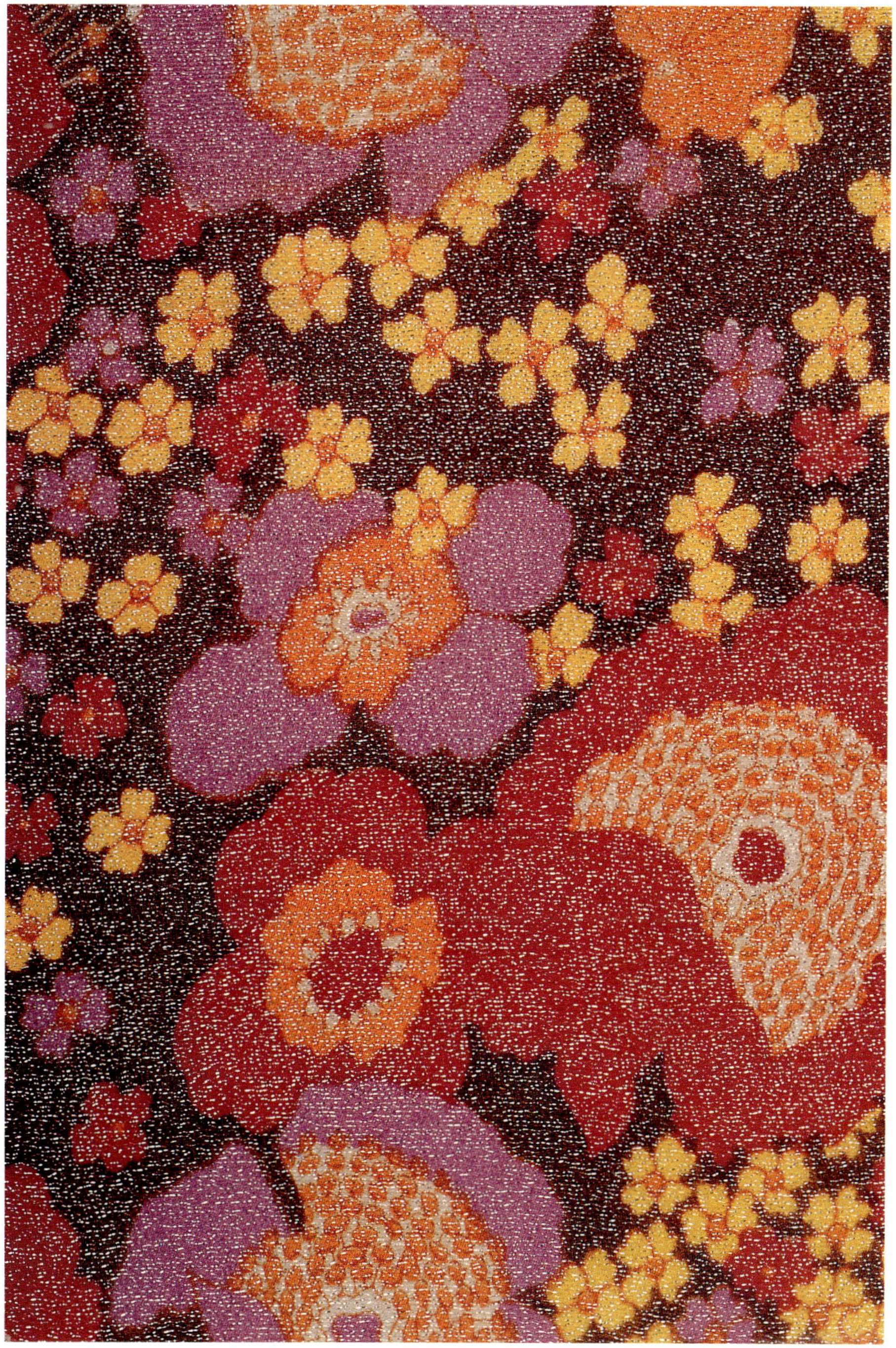

Floral design on brown ground silver gold flecks. Rayon/spun rayon, Japan, 1960s.

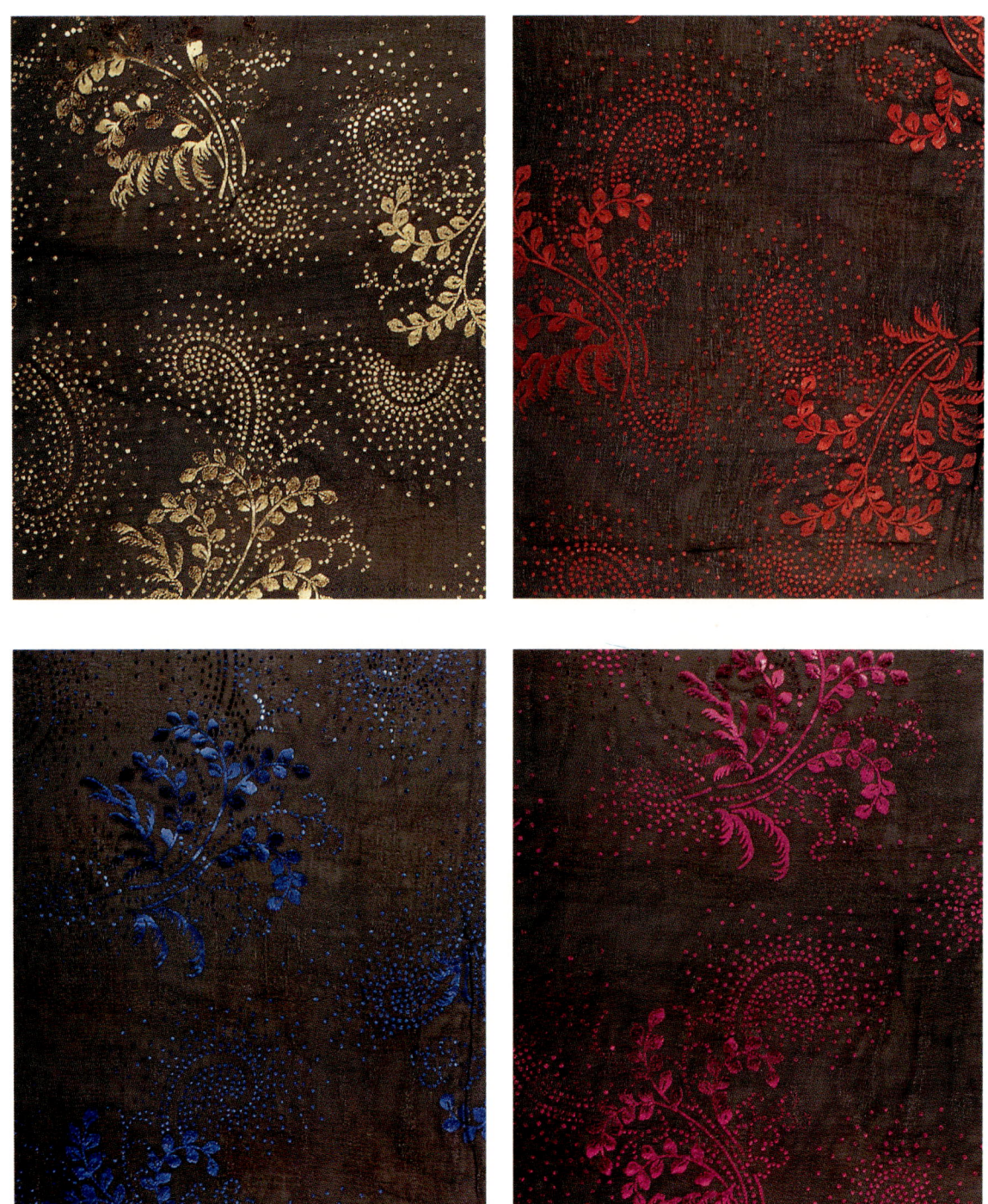

Four variations on black net with metallic gold foliage- and dot-motif print. Rayon sheer crepe with foil, Japan, 1980s.

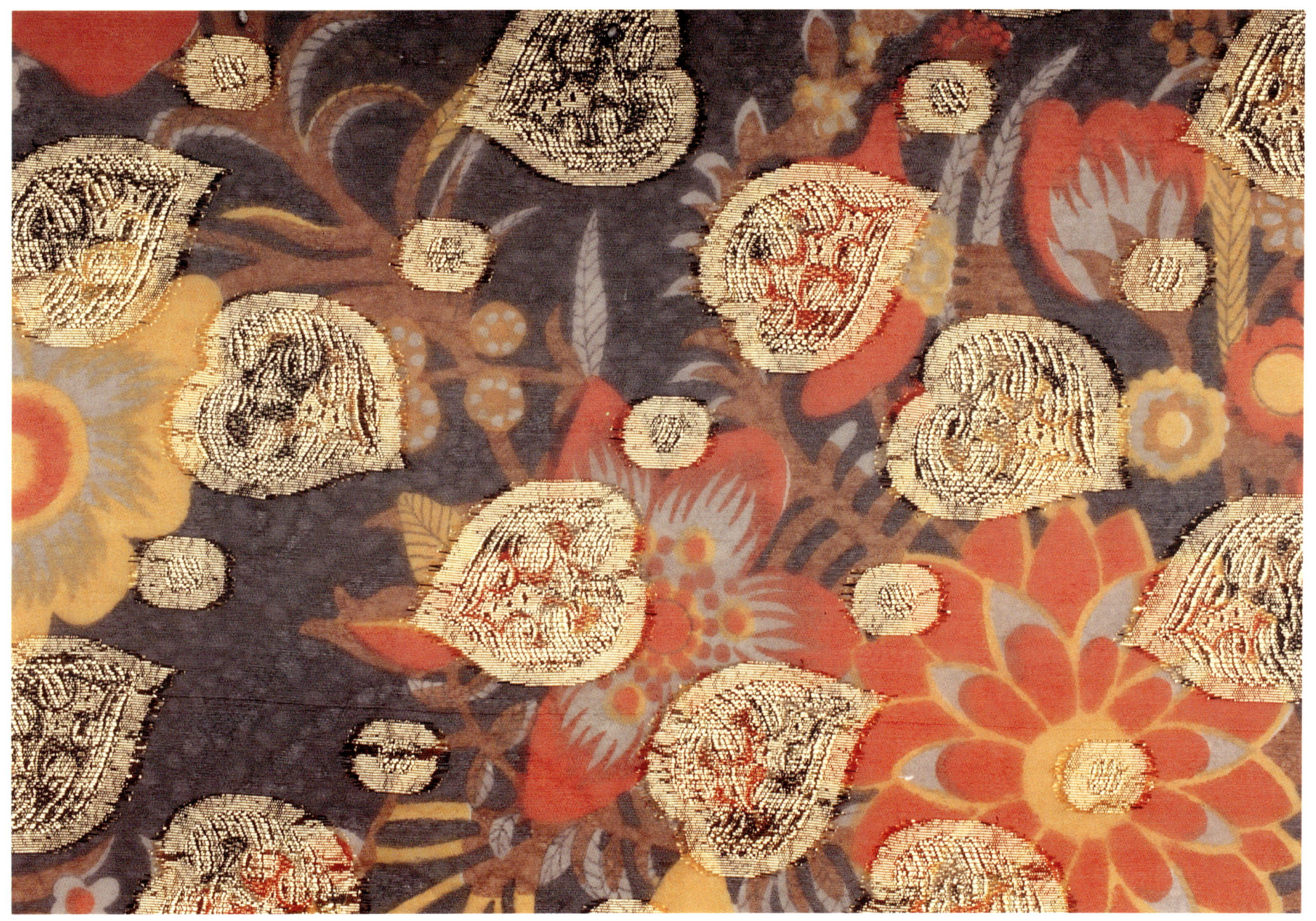
Floral print on film with gold hearts. Orange and yellow on black ground. Nylon/polyester, Japan, 1960s.

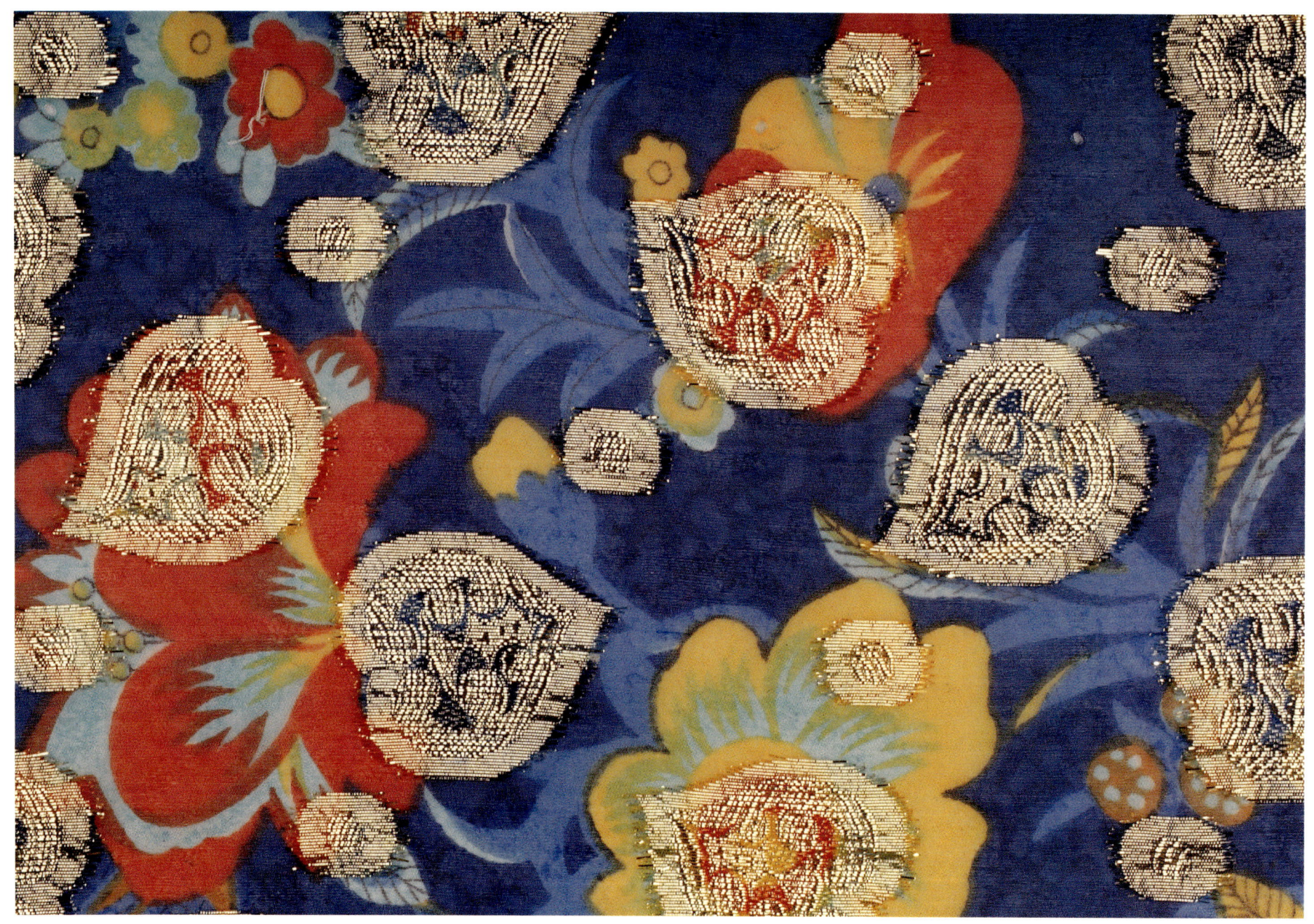
Floral print on film with gold hearts. Yellow and red on blue ground. Nylon/polyester, Japan, 1960s.

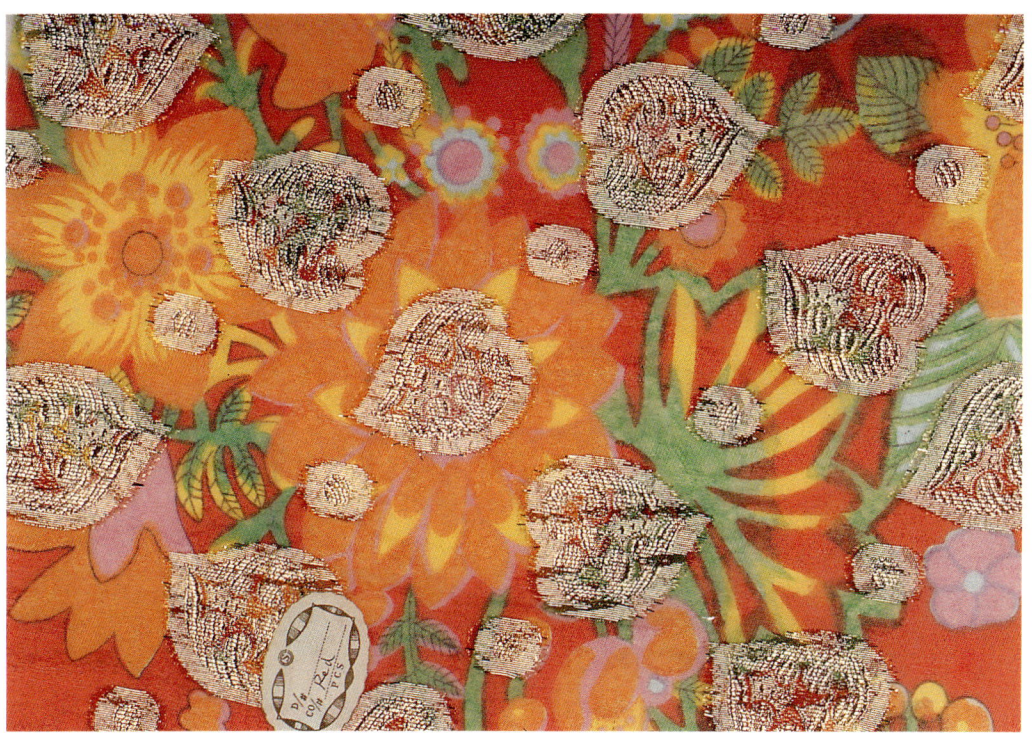

Floral print with gold hearts. Reds and green. Nylon/polyester, Japan, 1960s.

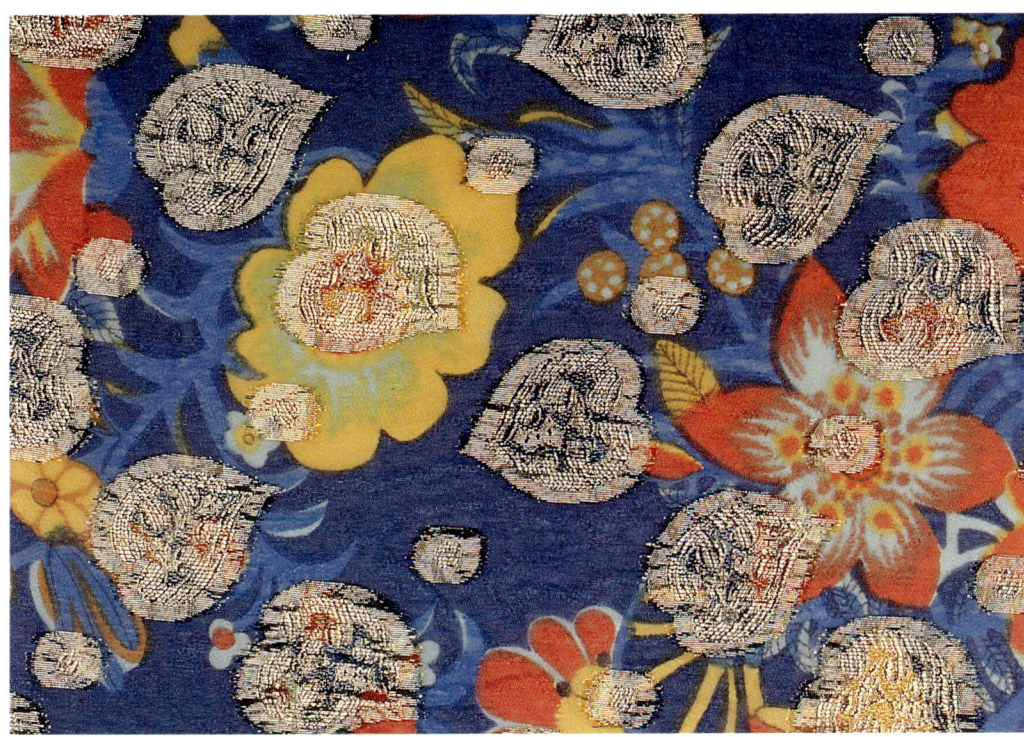

Floral print with gold hearts. Orange and blues. Nylon/polyester, Japan, 1960s.

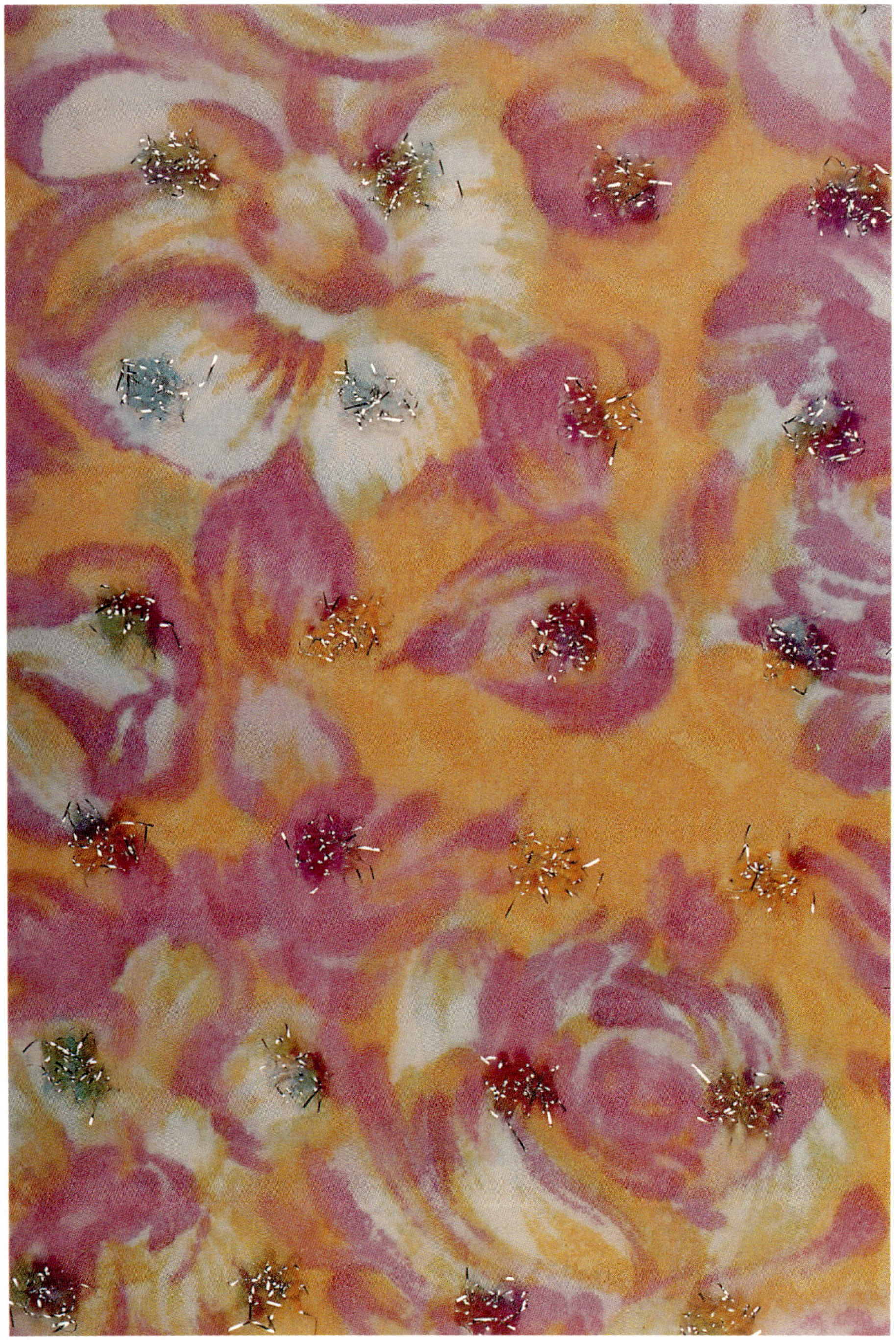

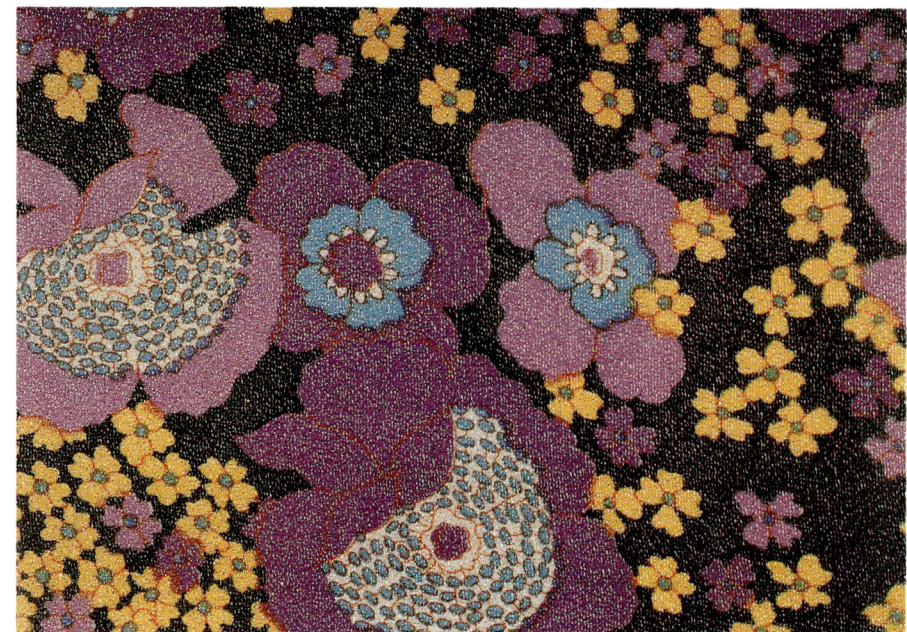

Floral design on dark green ground with silver flecks. Rayon/spun rayon, Japan, 1960s.

Floral print on film with metallic/velour dots. Nylon/polyester film, Japan, 1960s.

Chapter Five

PAISLEY

Silver threads form paisley pattern on black ground. Japan, 1970s.

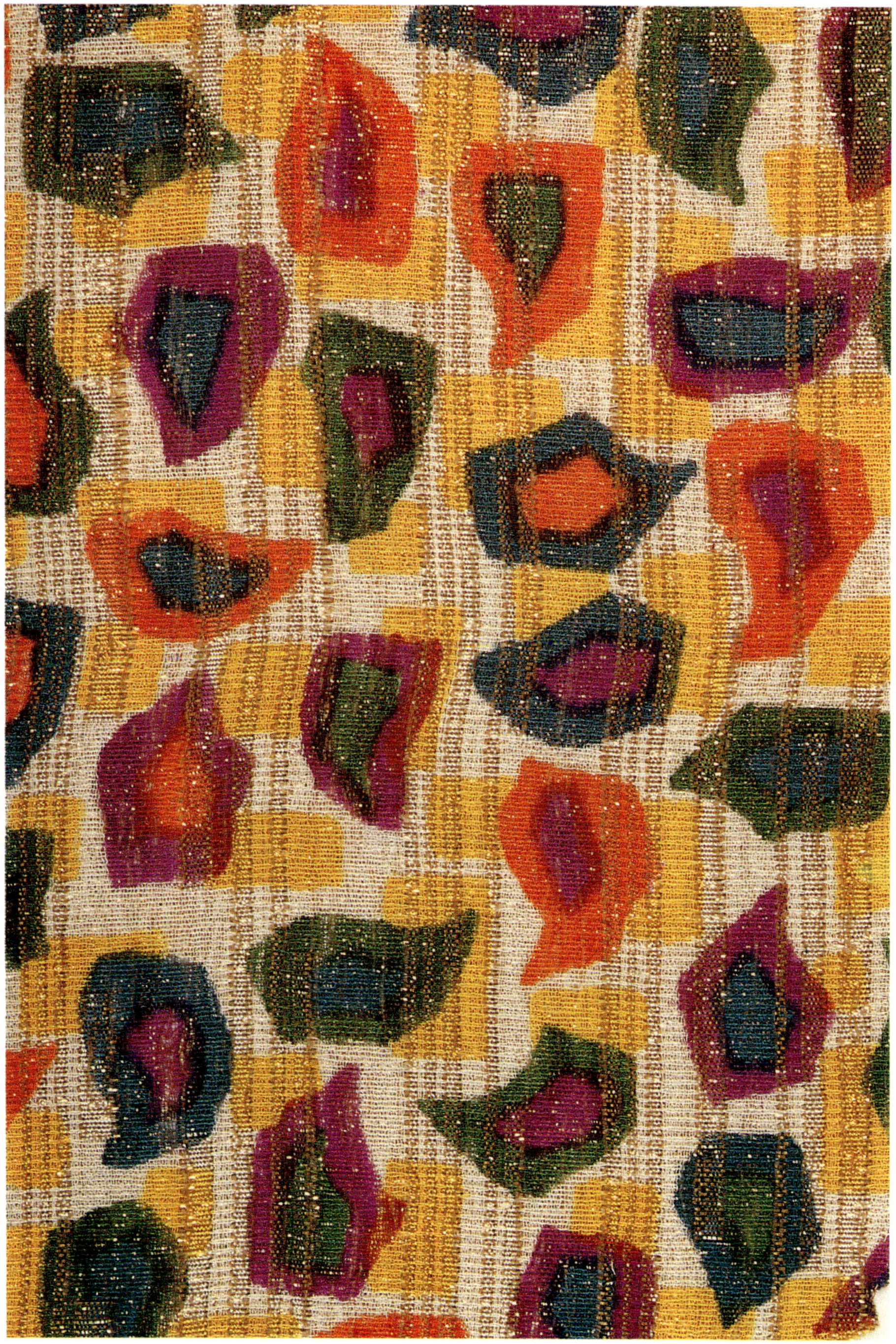

Vertical gold threads with geometric paisley print. Cotton/polyester, France, 1962.

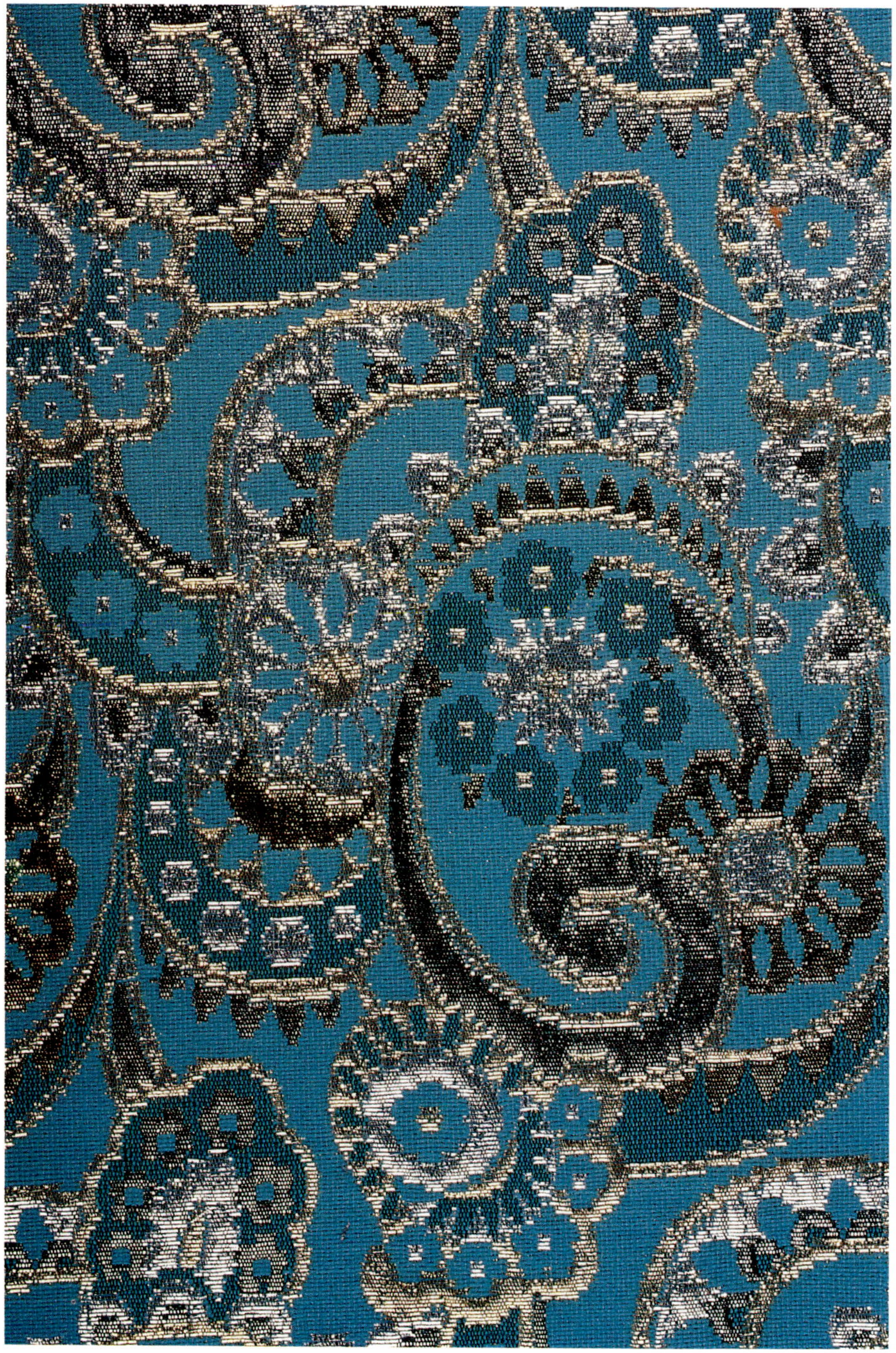

Gold, silver, and black metallic threads adorn brocade. Japan, 1970s.

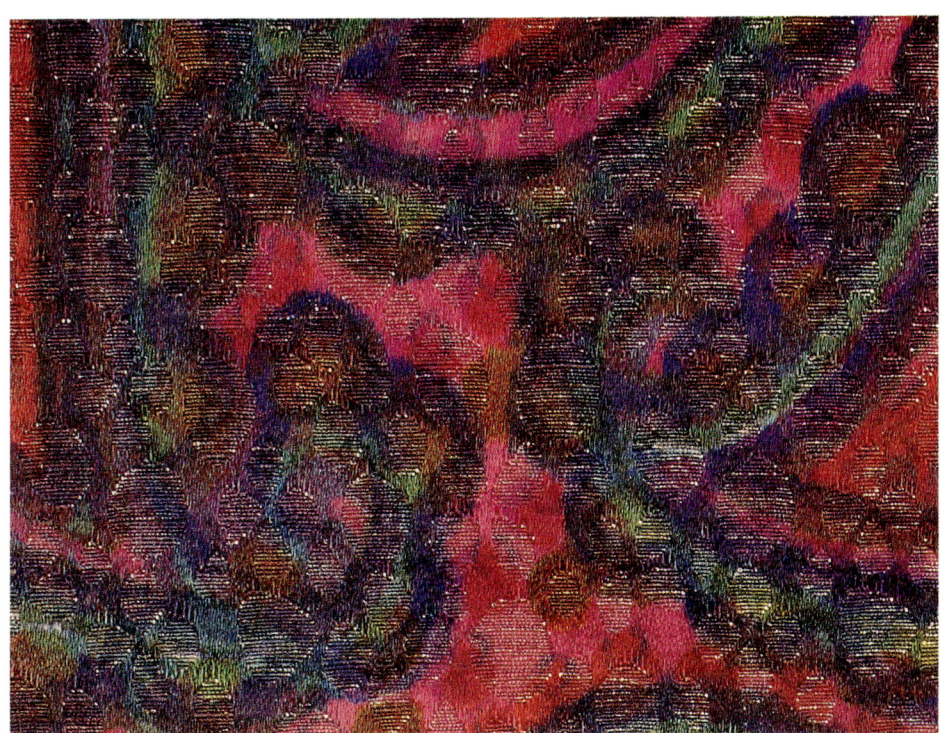

Purple, green, and brown paisley on pink with gold highlights. France, 1962.

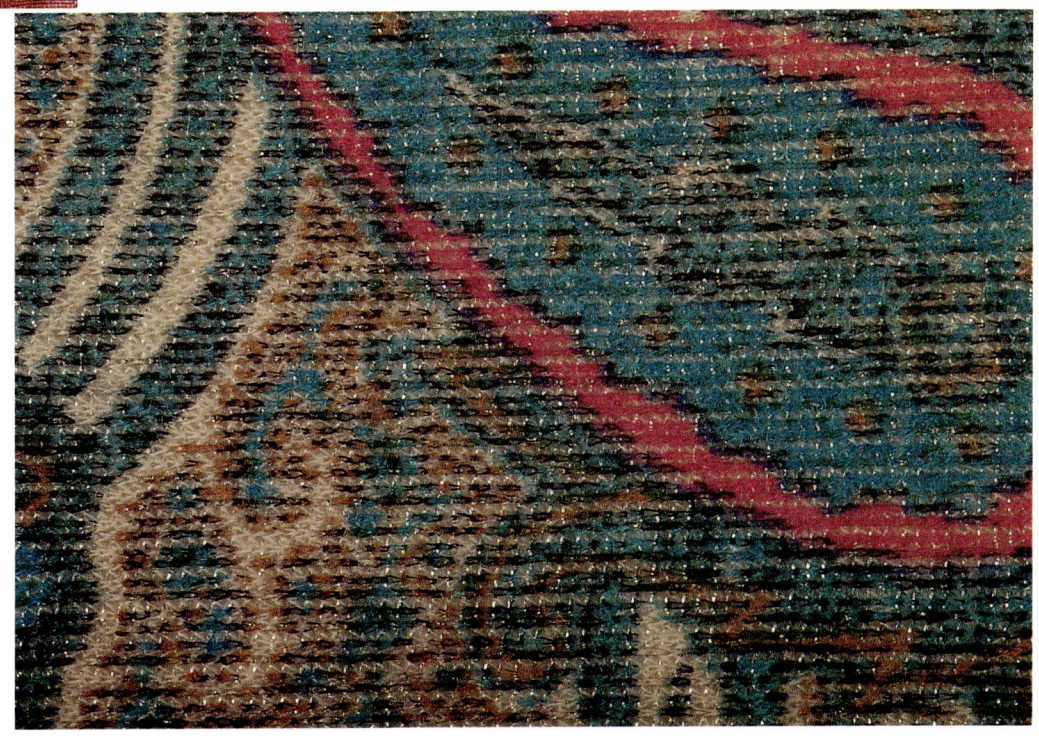

Vertical silver adds sparkle to olive and green design with hot pink paisley. Polyester blend, France. 1964.

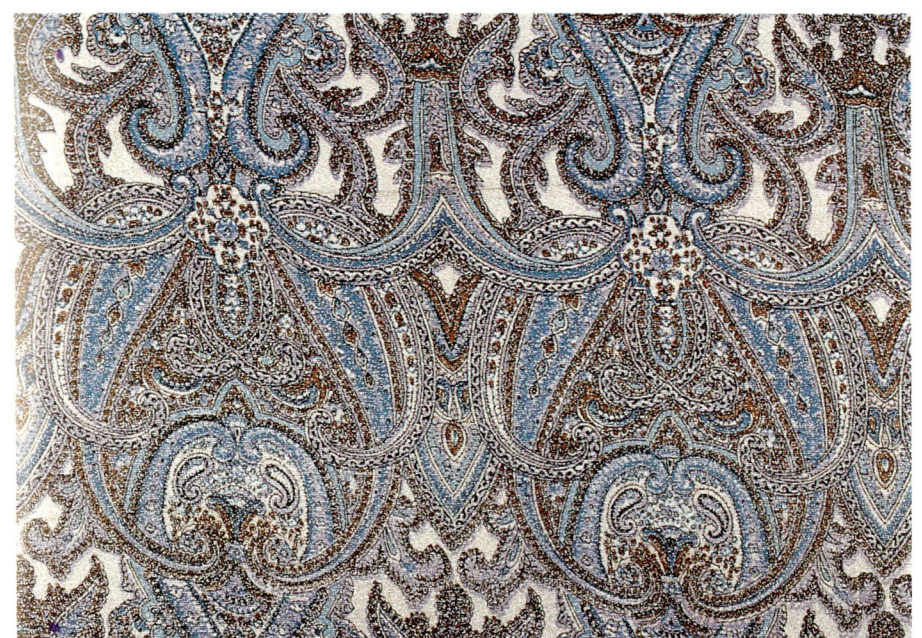
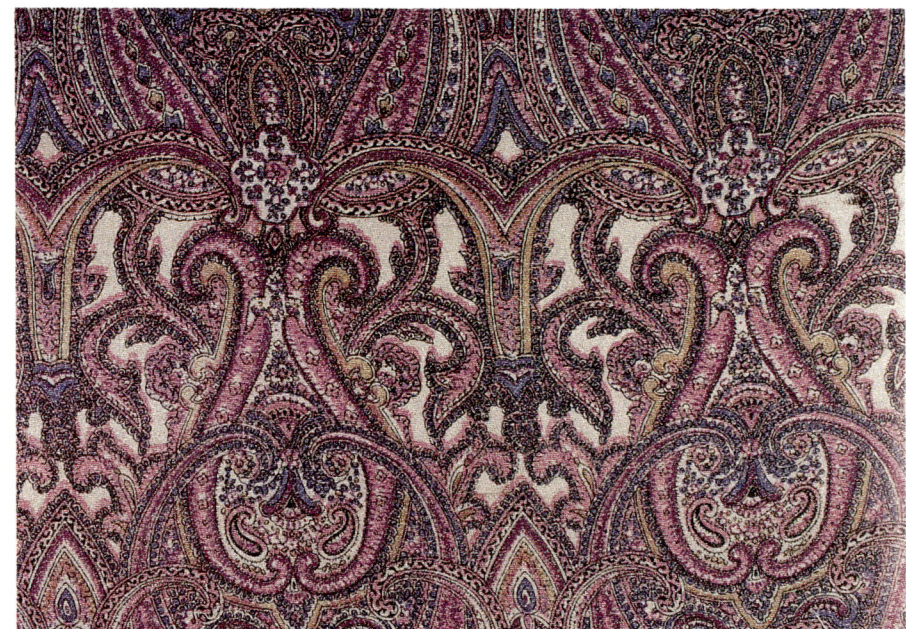

Three variations of elaborate paisley design with silver. Rayon/spun rayon, Japan, 1960s.

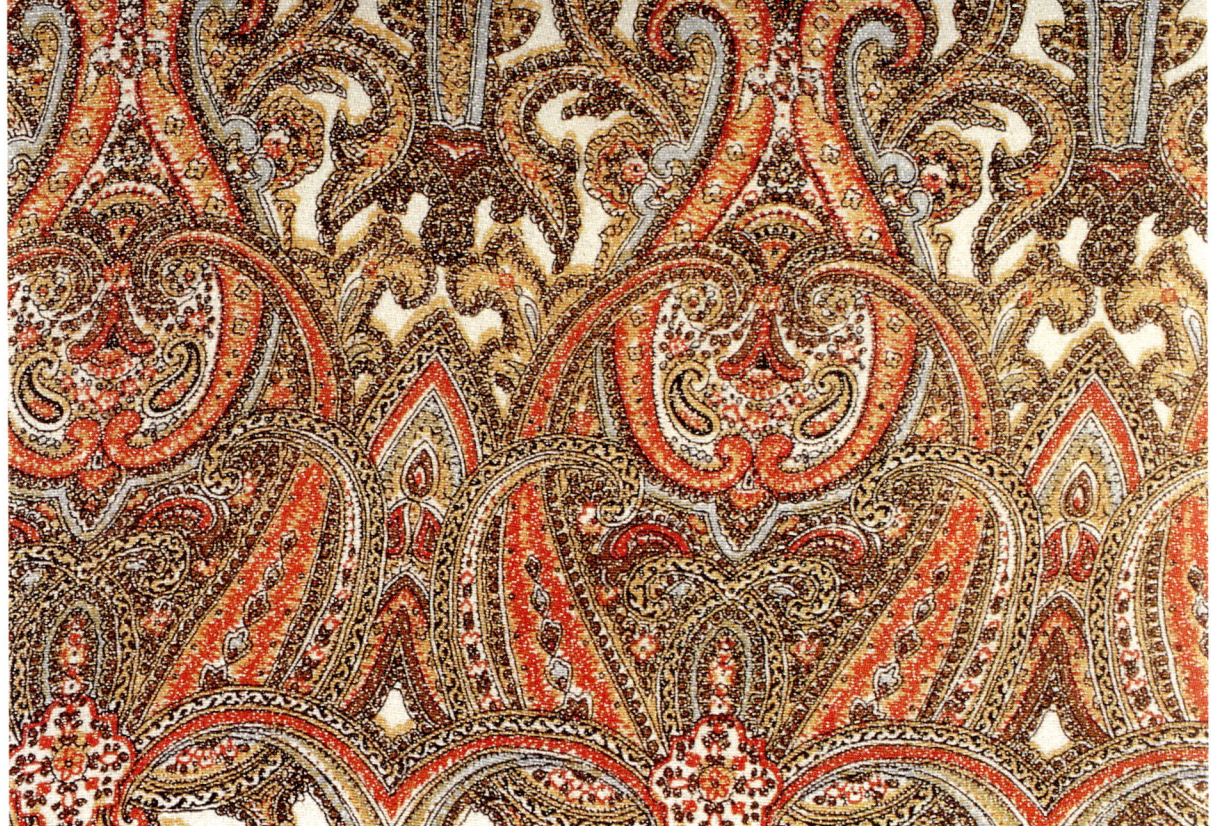

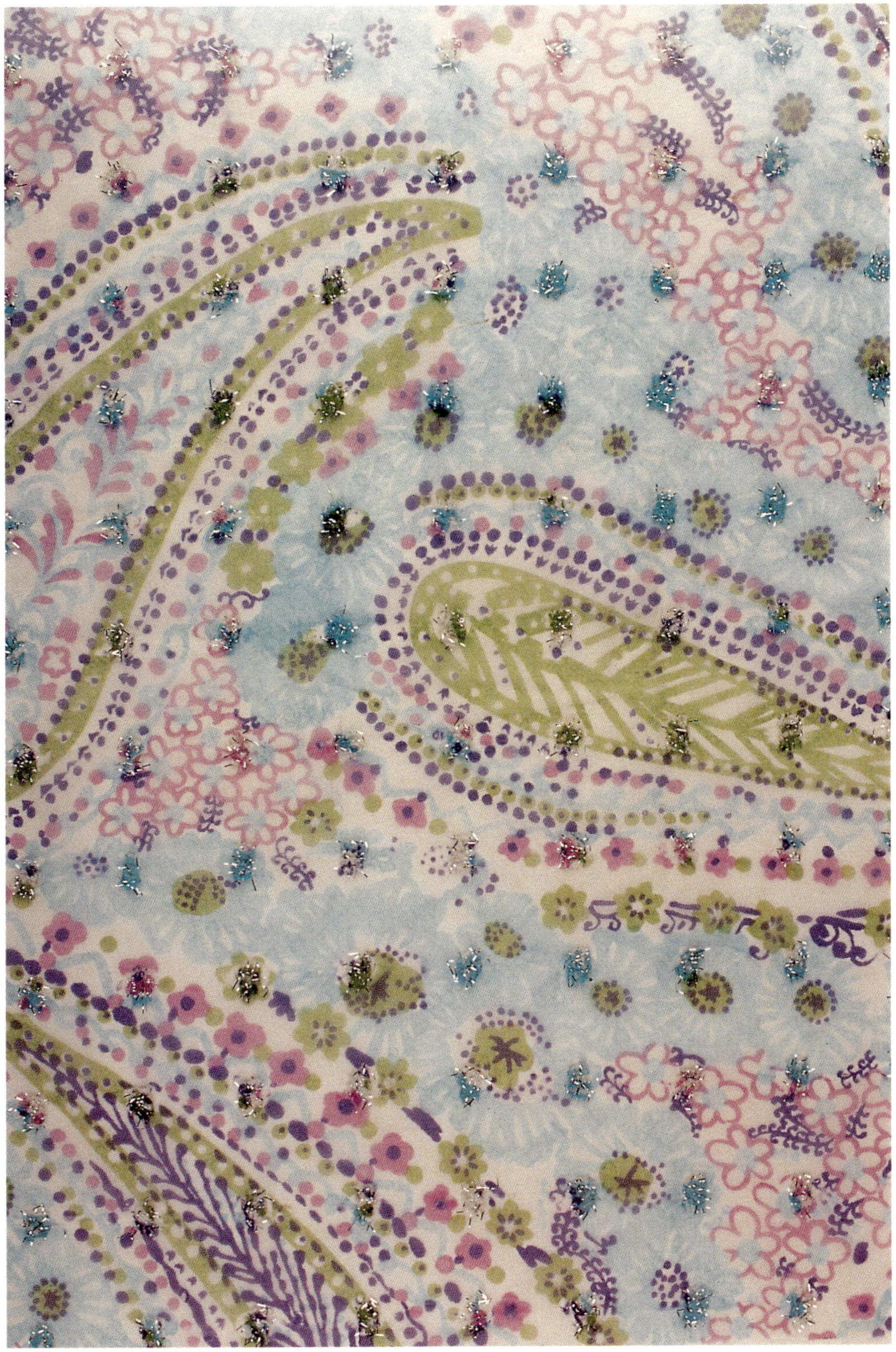

Raised silver and fiber dots on filmy print. Green, blue, and purple. Nylon/polyester film, Japan, 1960s.

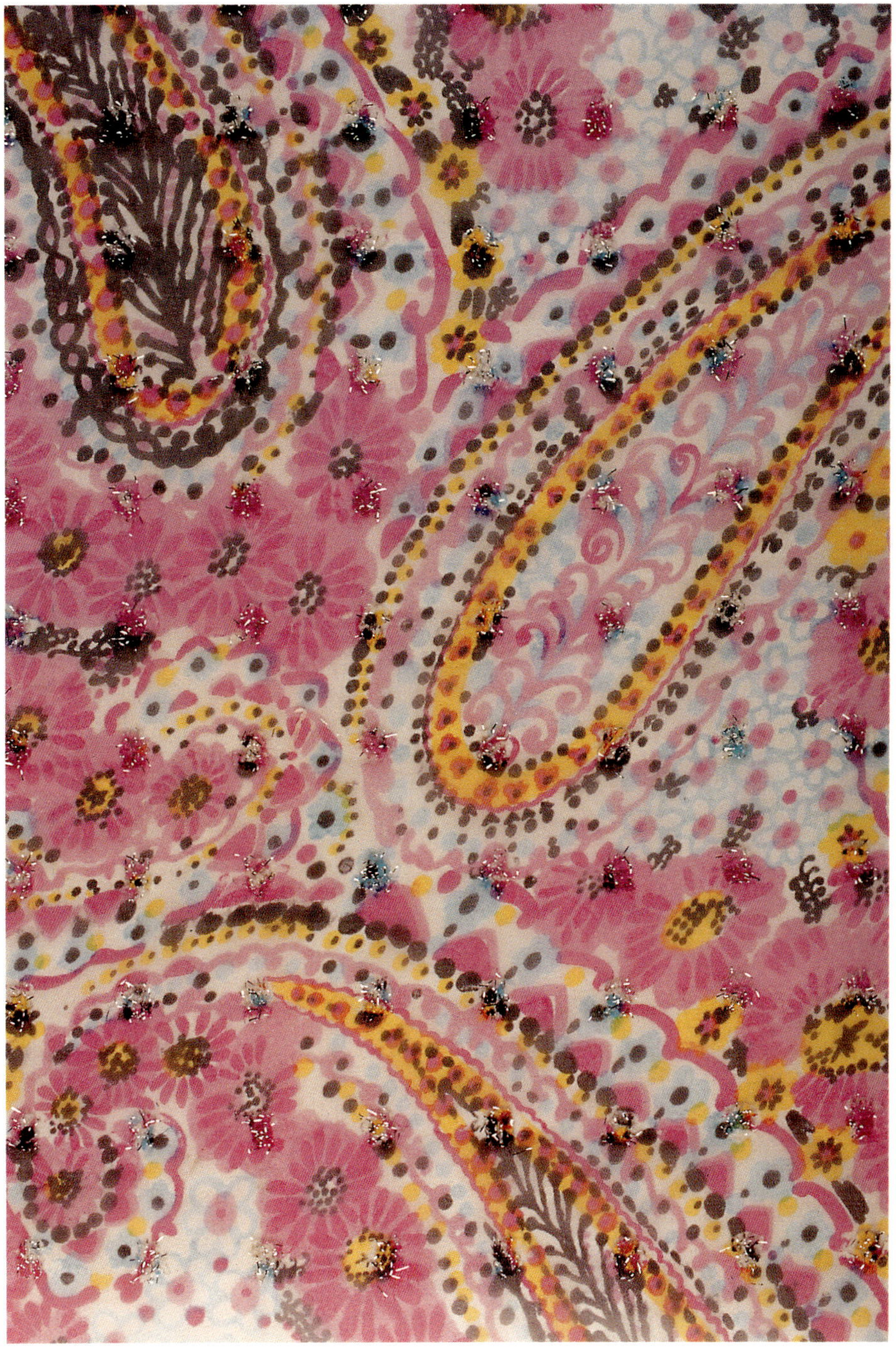

Raised silver and fiber dots on filmy print. Pink, blue, and yellow. Nylon/polyester film, Japan, 1960s.

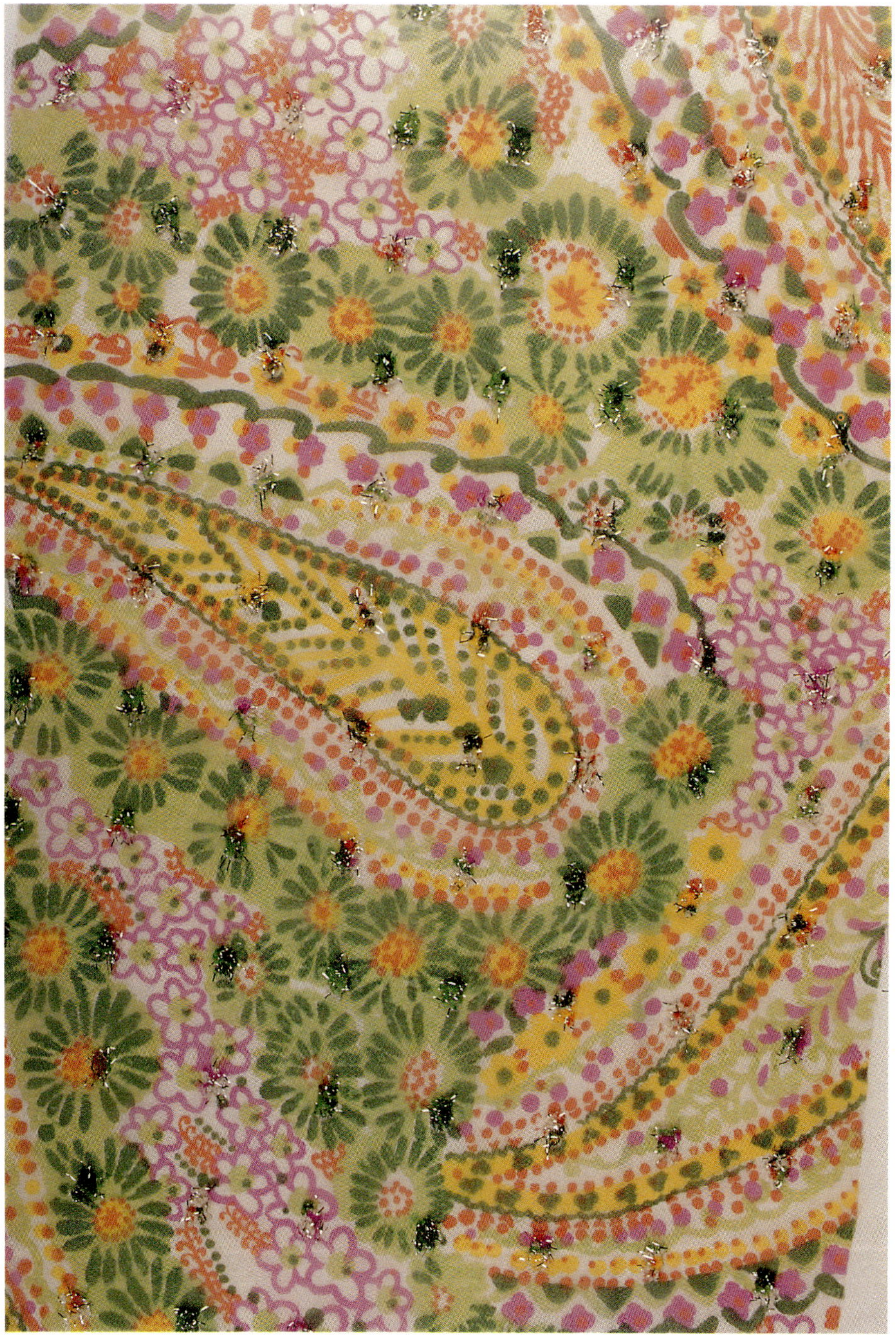

Raised silver and fiber dots on filmy print. Green, pink, and yellow. Nylon/polyester film, Japan, 1960s.

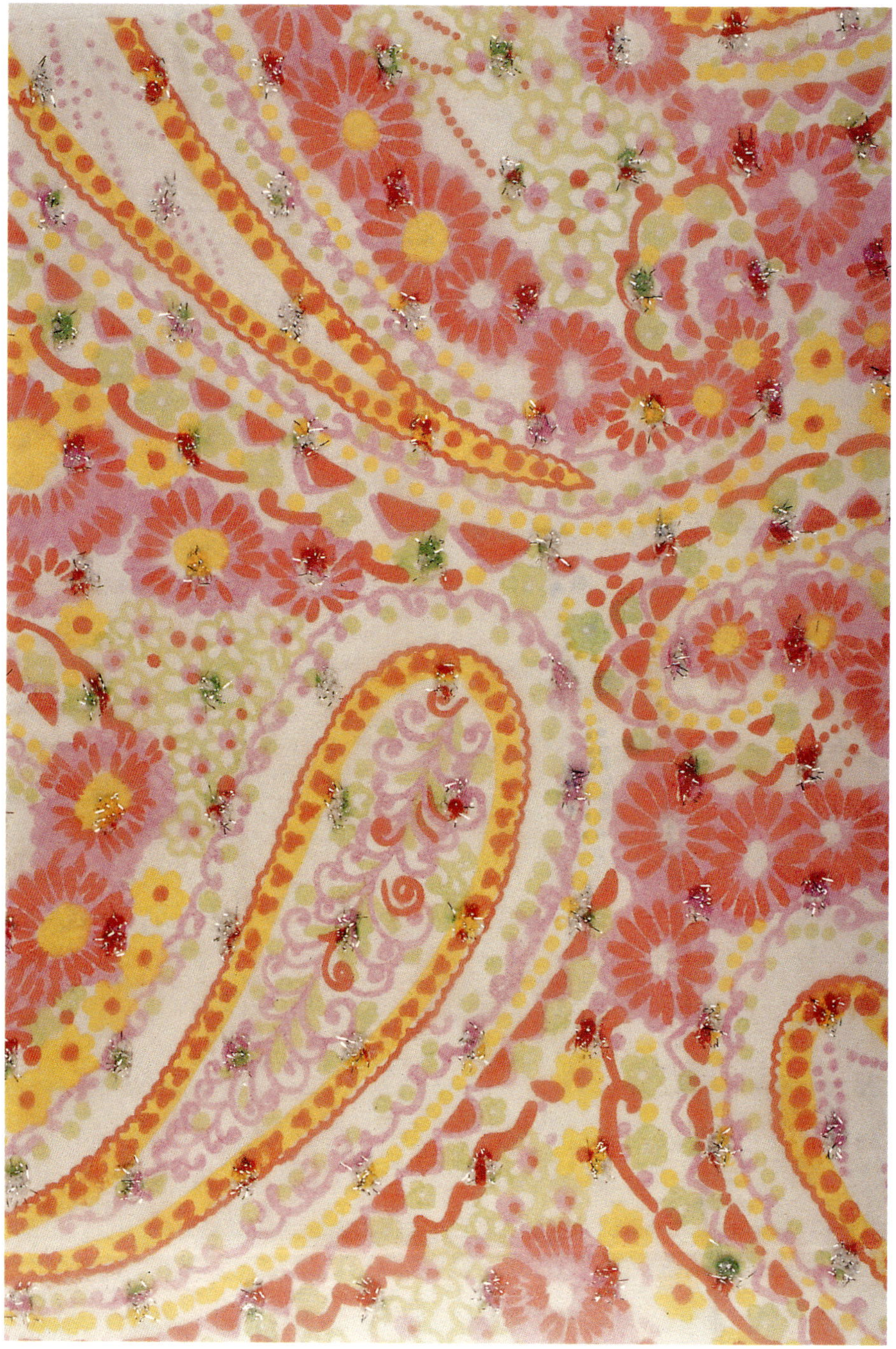

Raised silver and fiber dots on filmy print. Pink, orange, and yellow. Nylon/polyester film, Japan, 1960s.

Silver weave creates brocade effect. Paisley print in red, lime green, and yellow. Rayon/polyester/nylon, Japan, 1960s.

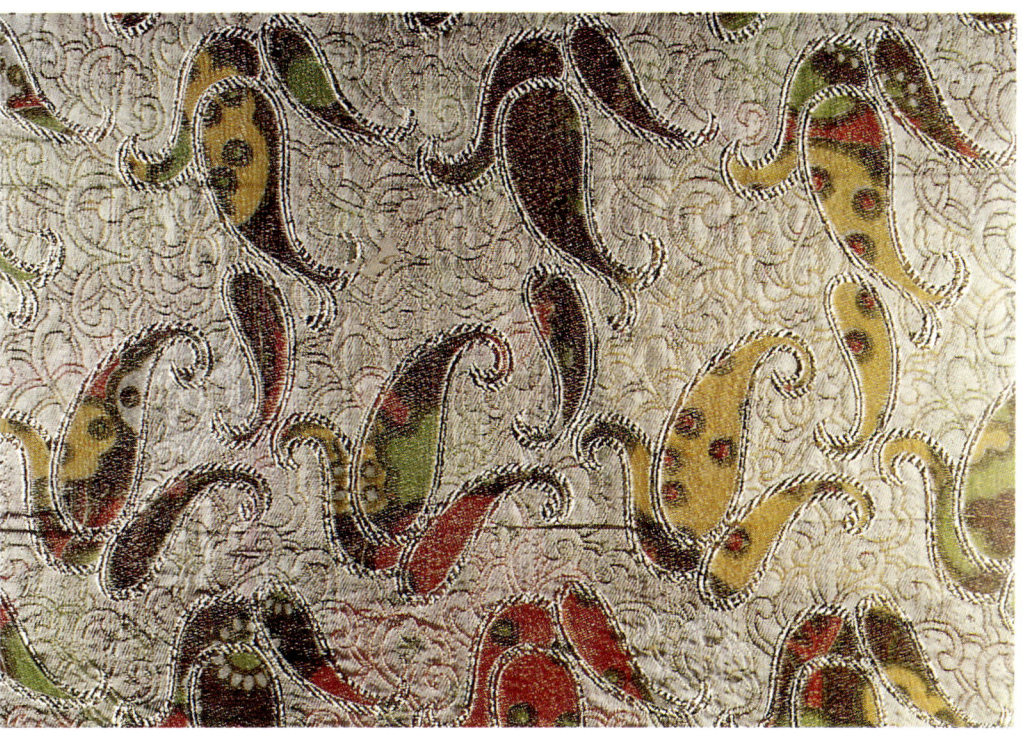

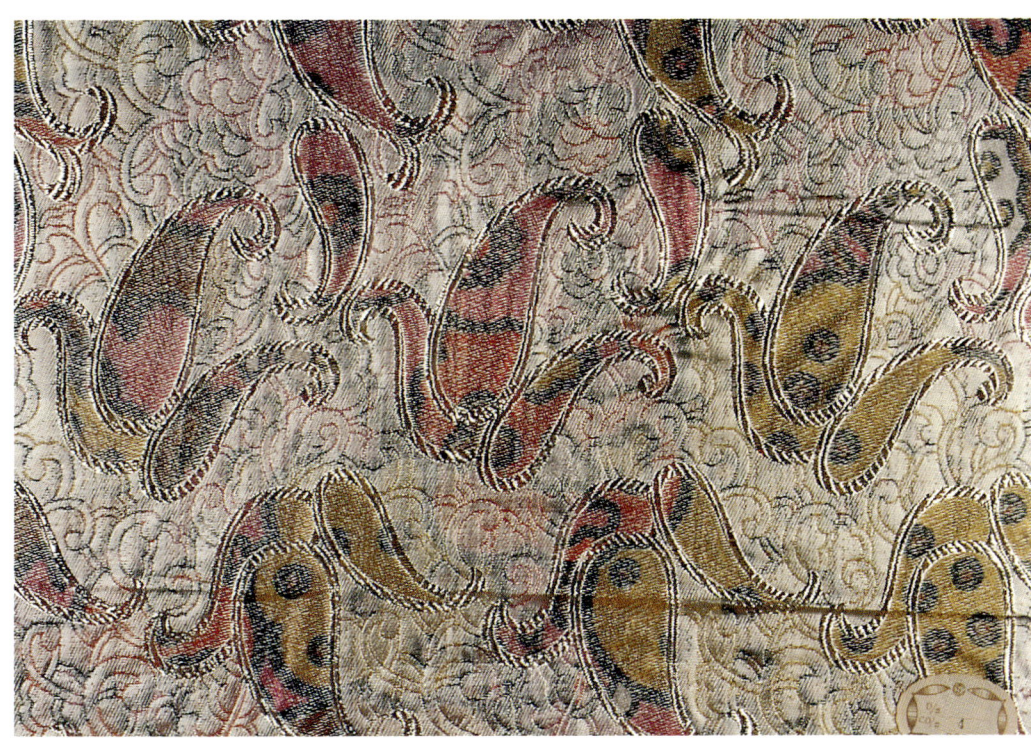

Silver weave creates brocade effect. Paisley print in hot pink, red, brown, and yellow. Rayon/polyester/nylon, Japan, 1960s.

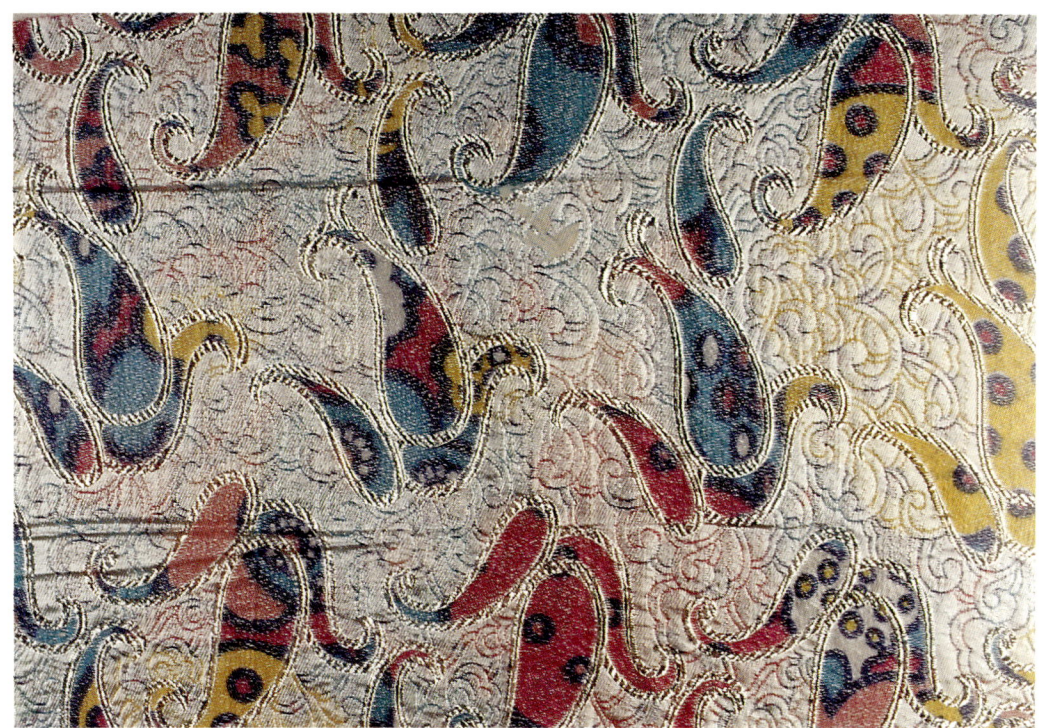

Silver weave creates brocade effect. Paisley print yellow, pink, and blues. Rayon/polyester/nylon, Japan, 1960s.

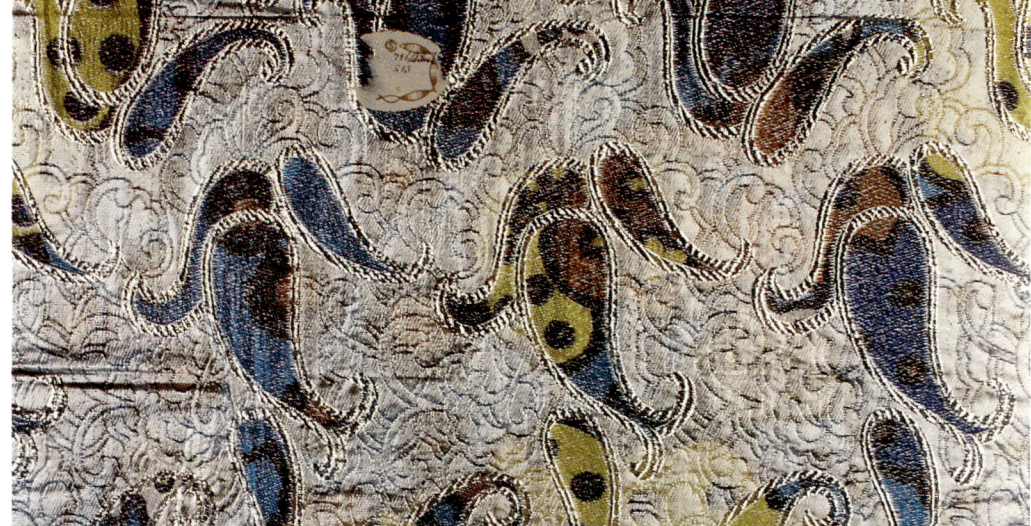

Silver weave creates brocade effect. Paisley print in blues, lime green, and brown. Rayon/polyester/nylon, Japan, 1960s.

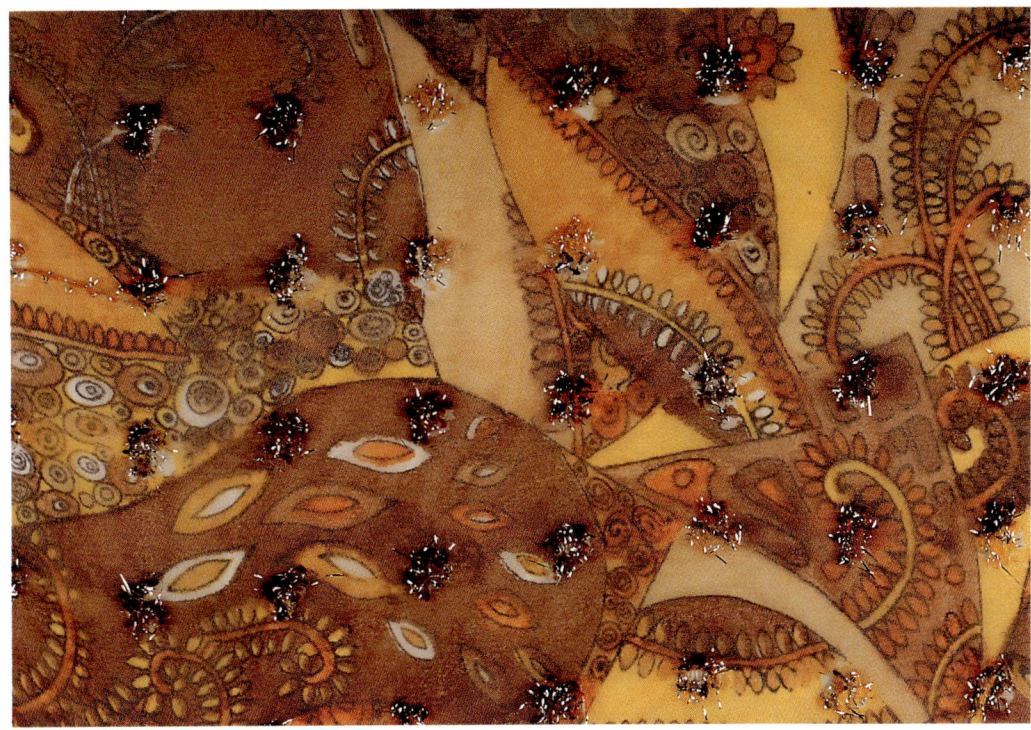

Psychedelic '60s print with metallic and velour dots. Printed orange, yellow, and brown. Nylon/polyester film, Japan, 1960s.

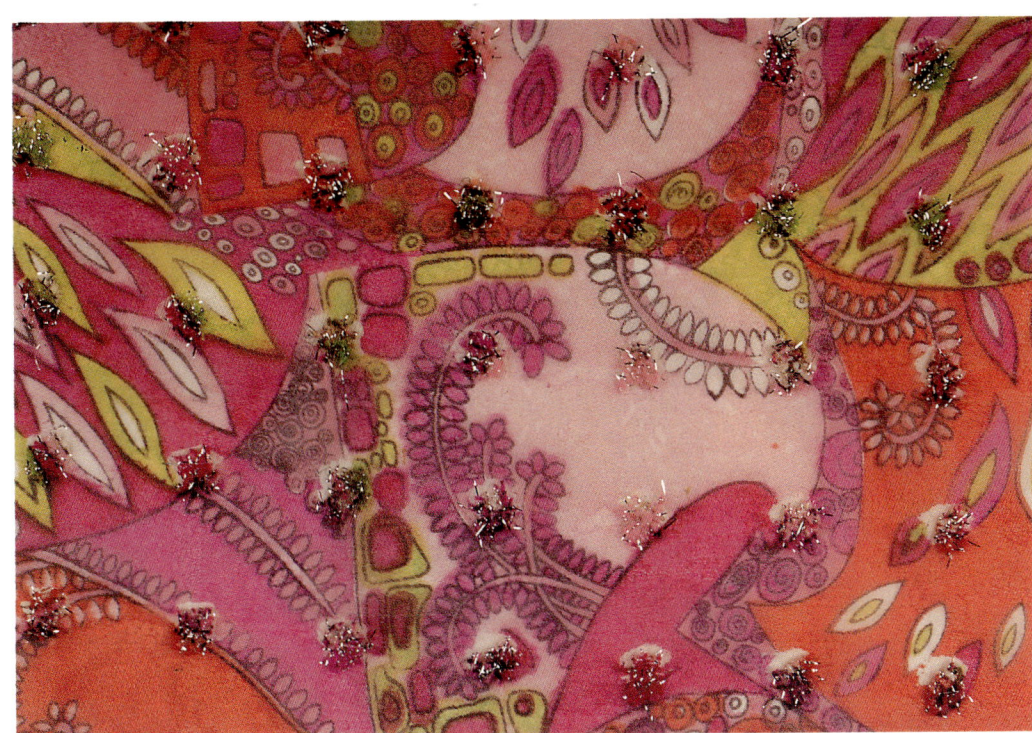

Psychedelic '60s print with metallic and velour dots. Printed purple, red, and green. Nylon/polyester film, Japan, 1960s.

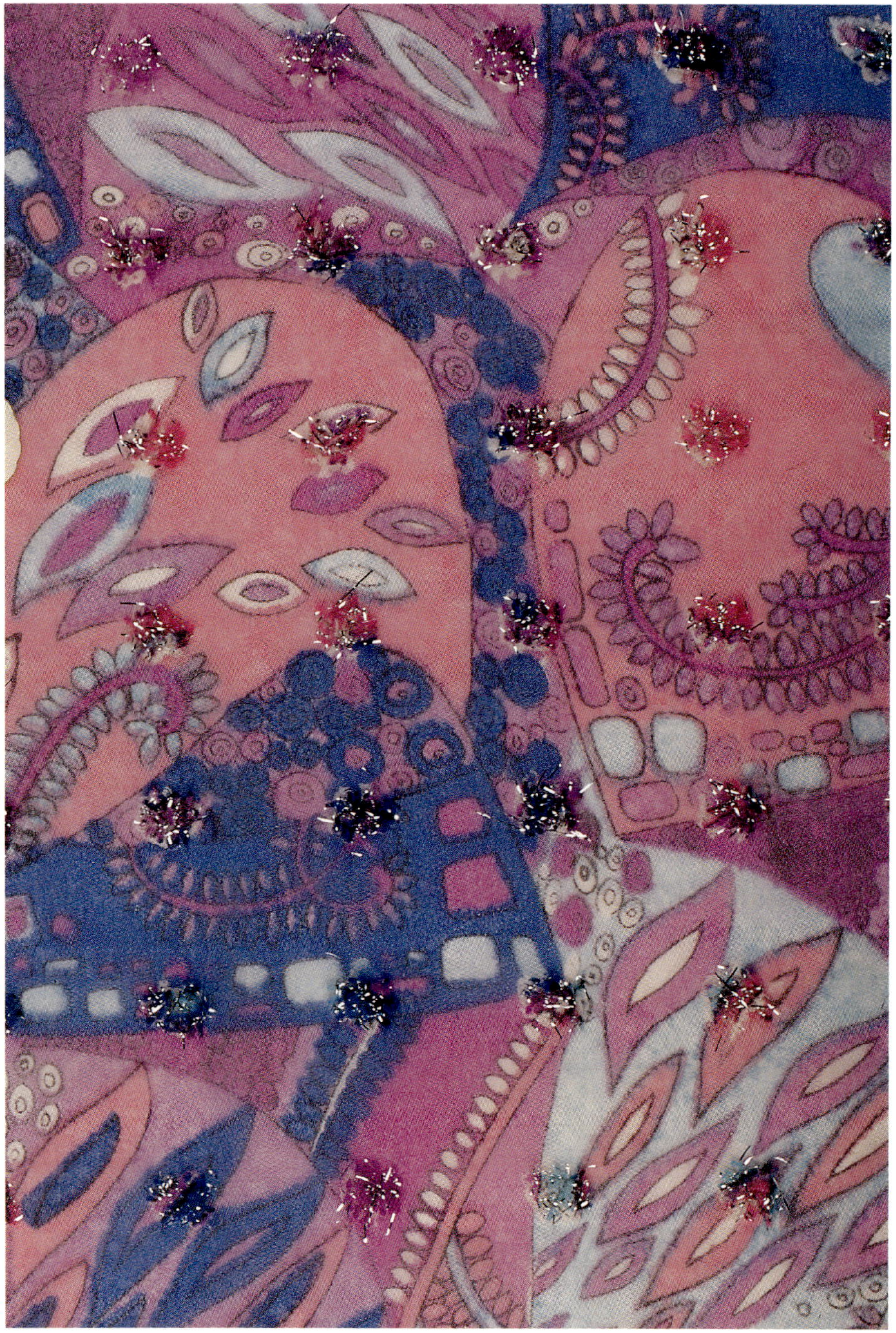

Psychedelic '60s print with metallic and velour dots. Printed purples, salmon, and blues. Nylon/polyester film, Japan, 1960s.

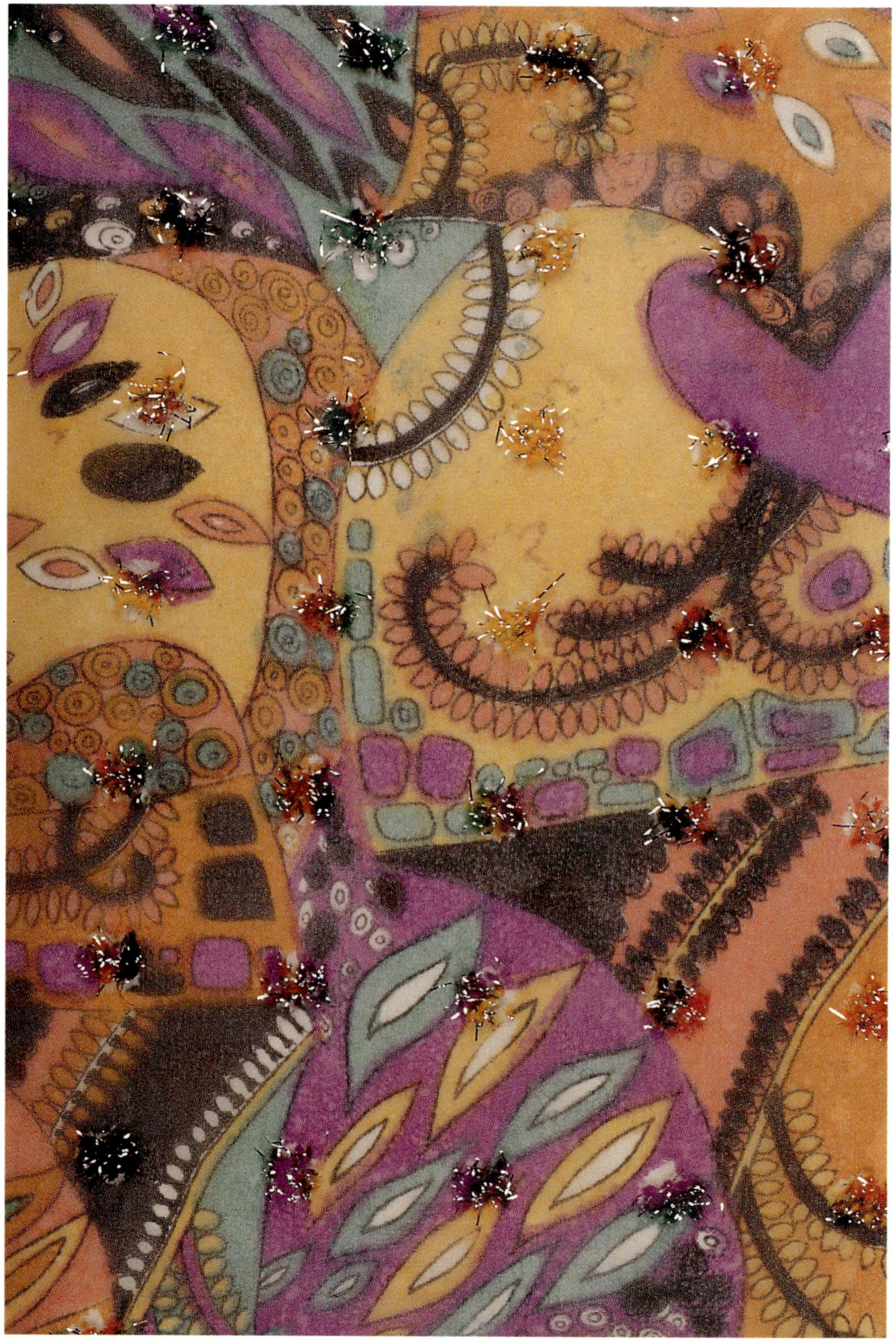

Psychedelic '60s print with metallic and velour dots. Printed purple, turquoise, and golds. Nylon/polyester film, Japan, 1960s.

Gold flowers and foliage over abstract design of block colors—blues, purple, and pinks. Rayon/polyester film/nylon, Japan, 1960s.

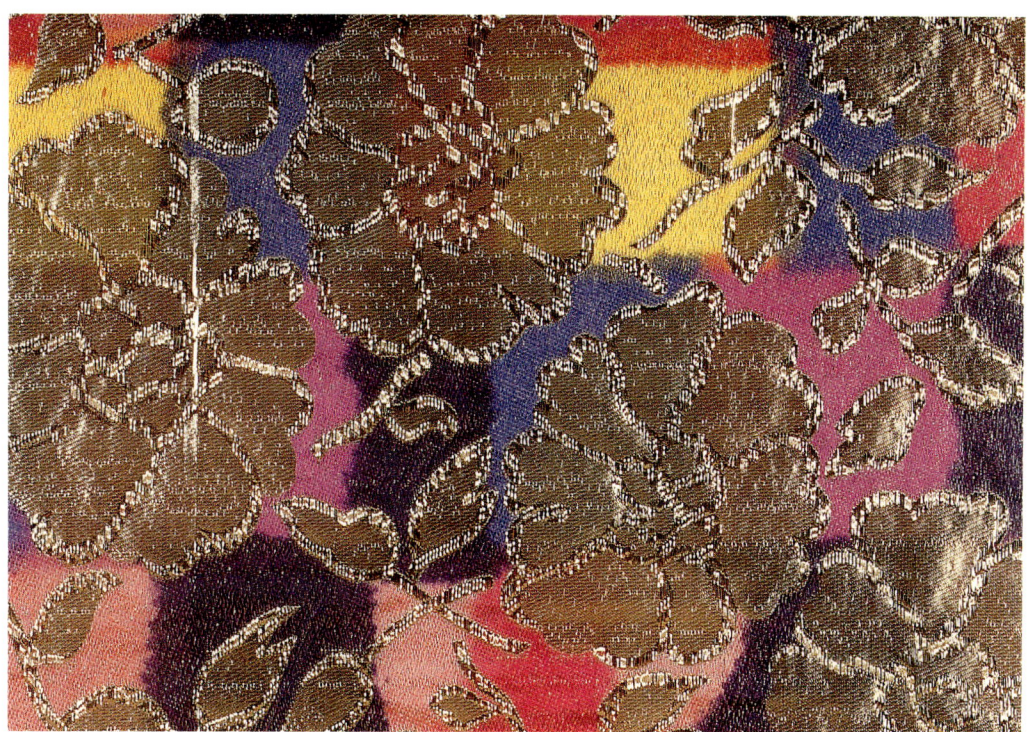

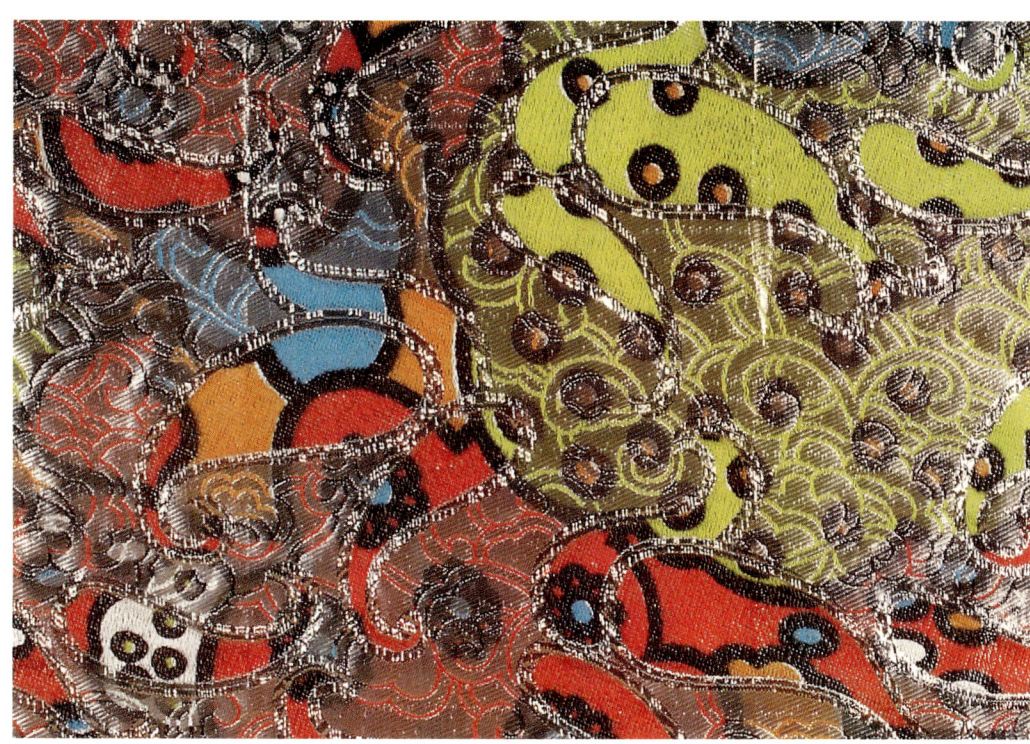

Silver weave creates brocade effect. Paisley print in lime green, red, yellow, and orange. Rayon/polyester/nylon, Japan, 1960s.

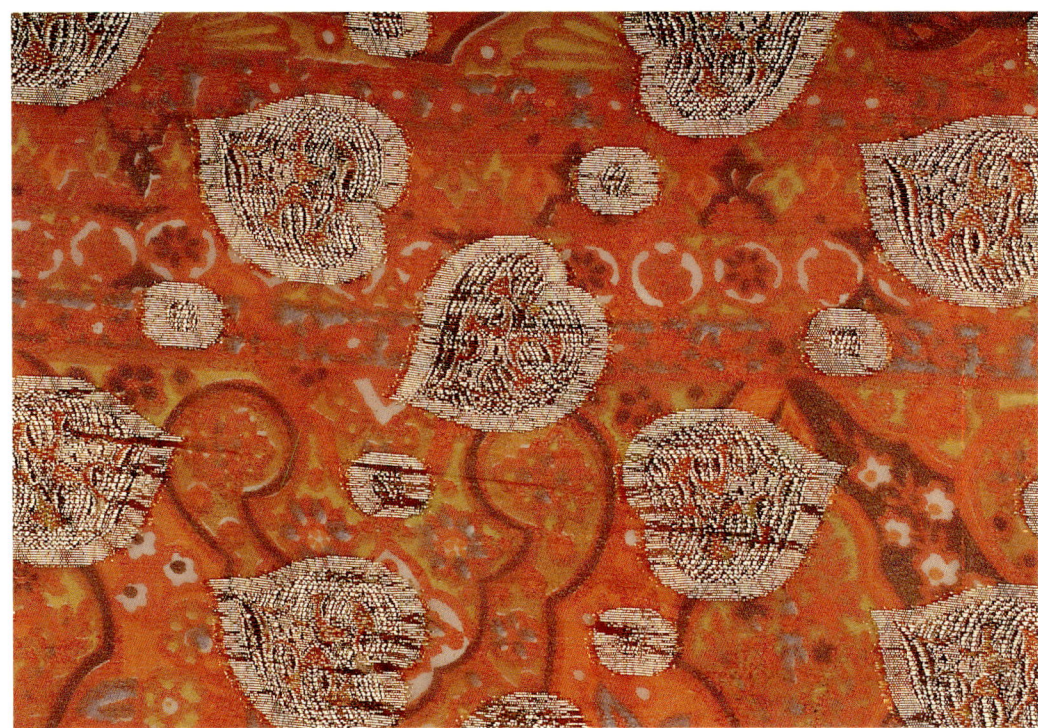

Abstract paisley printed motif with gold hearts. Nylon/polyester, Japan, 1960s.

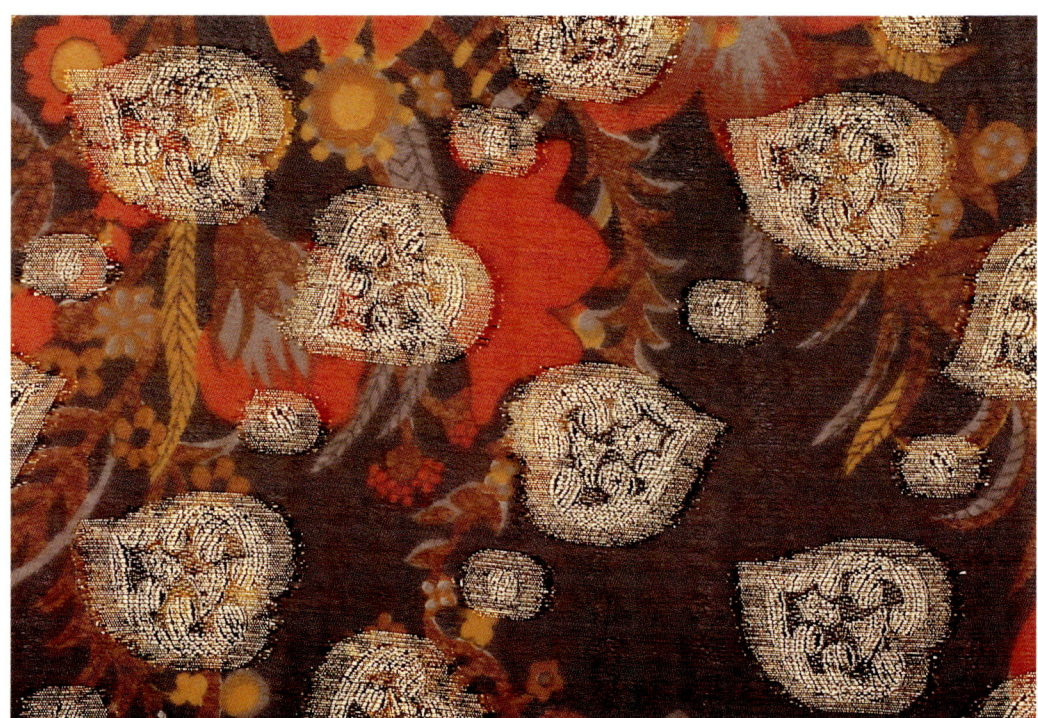

Floral and paisley print on film with gold hearts. Red, yellow, and slate blue on black ground. Nylon/polyester, Japan, 1960s.

Chapter Six

GEOMETRIC

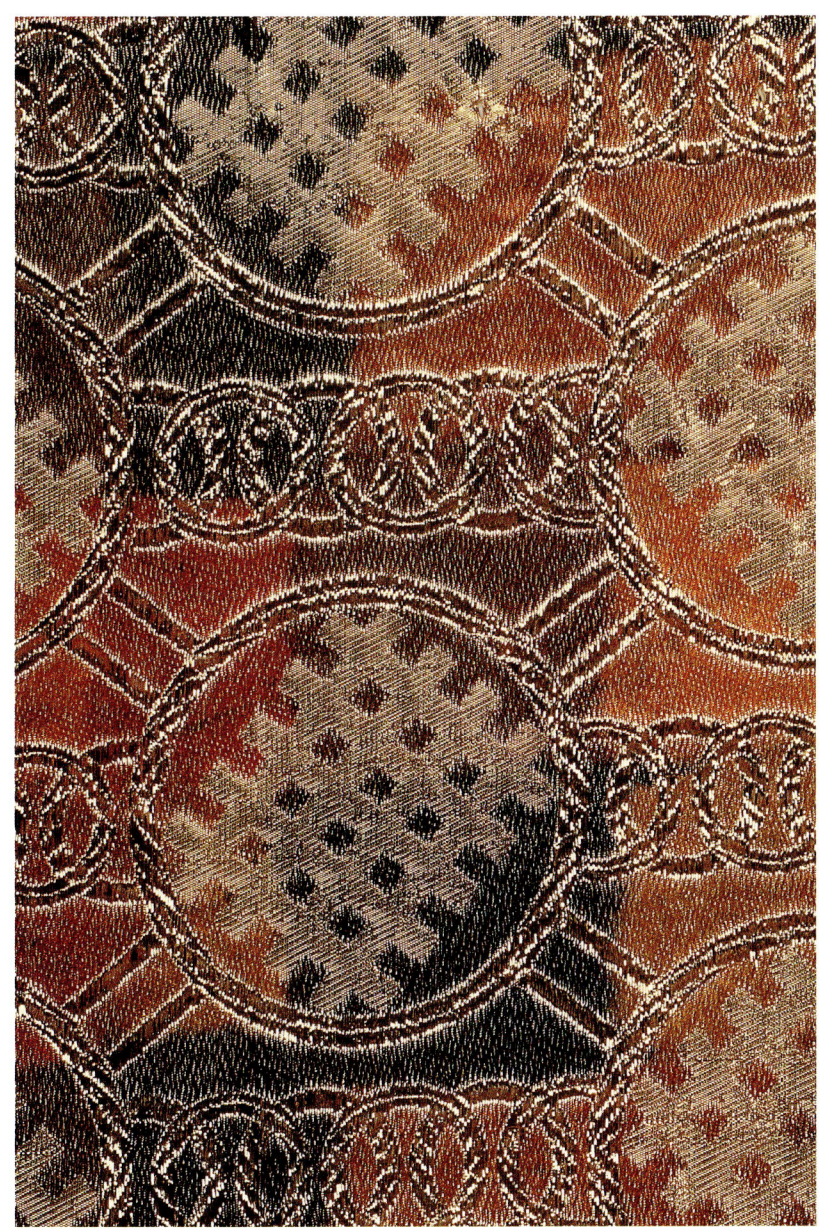
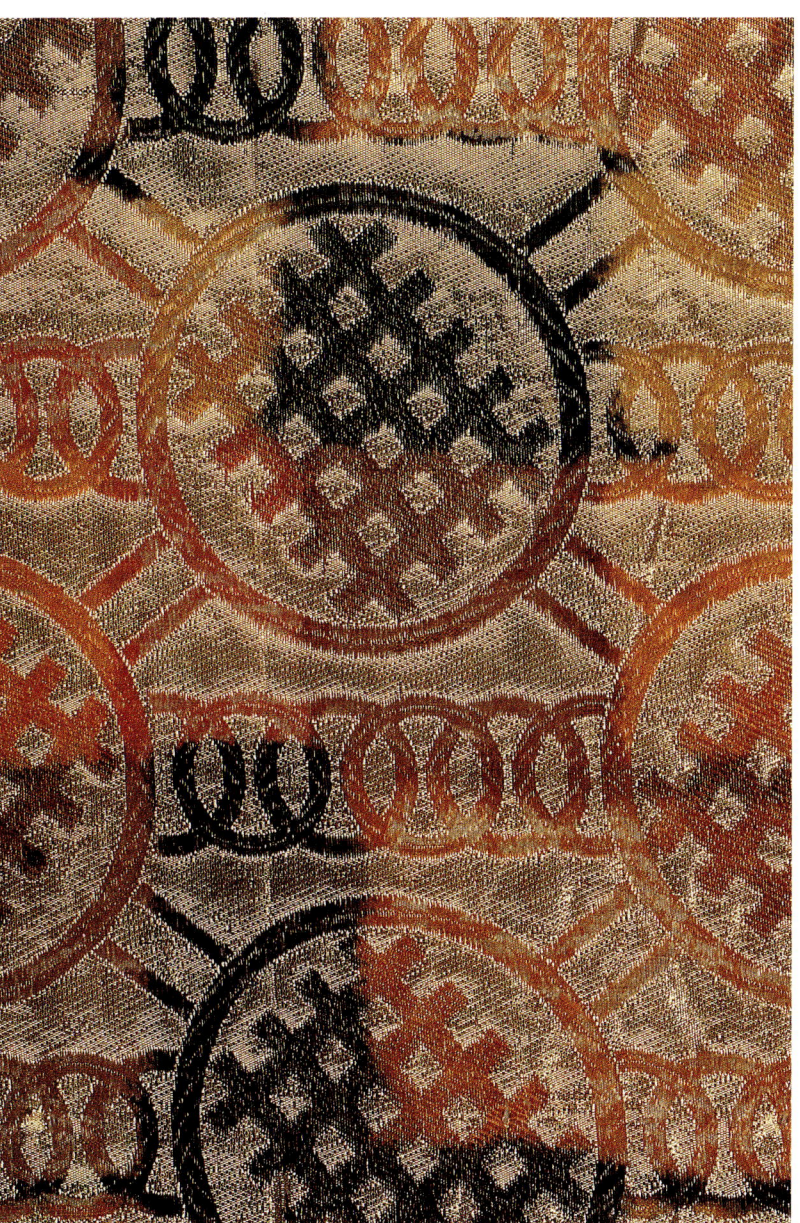

Both sides of a hand-printed rayon/polyester film with nylon mixed brocade. Black and gold tones. Japan, 1960s.

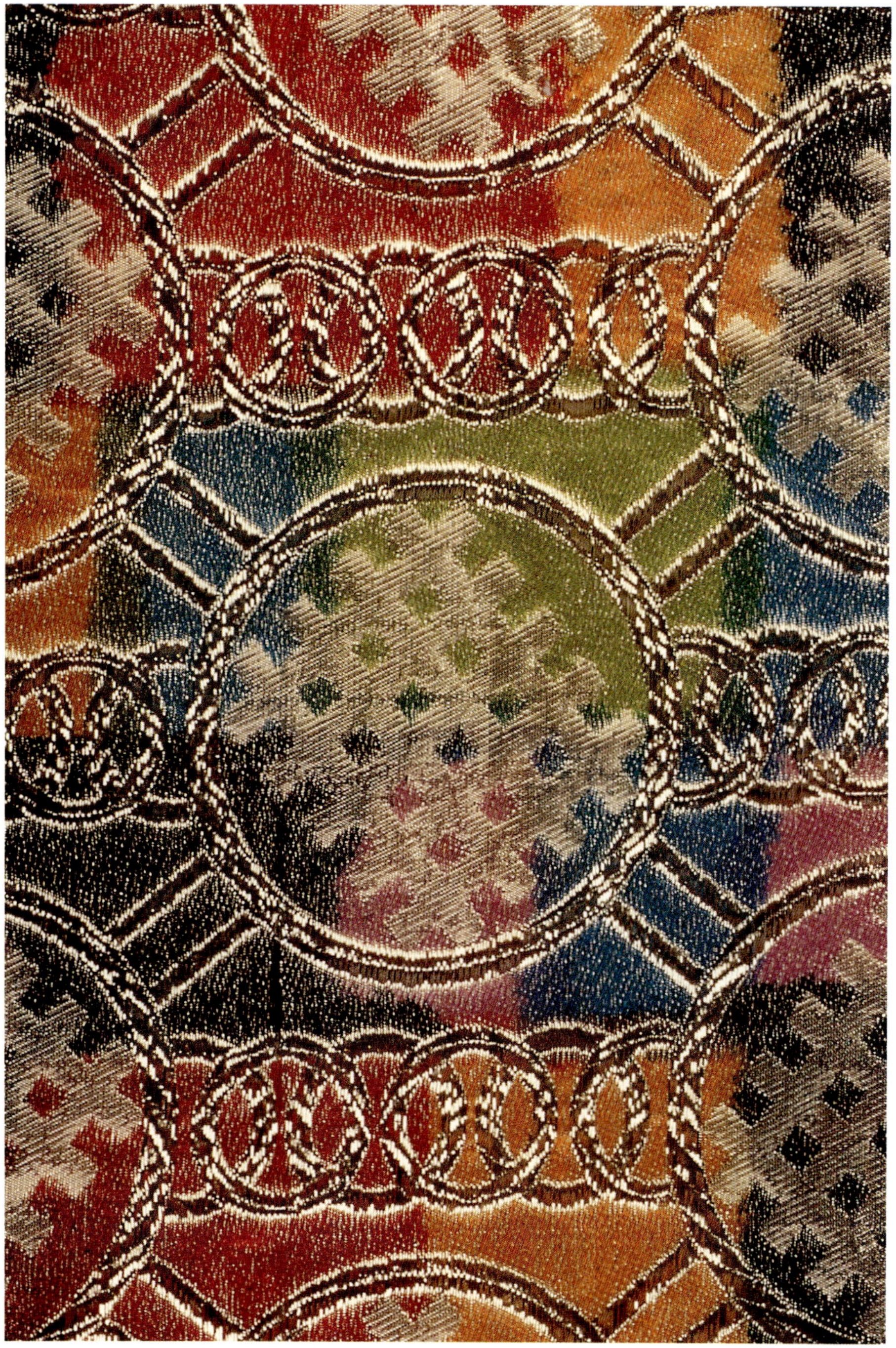

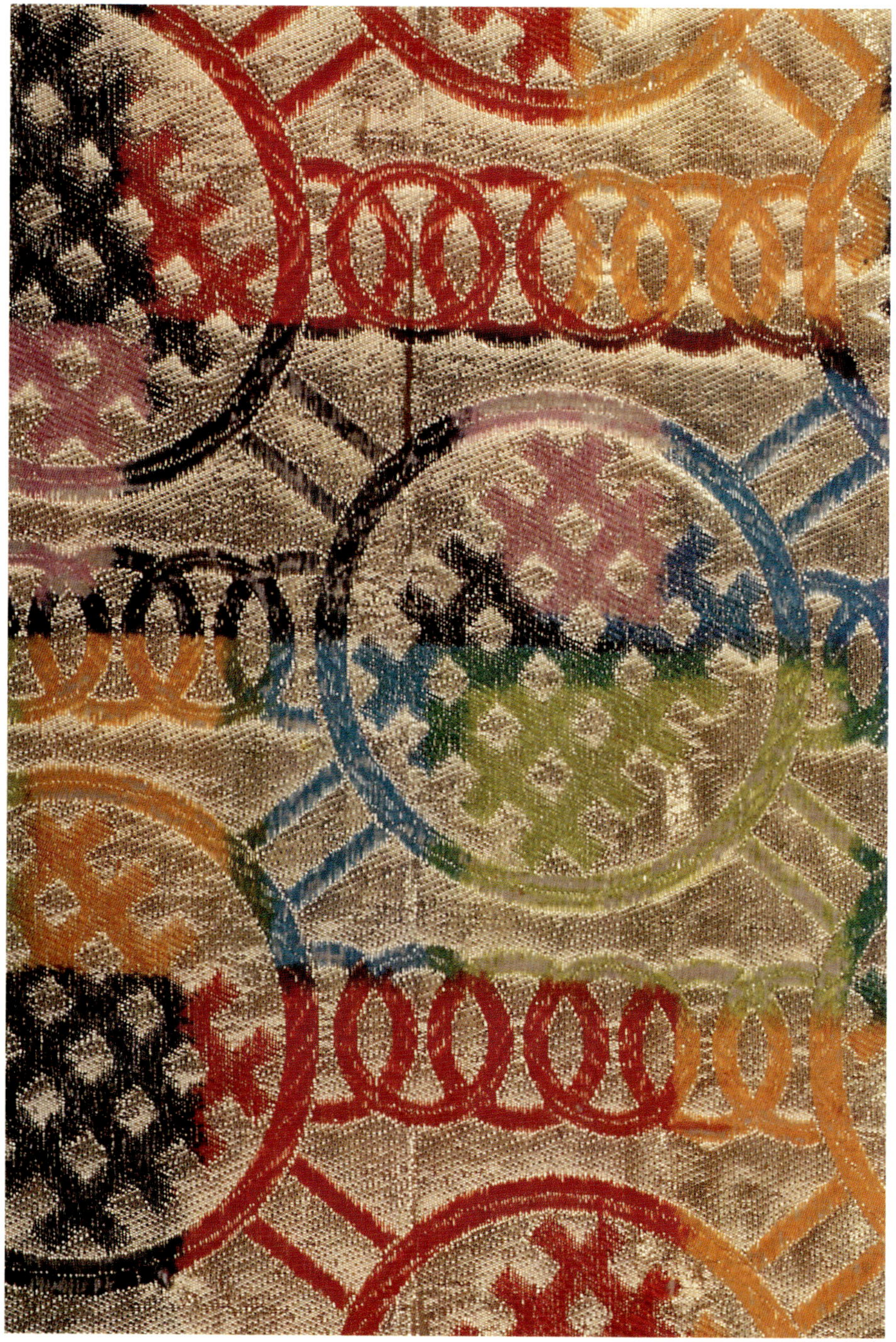

Both sides of a hand-printed rayon/polyester film with nylon mixed brocade. Multi-colored. Japan, 1960s.

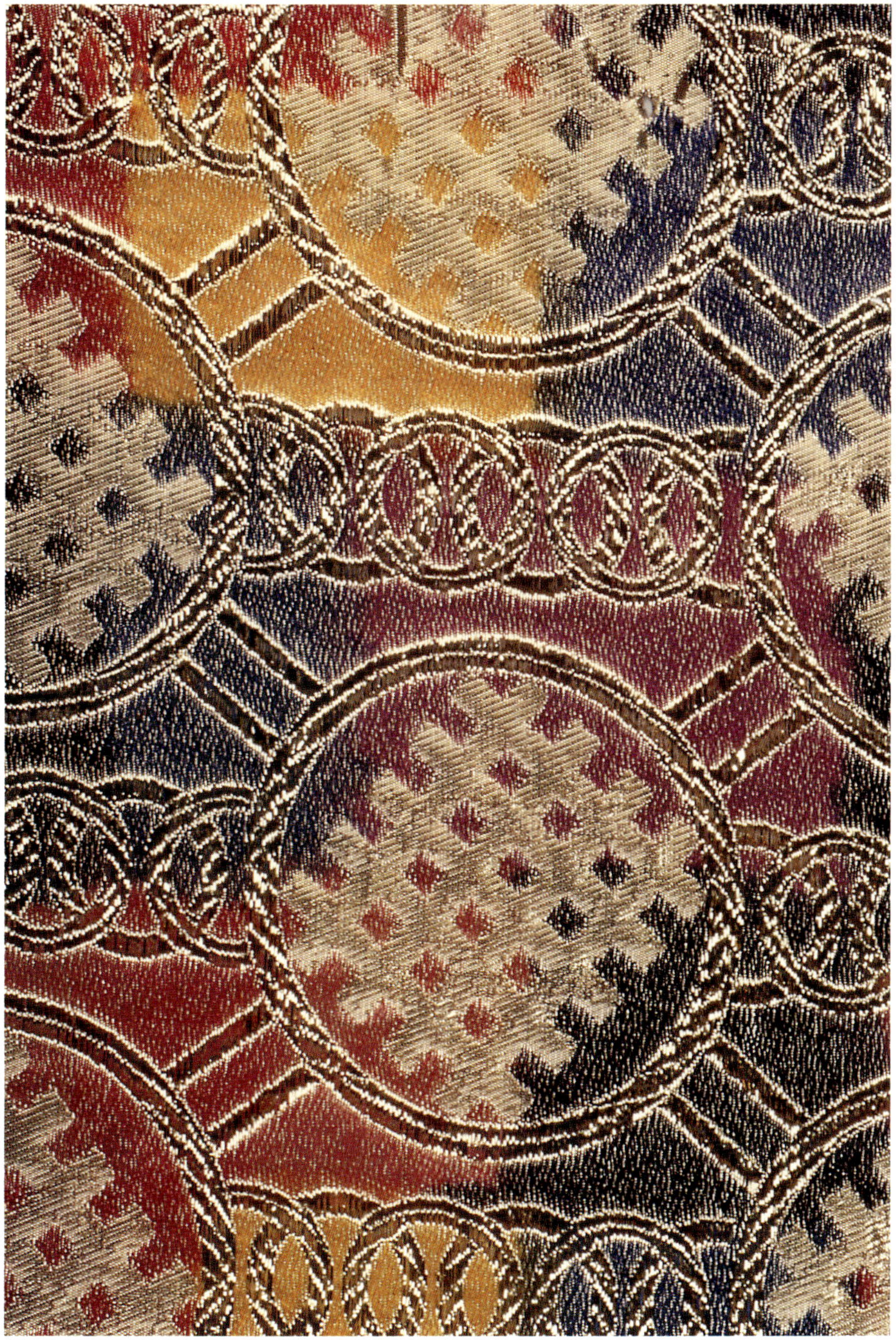

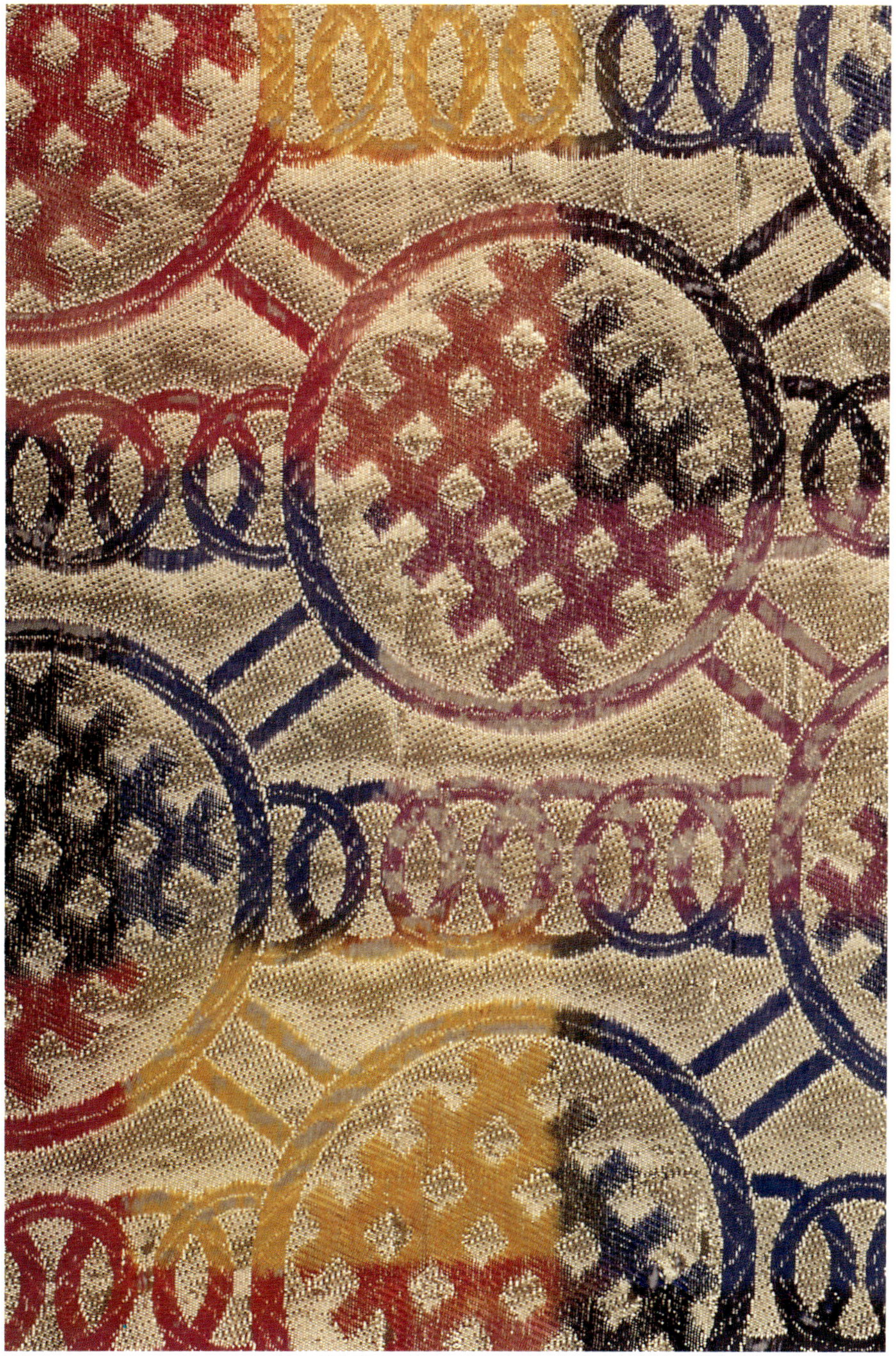

Both sides of a hand-printed rayon/polyester film with nylon mixed brocade. Purple, blue, pinks, black, and yellow. Japan, 1960s.

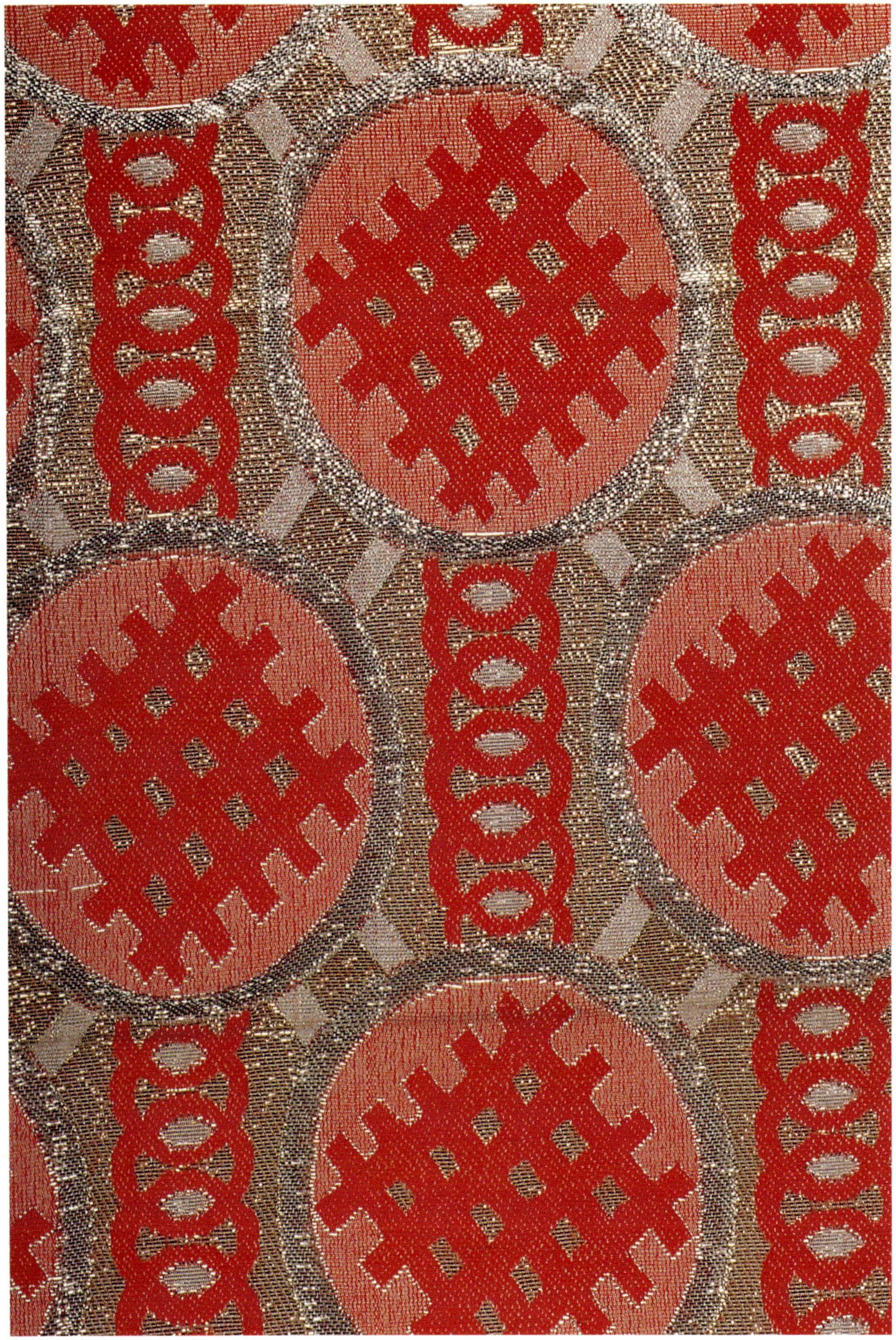

Circles and squares on gold ground with silver highlights, with red. Acrylic/acetate/polyester, Japan, 1960s.

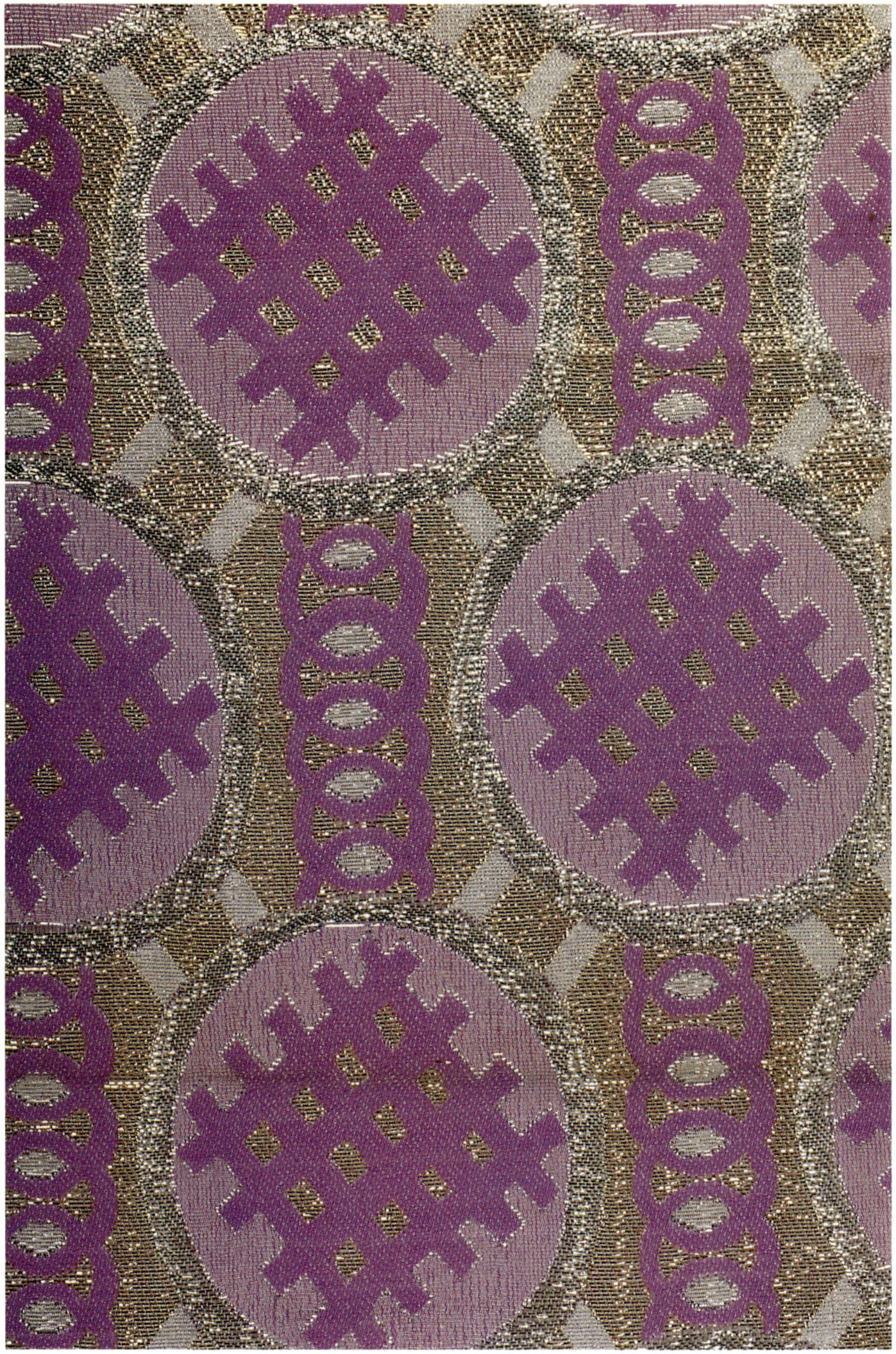

Circles and squares on gold ground with silver highlights, with purple. Acrylic/acetate/polyester, Japan, 1960s.

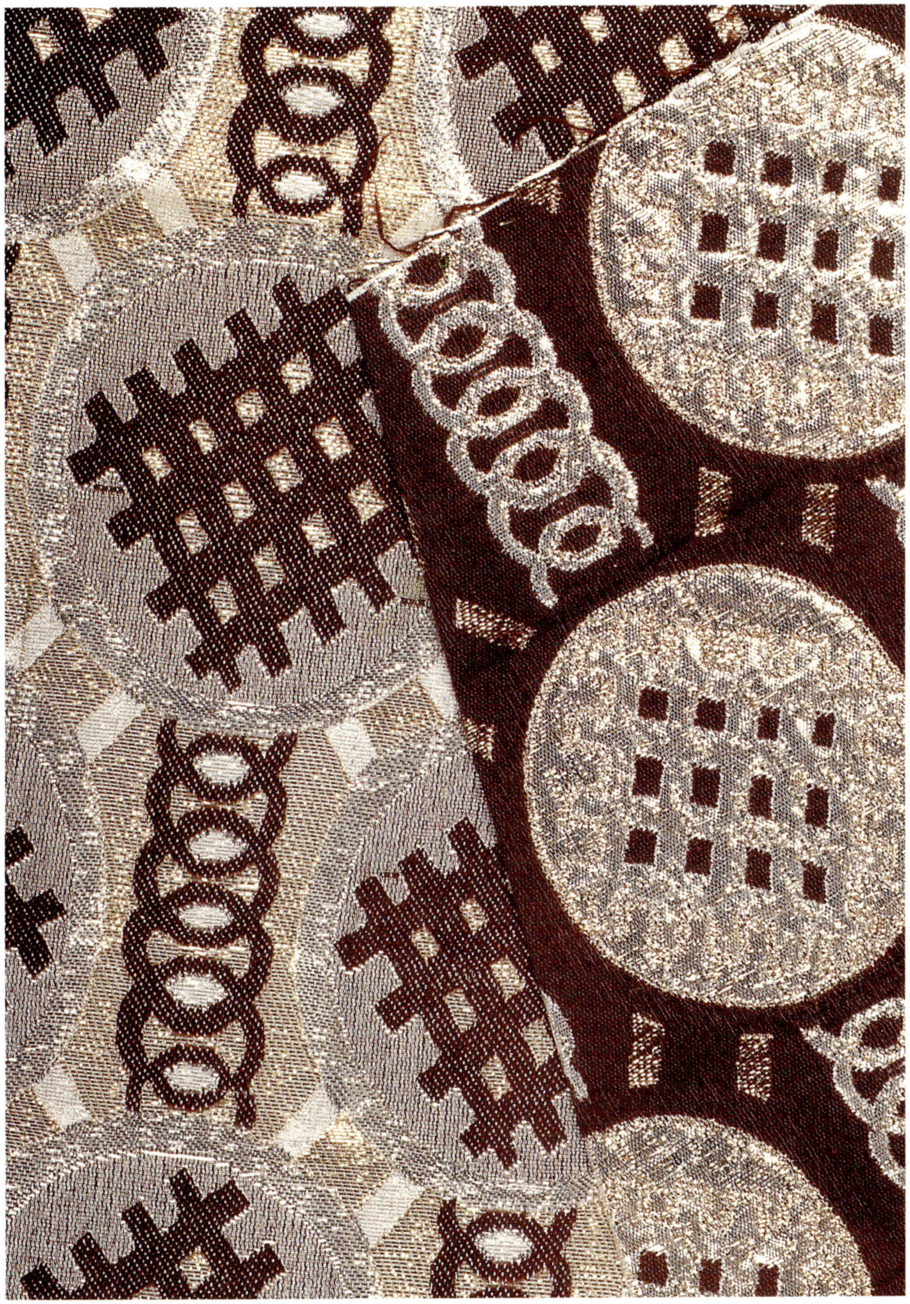

Circles and squares on gold ground with silver highlights, with brown. Fold back reveals reverse. Acrylic/acetate/polyester, Japan, 1960s.

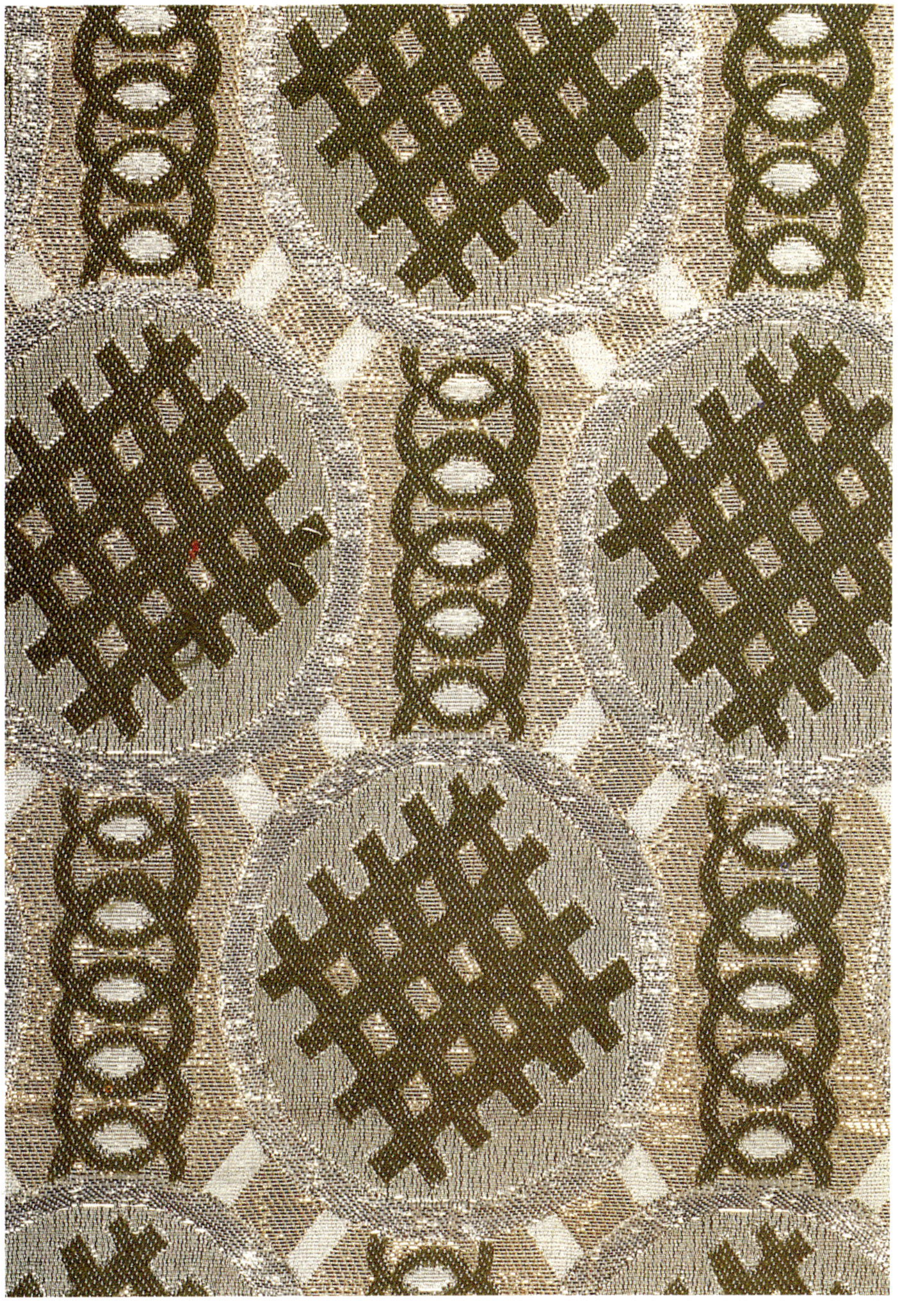

Circles and squares on gold ground with silver highlights, with green. Acrylic/acetate/polyester, Japan, 1960s.

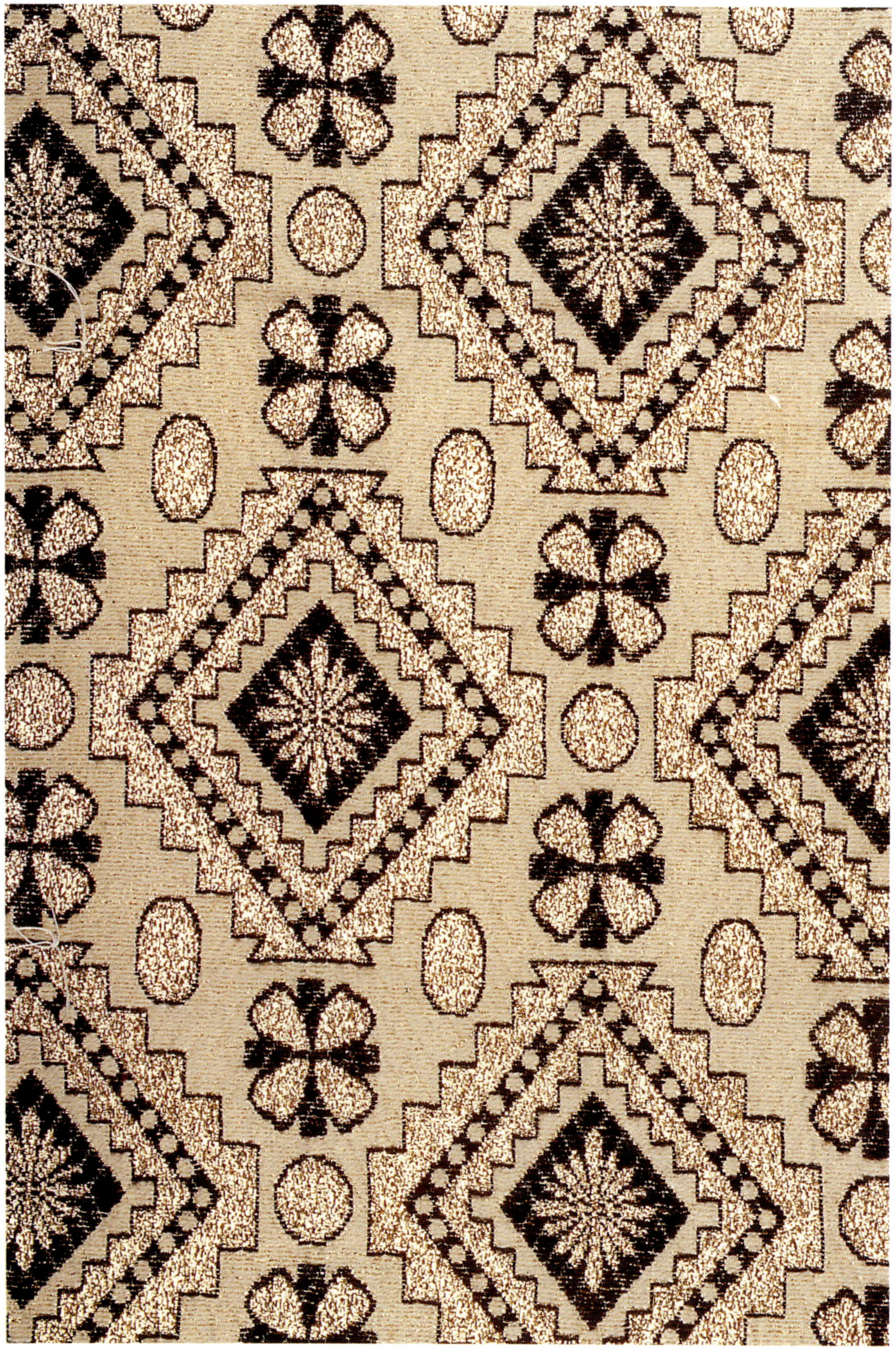

Aztec-like design in gold with black on tan ground. Acrylic/polyester, Japan, 1960s.

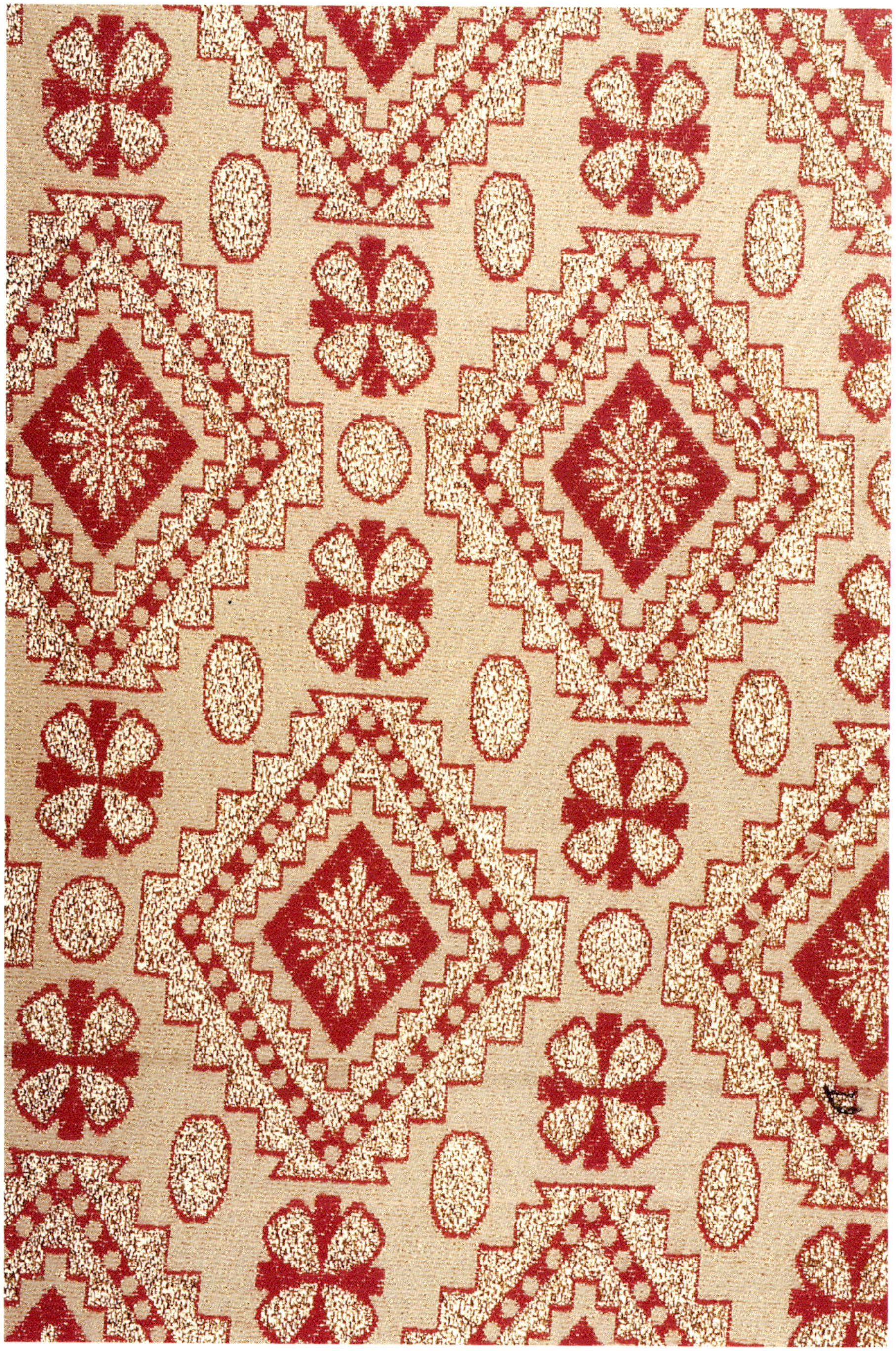

Aztec-like design in gold with magenta on tan ground. Acrylic/polyester, Japan, 1960s.

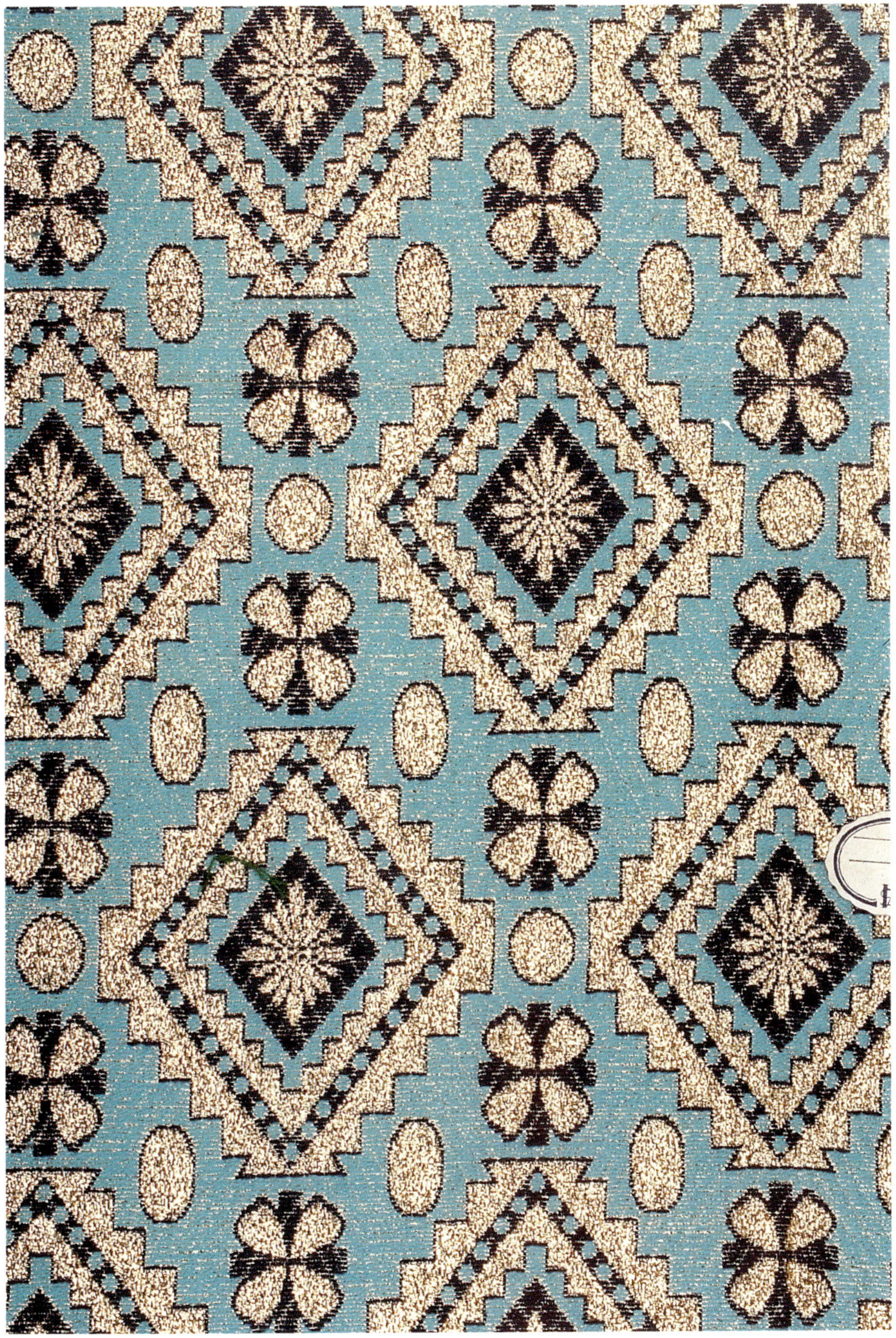

Aztec-like design in gold with black on blue ground. Acrylic/polyester, Japan, 1960s.

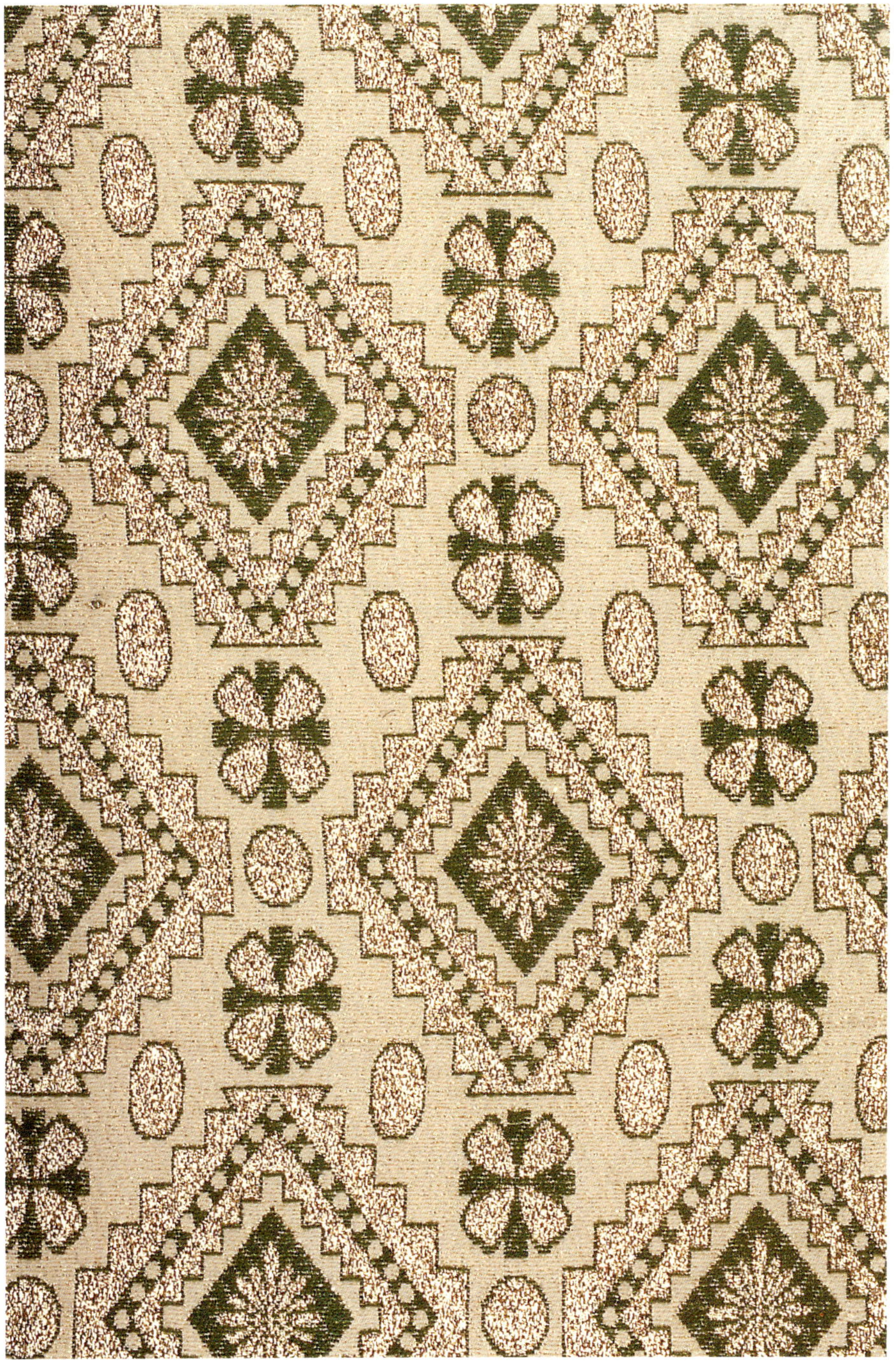

Aztec-like design in gold with green on tan ground. Acrylic/polyester, Japan, 1960s.

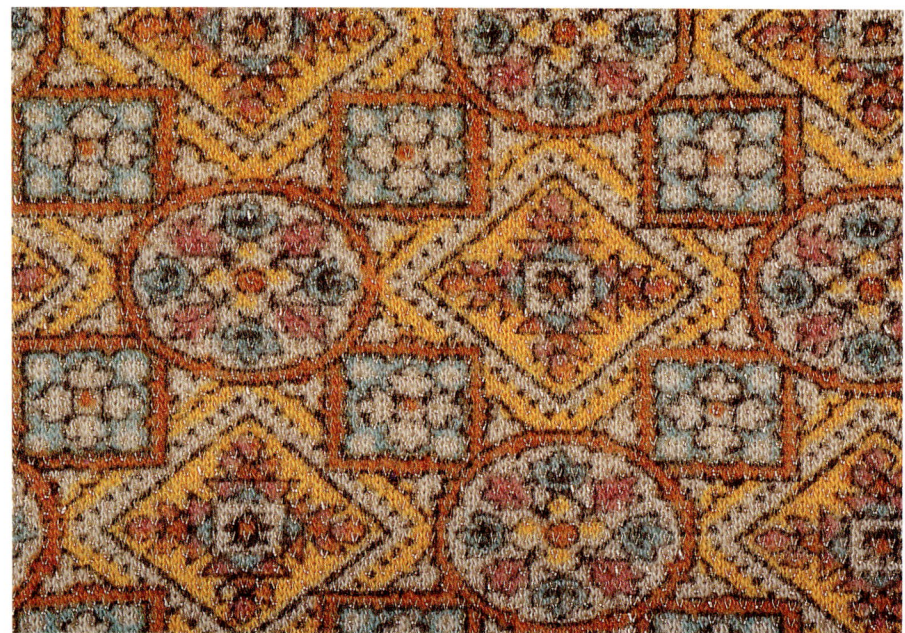

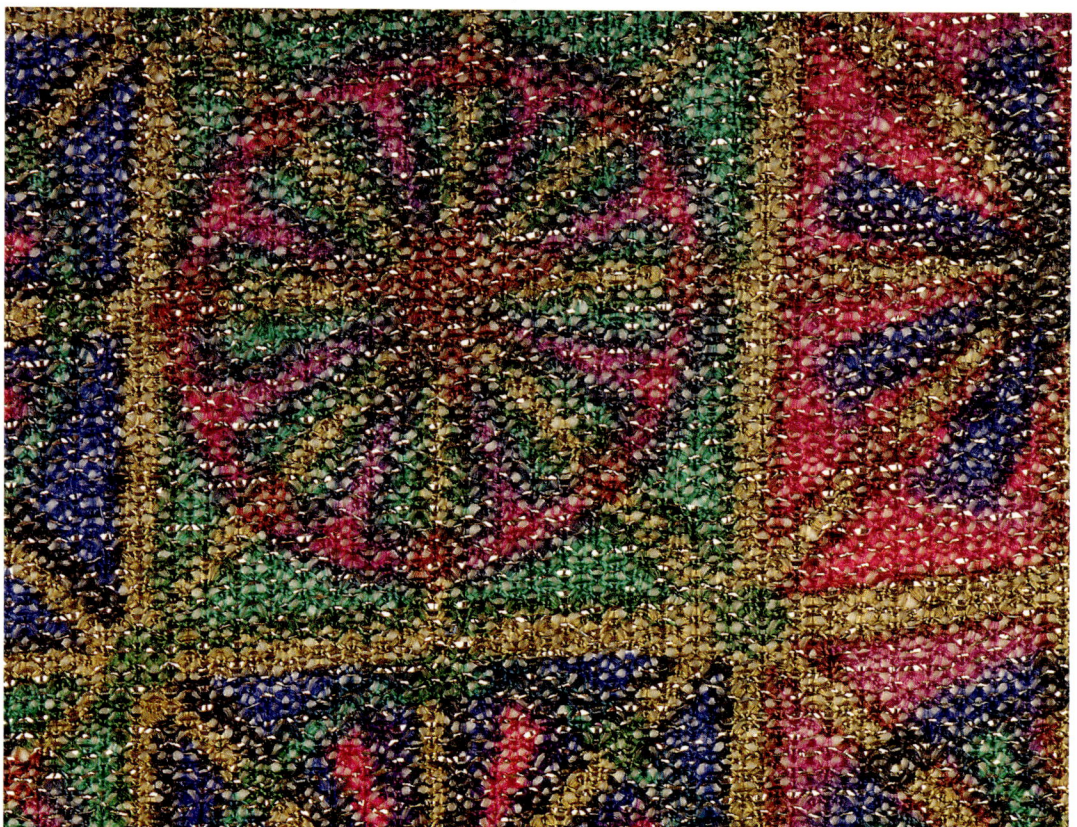

Top left; Geometric design in golden yellow tones. Wool/nylon, France, 1963.

Top right: Gold metallic threads interwoven with bone white serve as foil to geometric brown overprint. Polyester/acetate, France, 1964.

Bottom right: Gold threads in open weave add luster to wagon spoke pattern. Nylon/polyester, France, 1967.

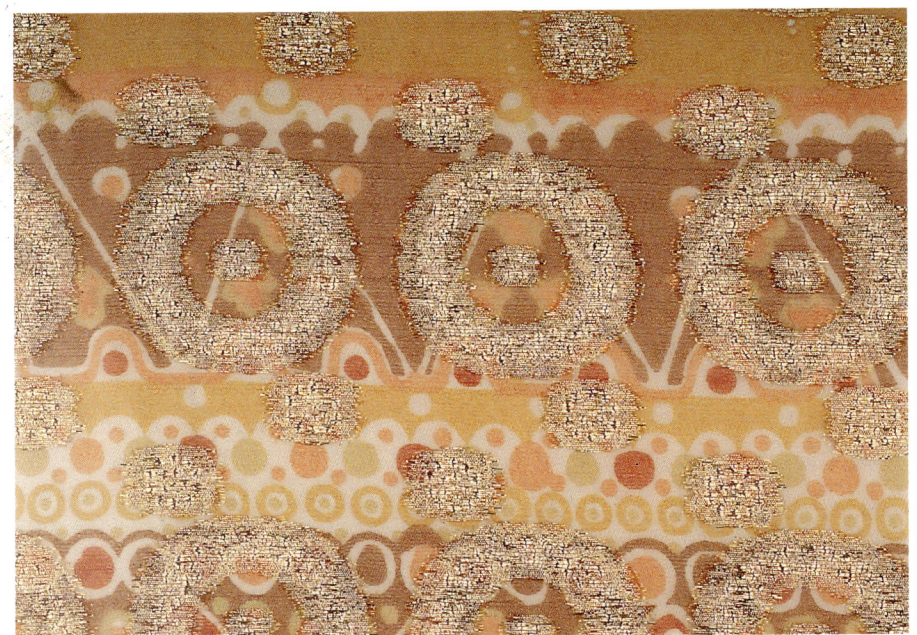
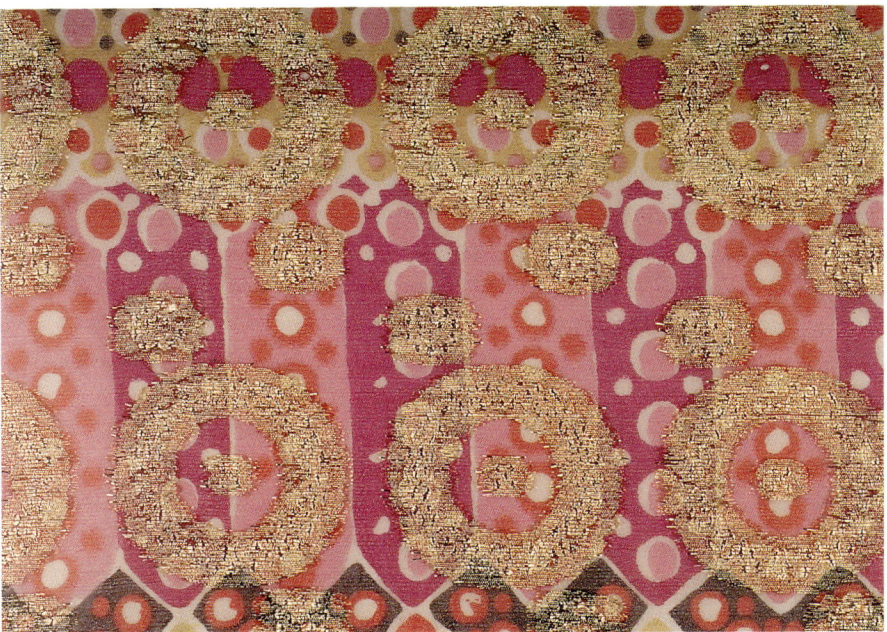

Metallic circles and dots line up over printed circles and lines, shown in three color variations. Nylon/polyester film mixed brocade, Japan, 1960s.

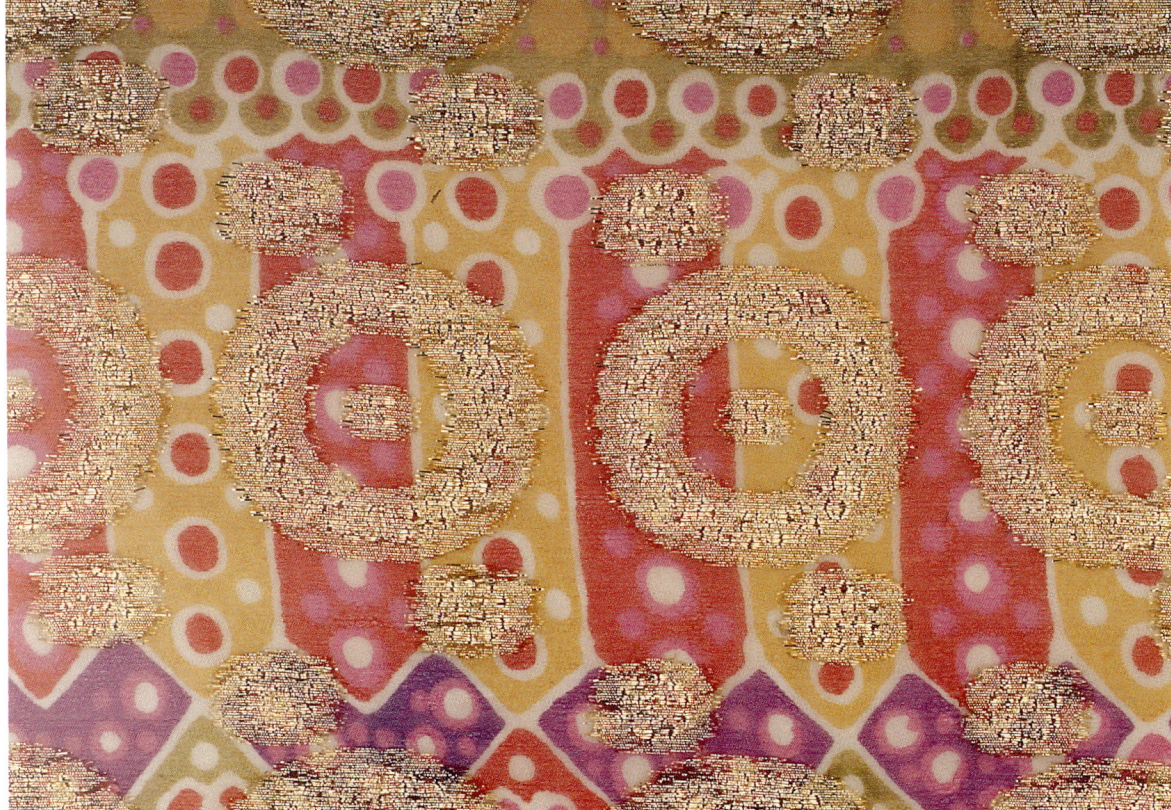

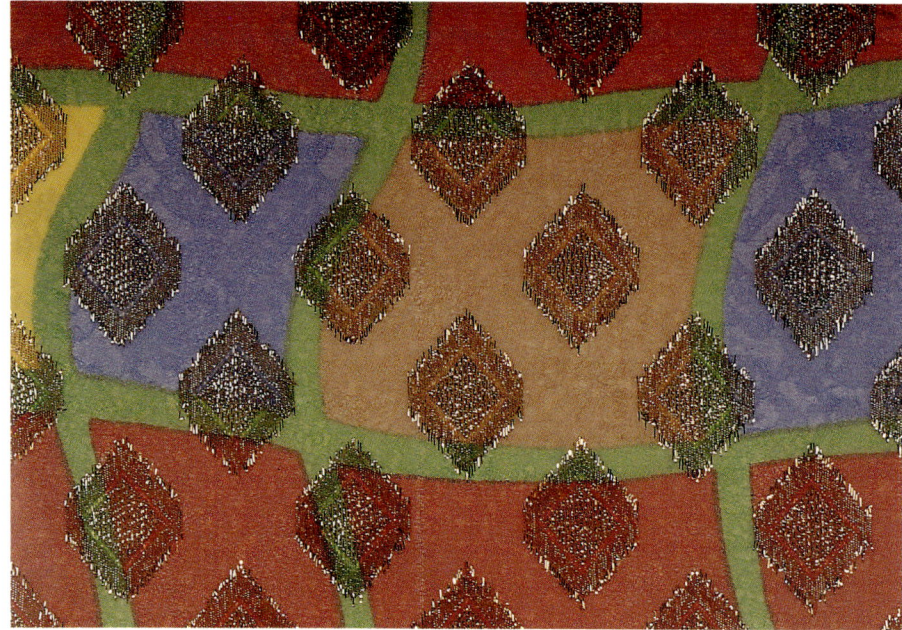

Gold diamonds ornament film with printed, multi-color windowpane check. Nylon/spun rayon, Japan, 1960s.

Blue and silver geometric brocade. Japan, 1970s.

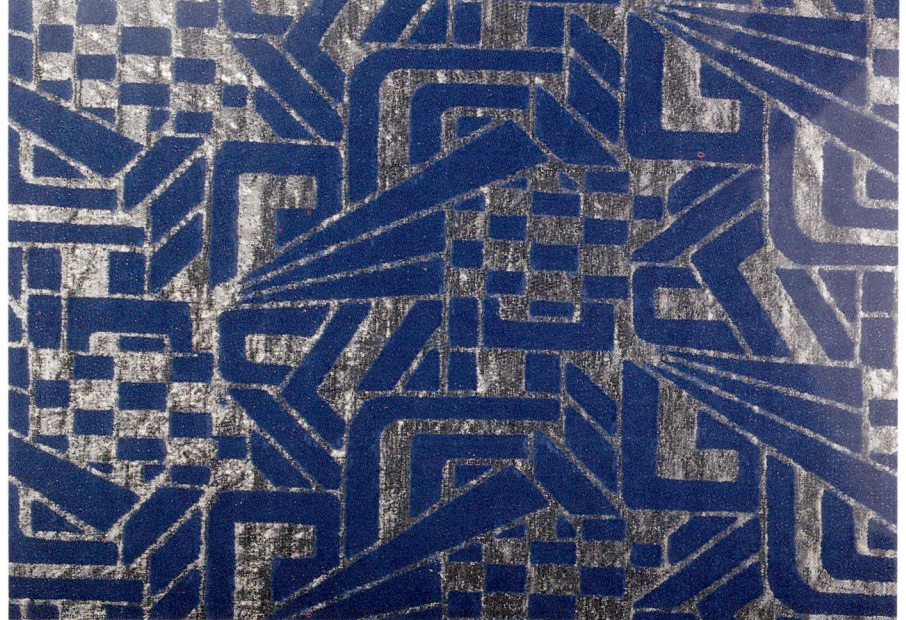

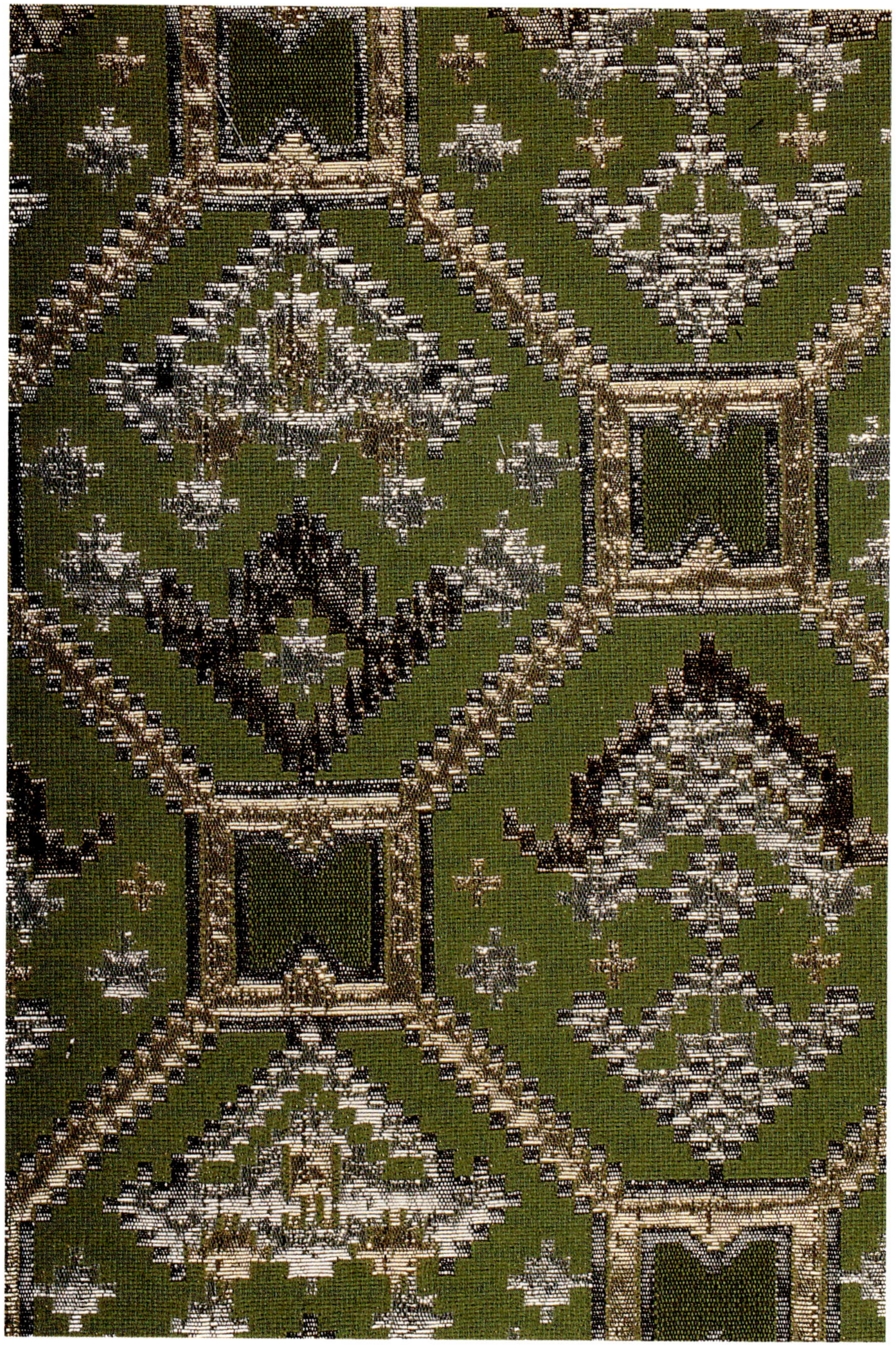

Metallic tones create geometric design against greens. Japan, 1970s.

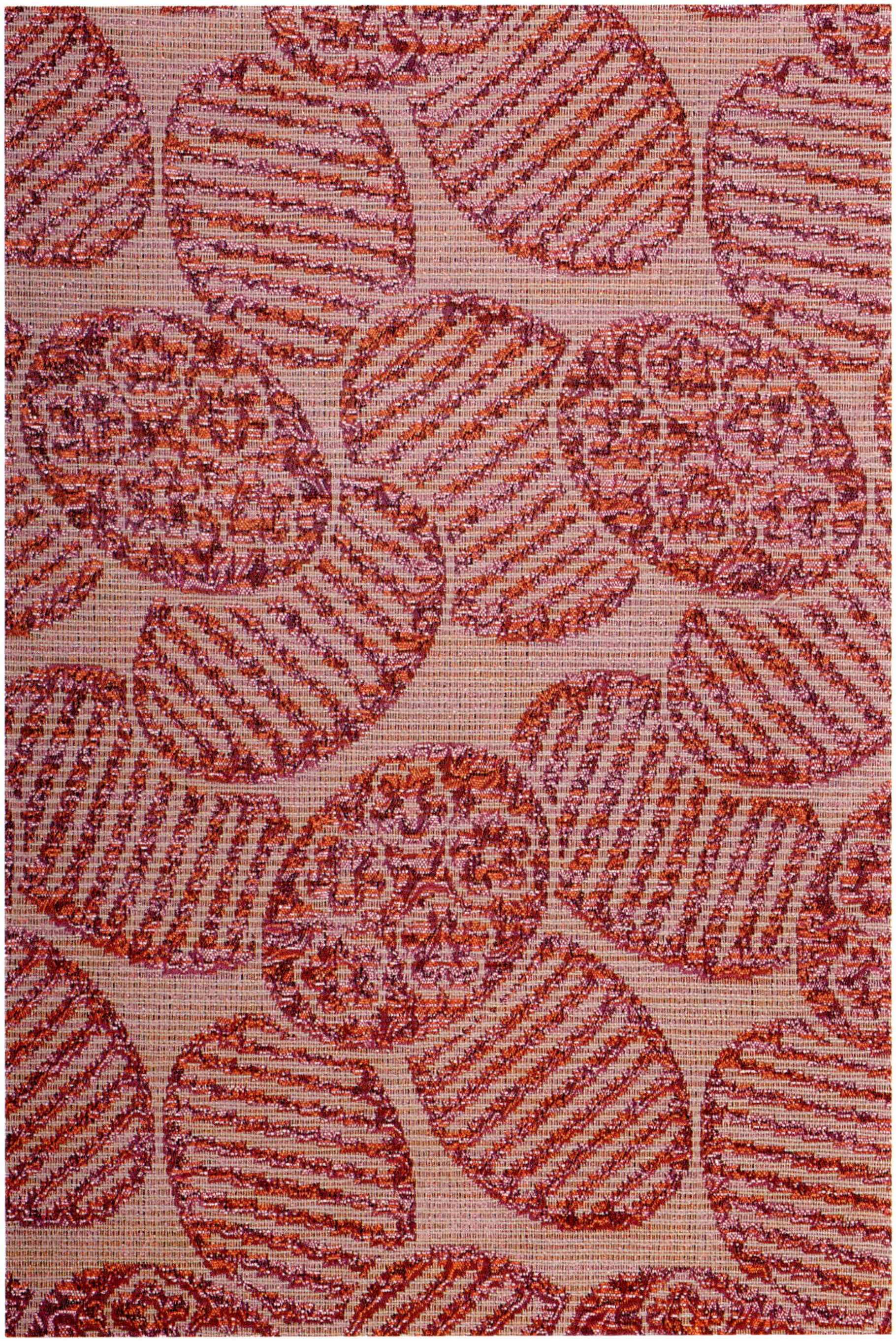

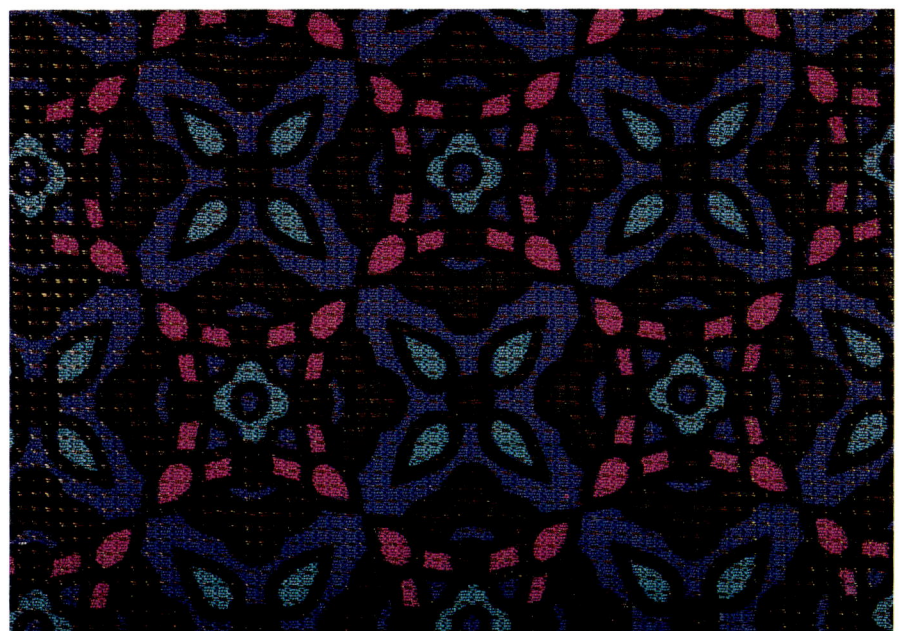

Horizontal gold in mod floral design. France, 1961.

Easter-egg effect in metallic pink. Japan, 1970s.

87

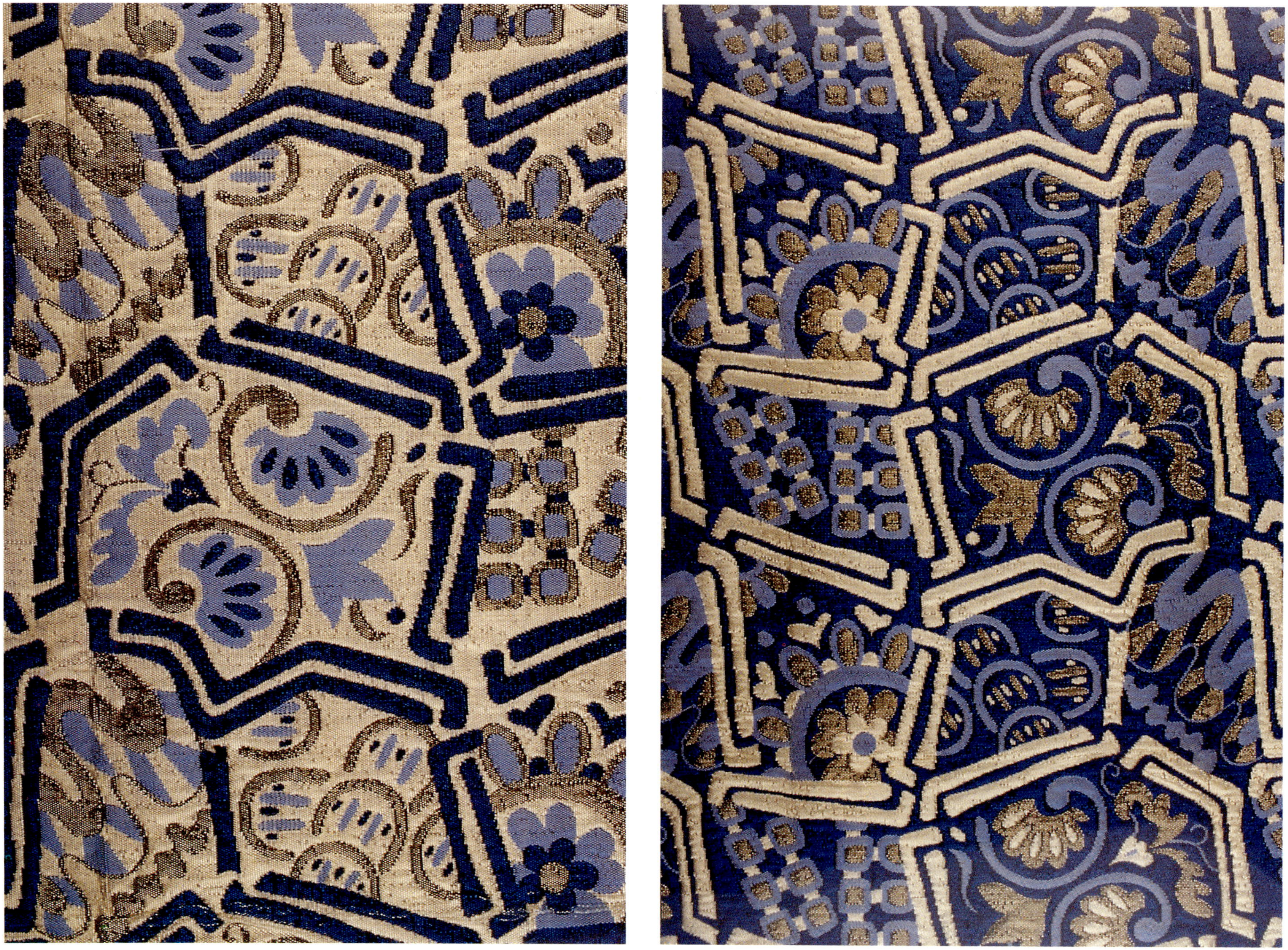

Front and back of mixed brocade with geometric patterns sparked by gold blocks and metallic light and dark blue threads. Acetate/acrylic/polyester film, Japan, 1960s.

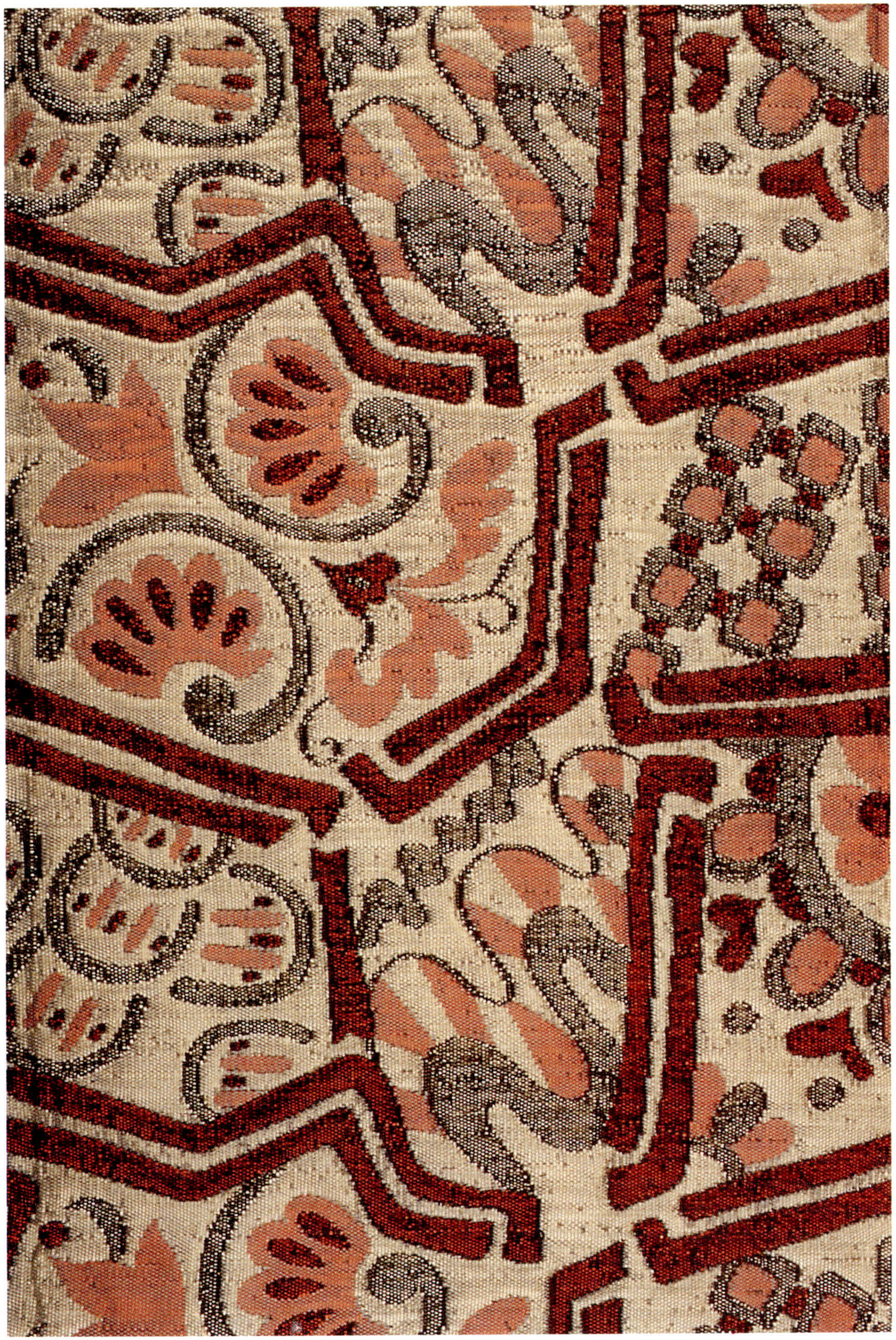

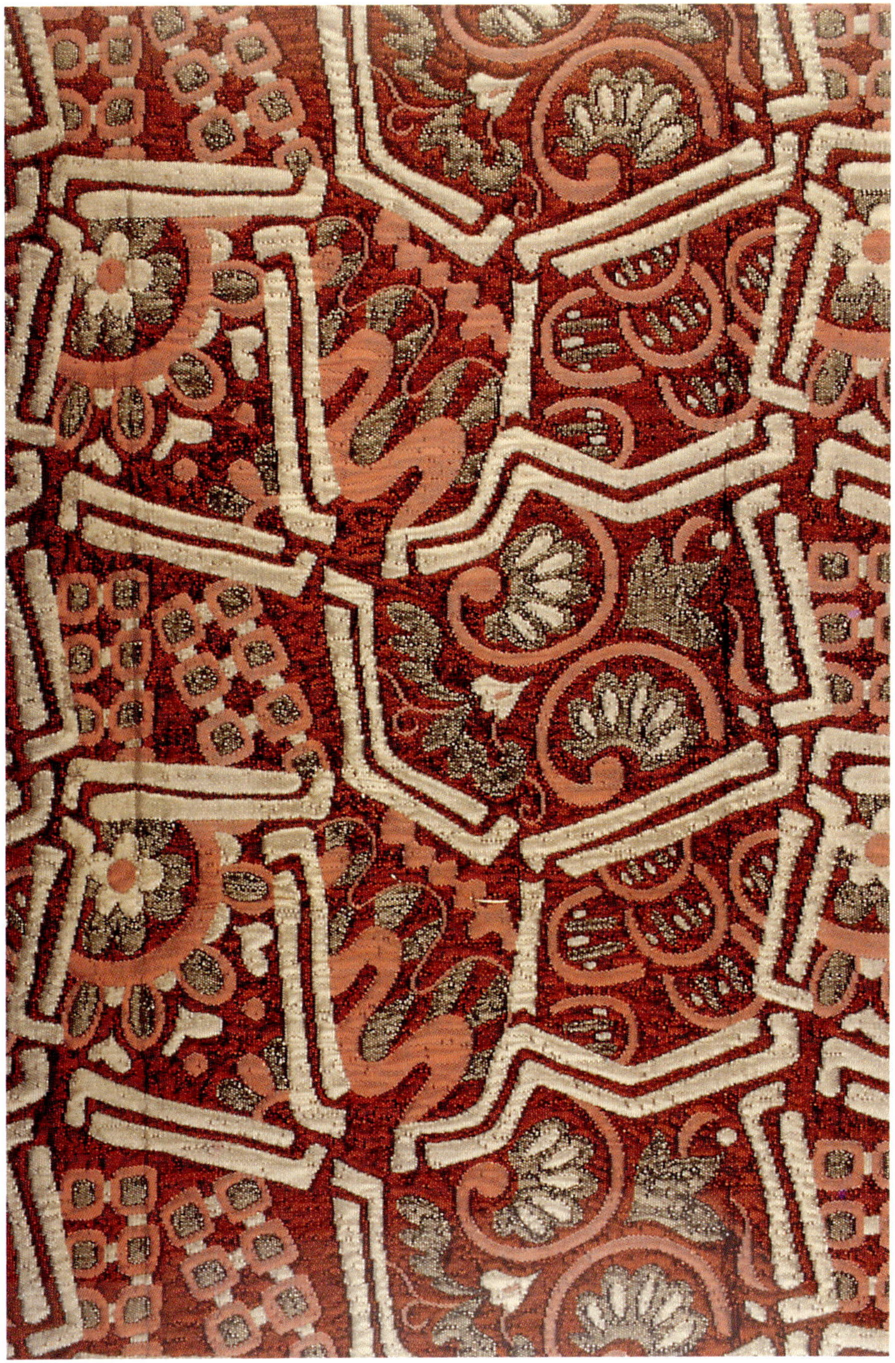

Front and back of mixed brocade with geometric patterns sparked by two shades of gold blocks and metallic peach and copper threads. Acetate/acrylic/polyester film, Japan, 1960s.

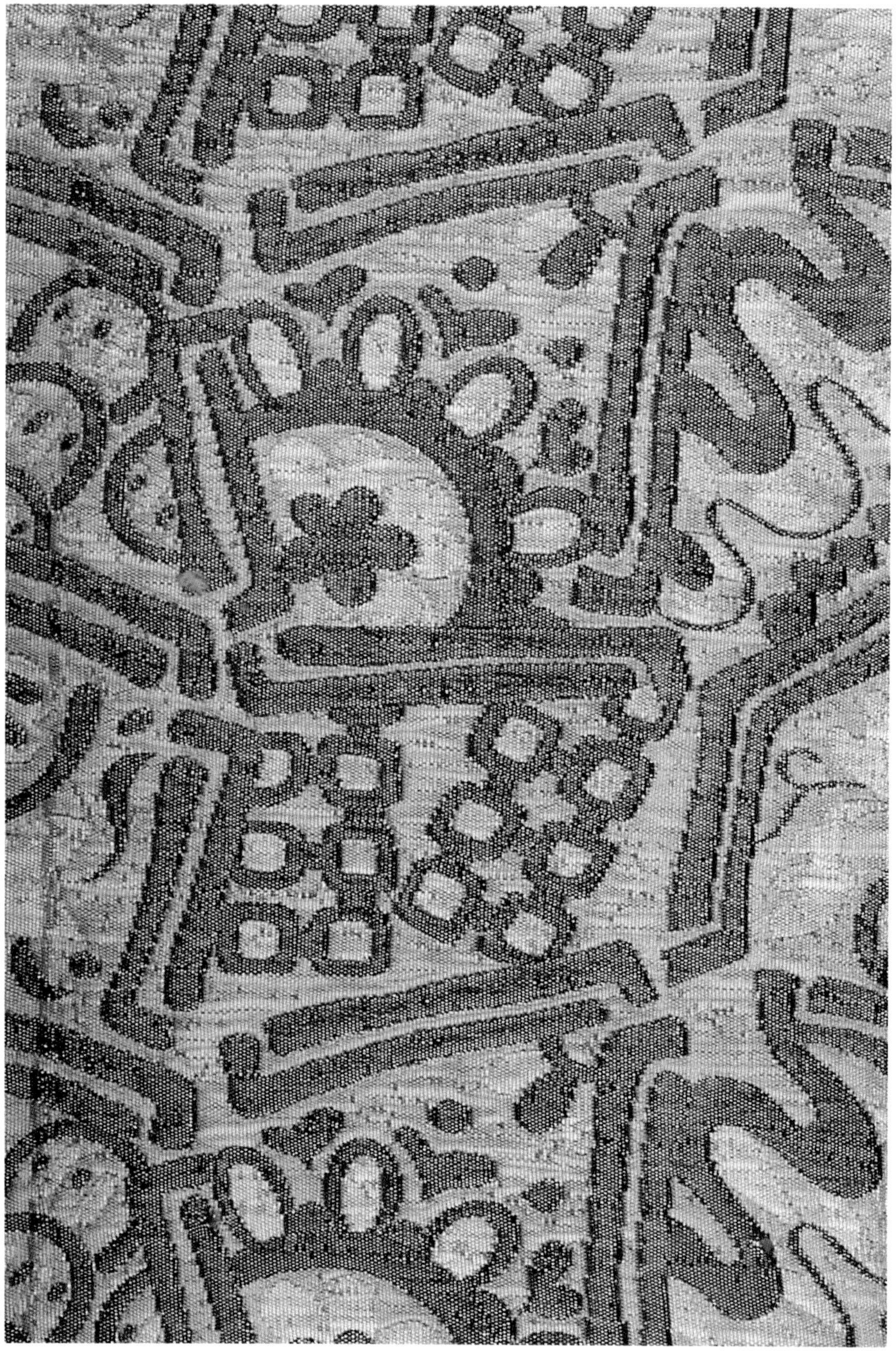

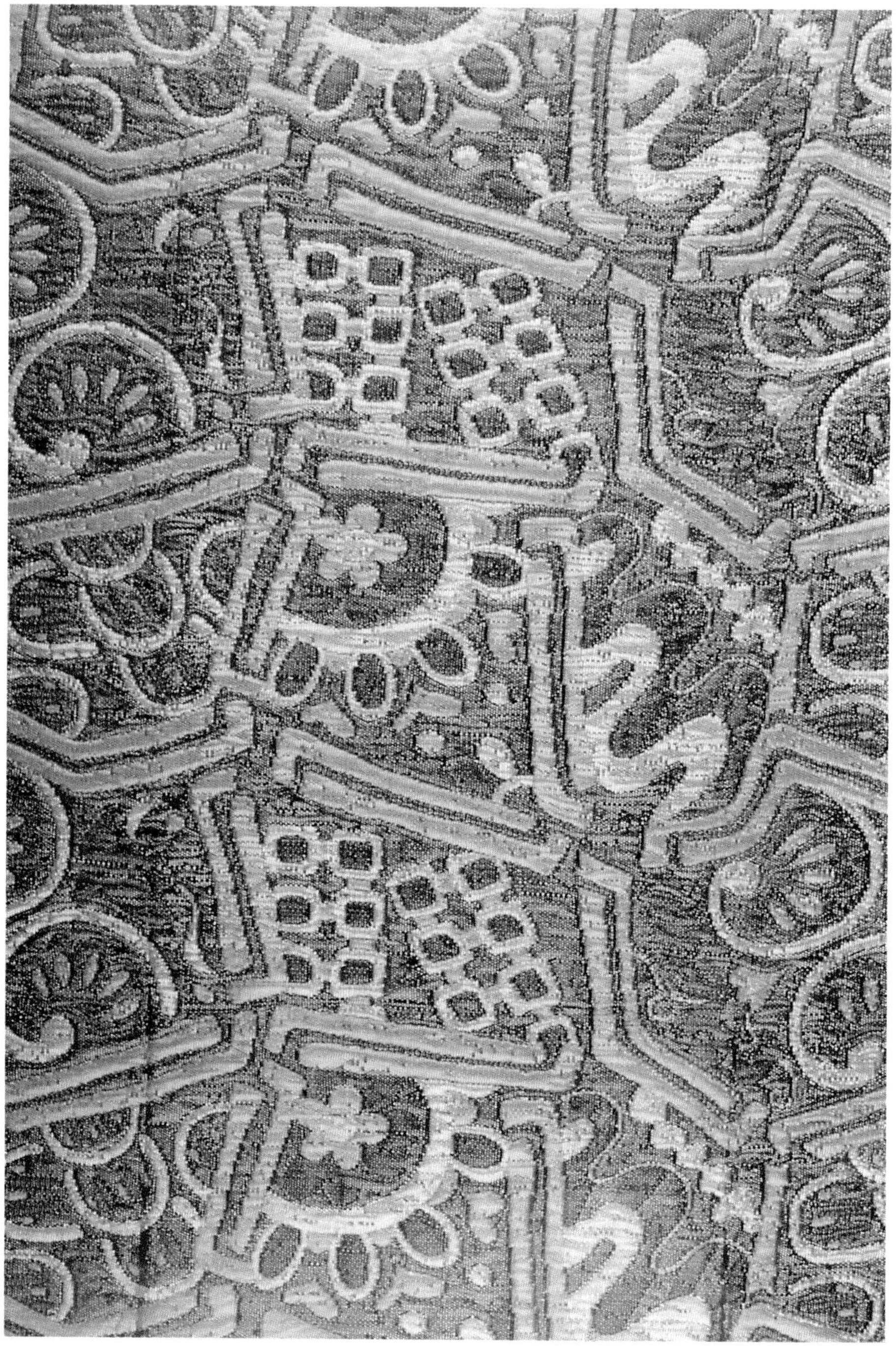

Front and back of mixed brocade with geometric patterns sparked by gold and silver blocks and metallic gray threads. Acetate/acrylic/polyester film, Japan, 1960s.

Chapter Seven

EXOTICS

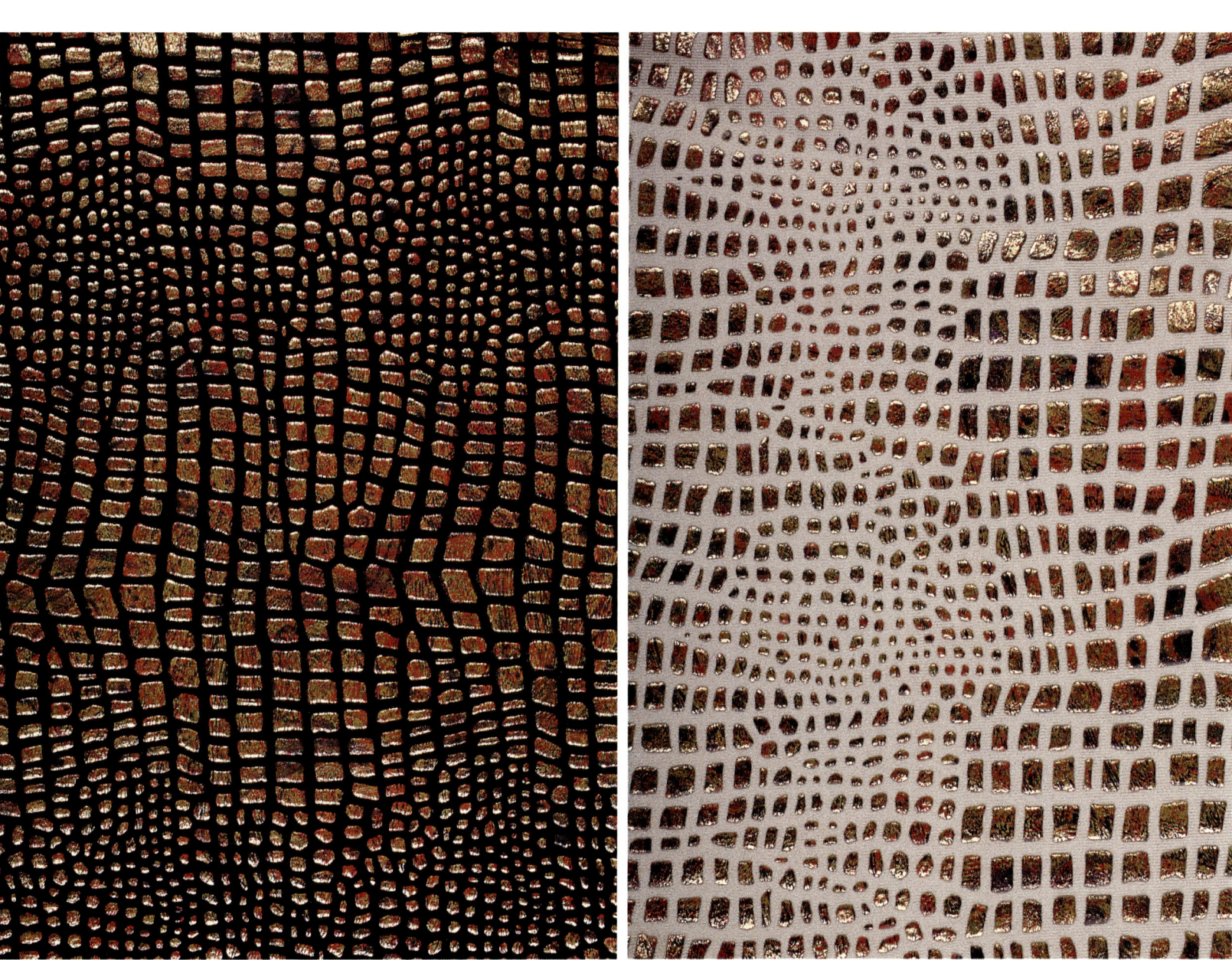

Left: Metallic red and gold snakeskin on black. *Courtesy of Tessitura Taiana Virgilio, Olgiate Comasco, Italy.*

Right: Metallic red and gold snakeskin on white. *Courtesy of Tessitura Taiana Virgilio. Olgiate Comasco Italy.*

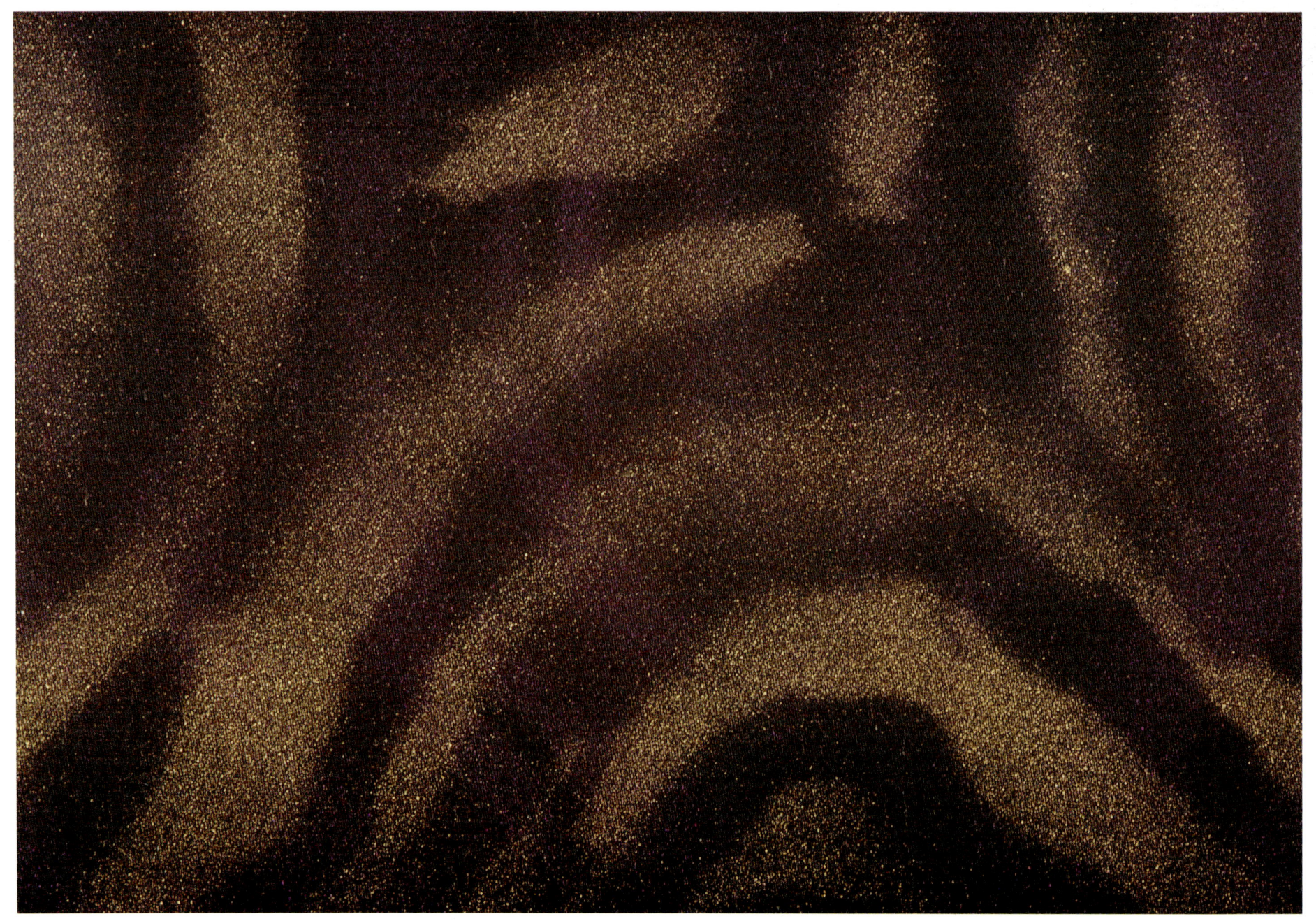

Gold flecks in animal print swirl. Cotton/rayon, Italy 1956.

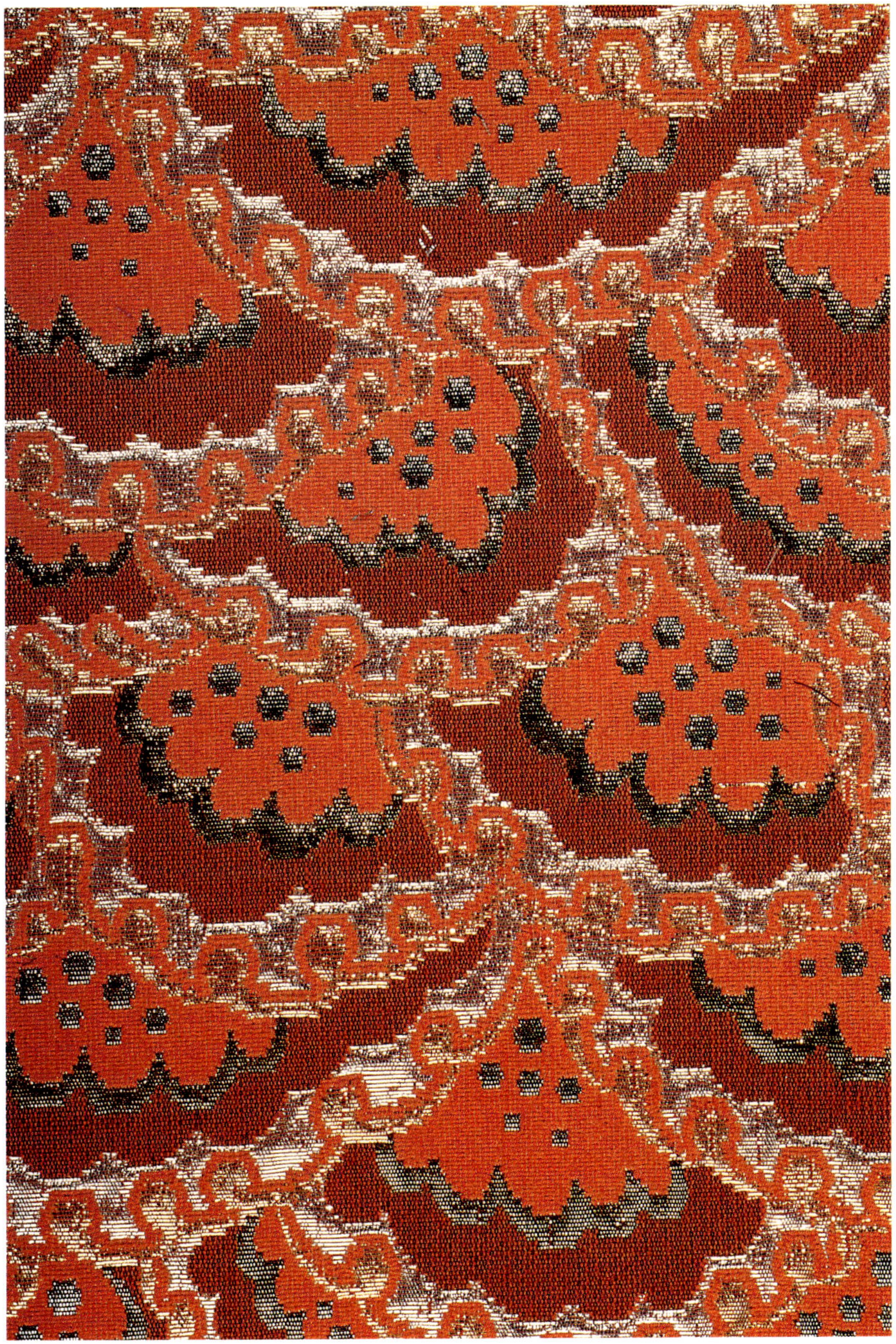

Gold, silver, and black metallic threads adorn brocade with two shades of orange. Japan, 1970s.

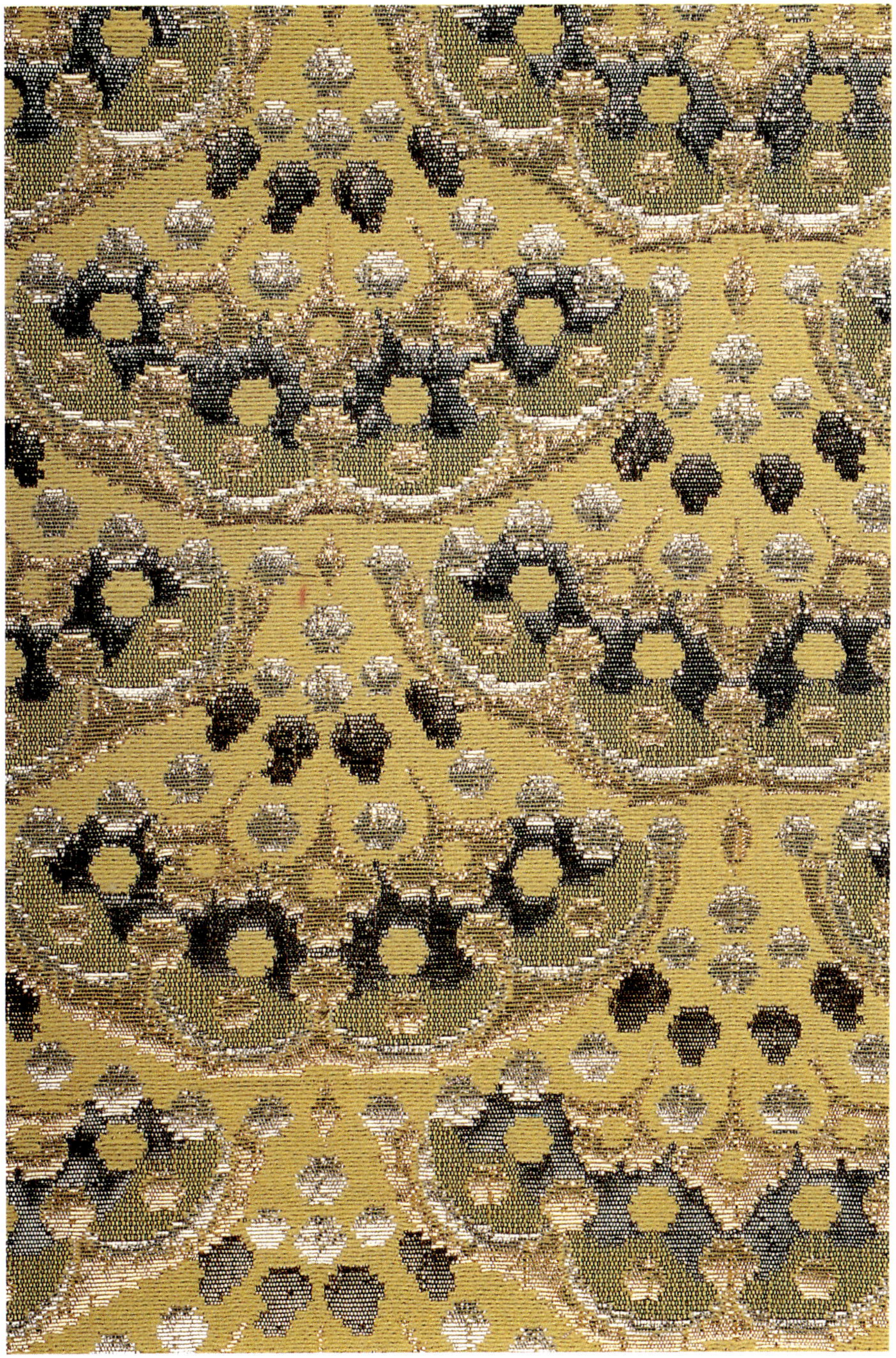

Gold and silver highlight green and black brocade. Japan, 1970s.

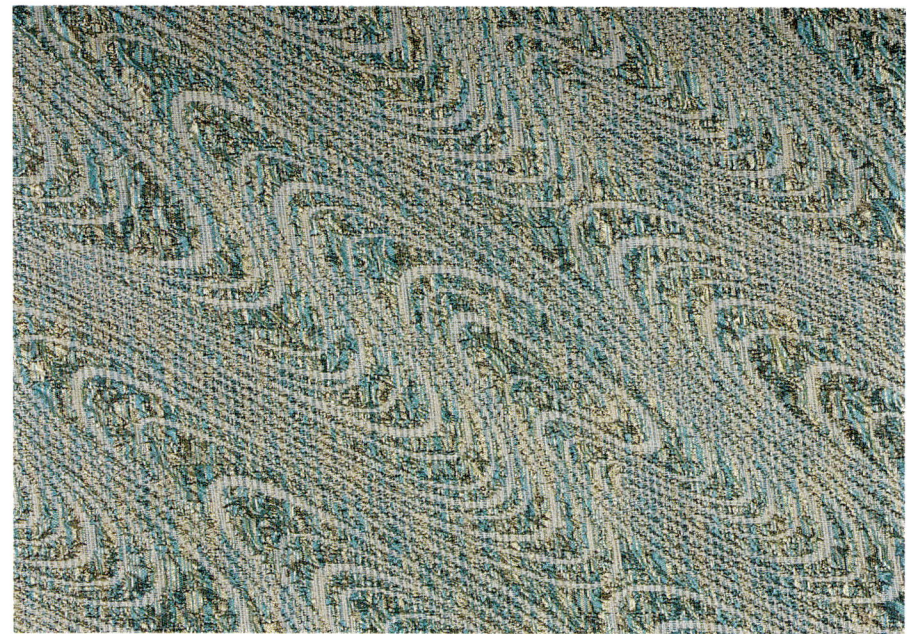

Raised green and gold creates psychedelic relief against like-colored ground. Japan, 1970s.

Quilted effect with blue and golds. Japan, 1970s.

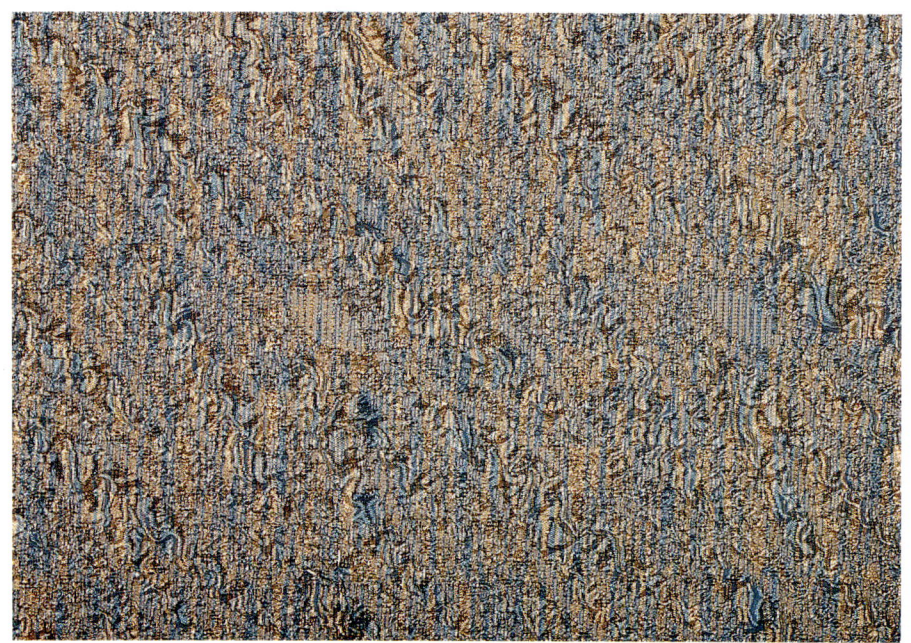

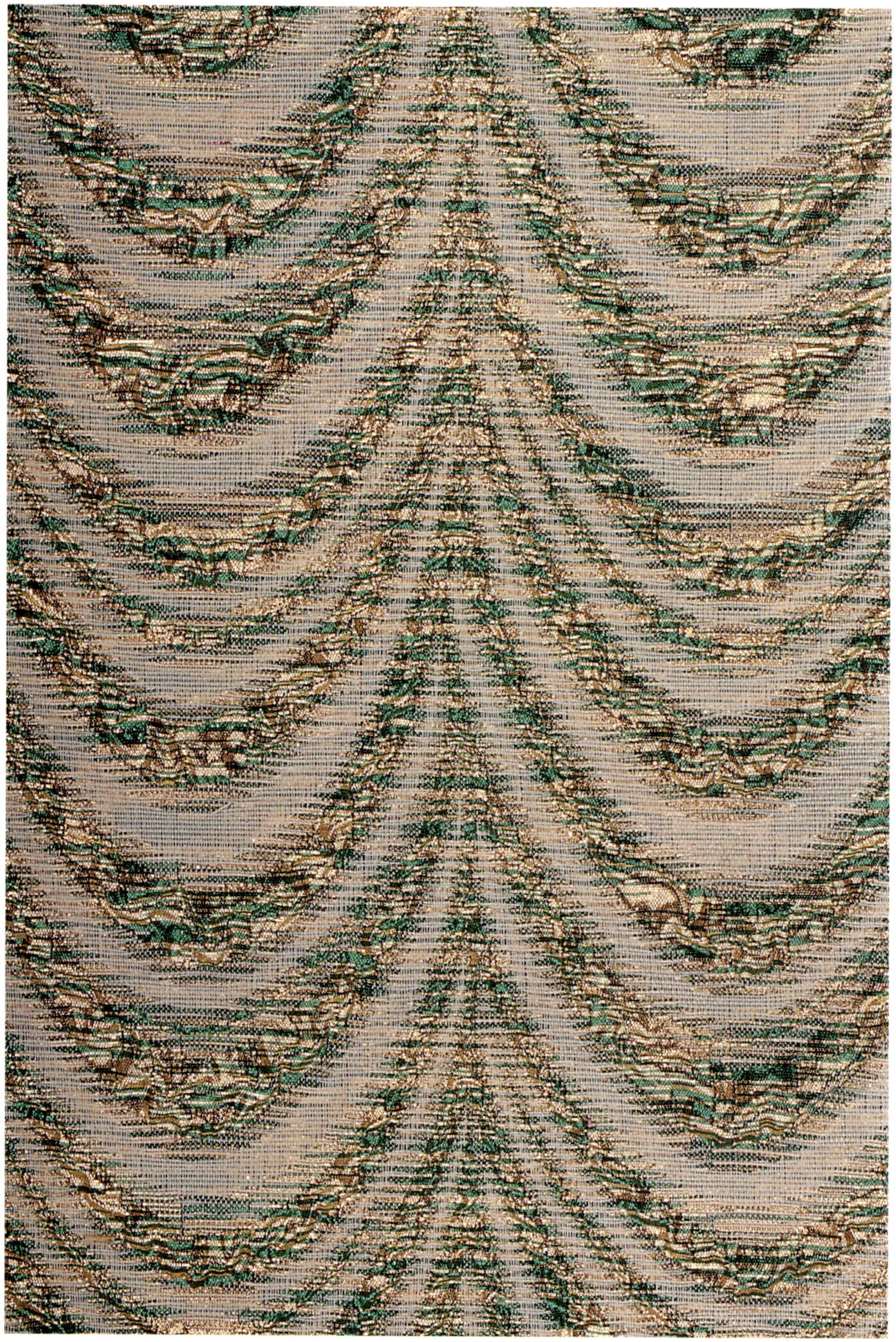

Draped effect is created in gold and green. Japan, 1970s.

Gold threads add lift to areas on abstract print of orange, olive, and browns. France, 1965.

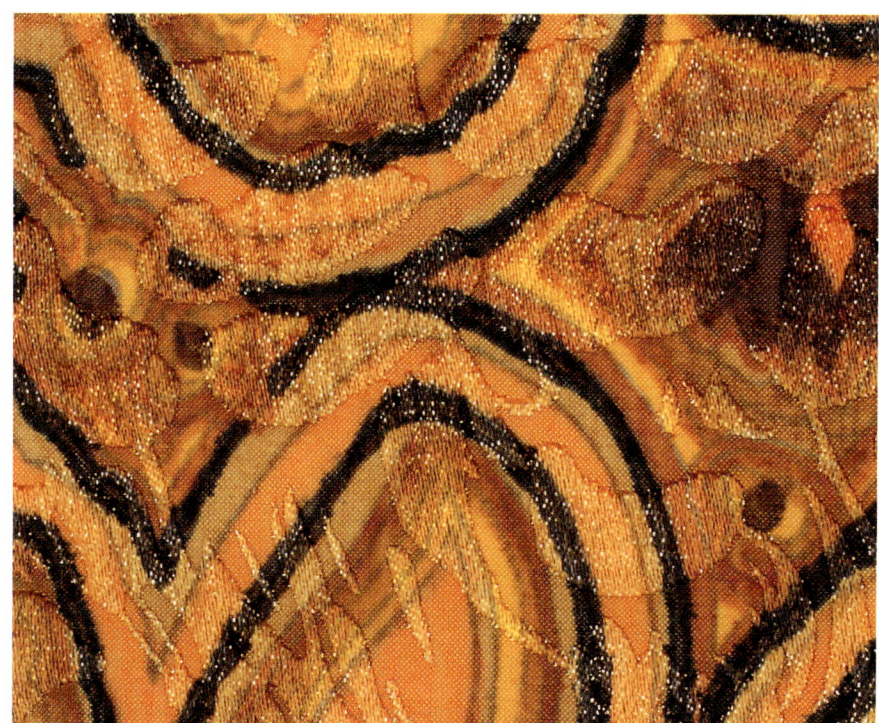

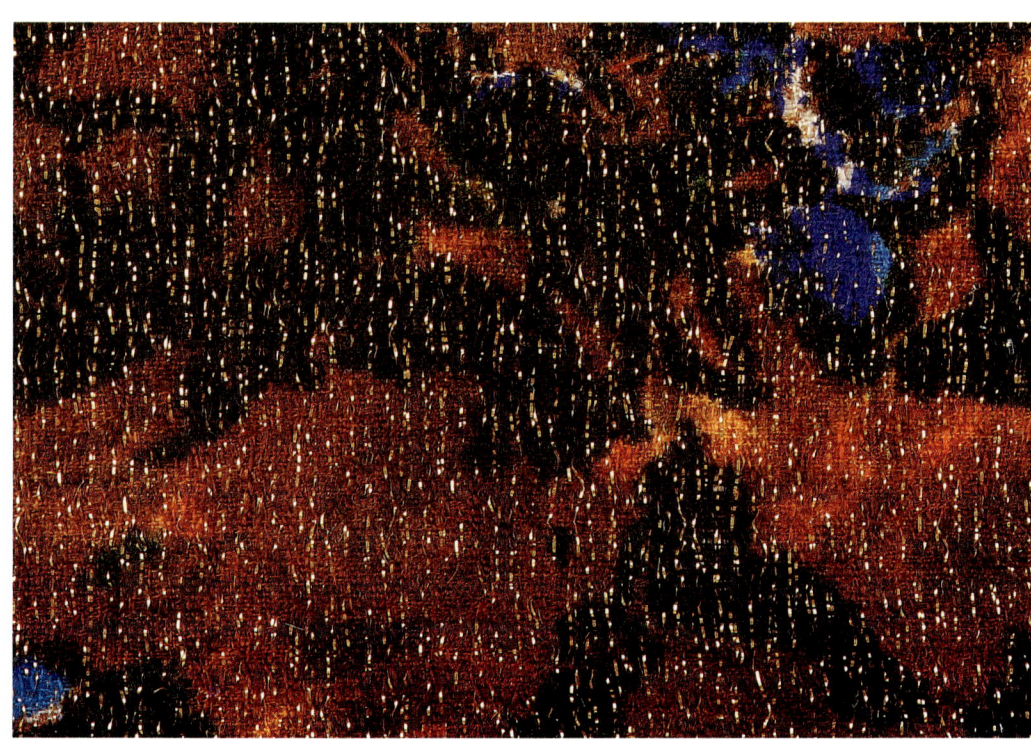

Gold flecks on mottled brown and black with blue accents. Polyester/cotton, France, 1962.

Chapter Eight

LACE

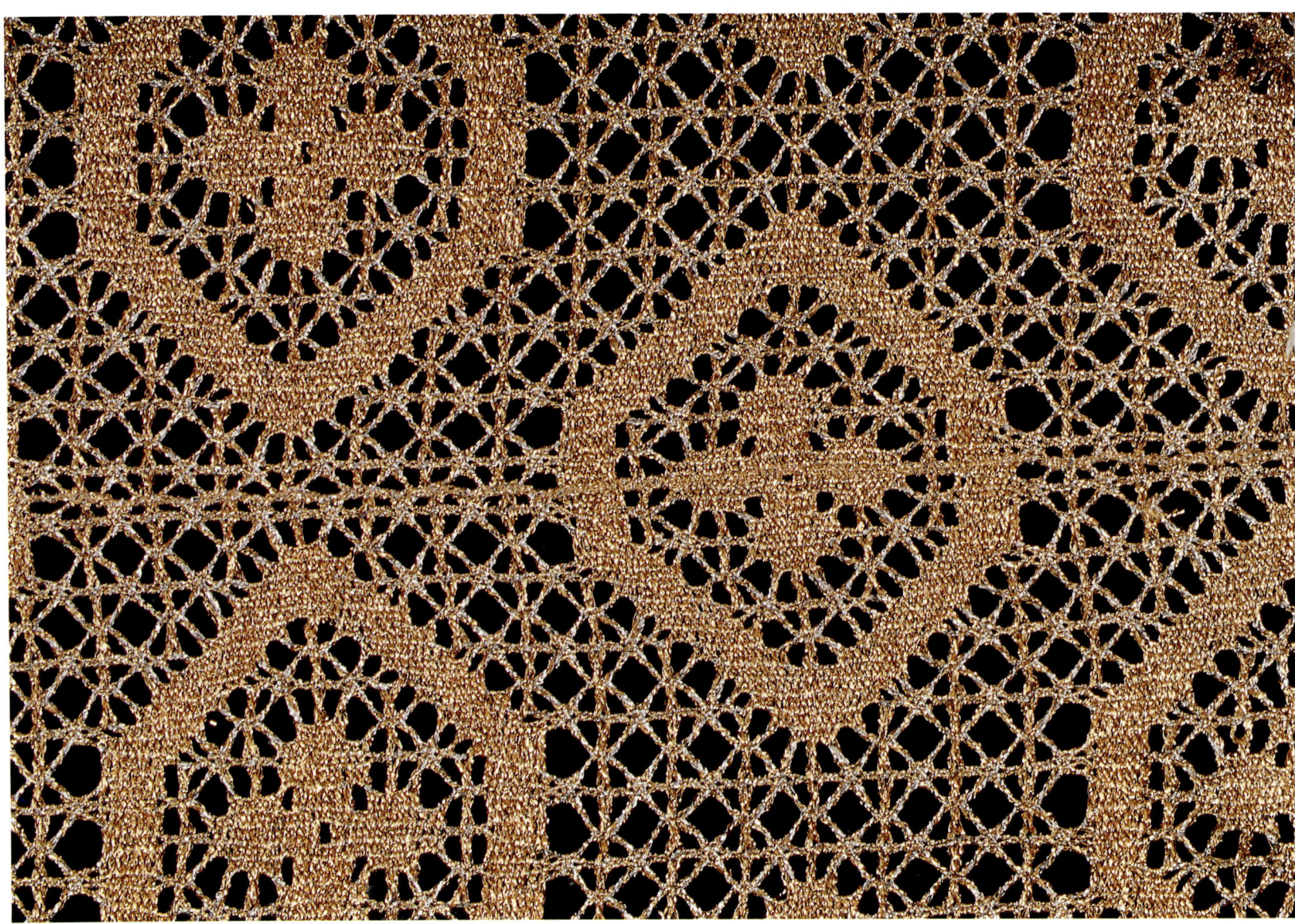

Gold lace design.
Japan, 1960s.

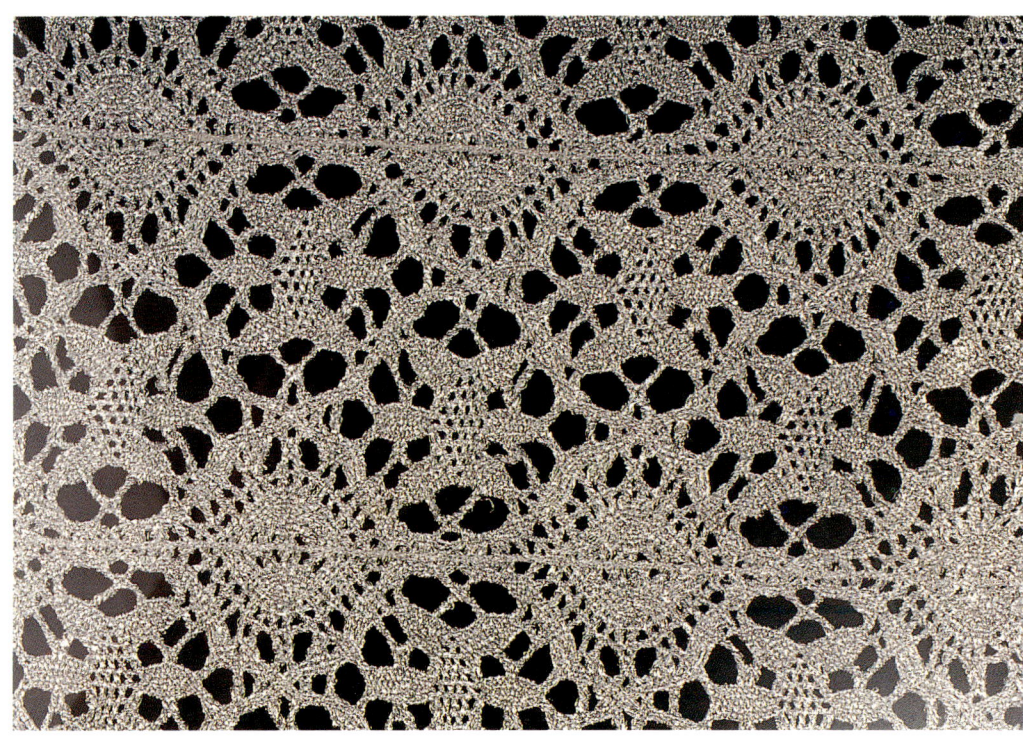

Silver lace. Japan, 1960s.

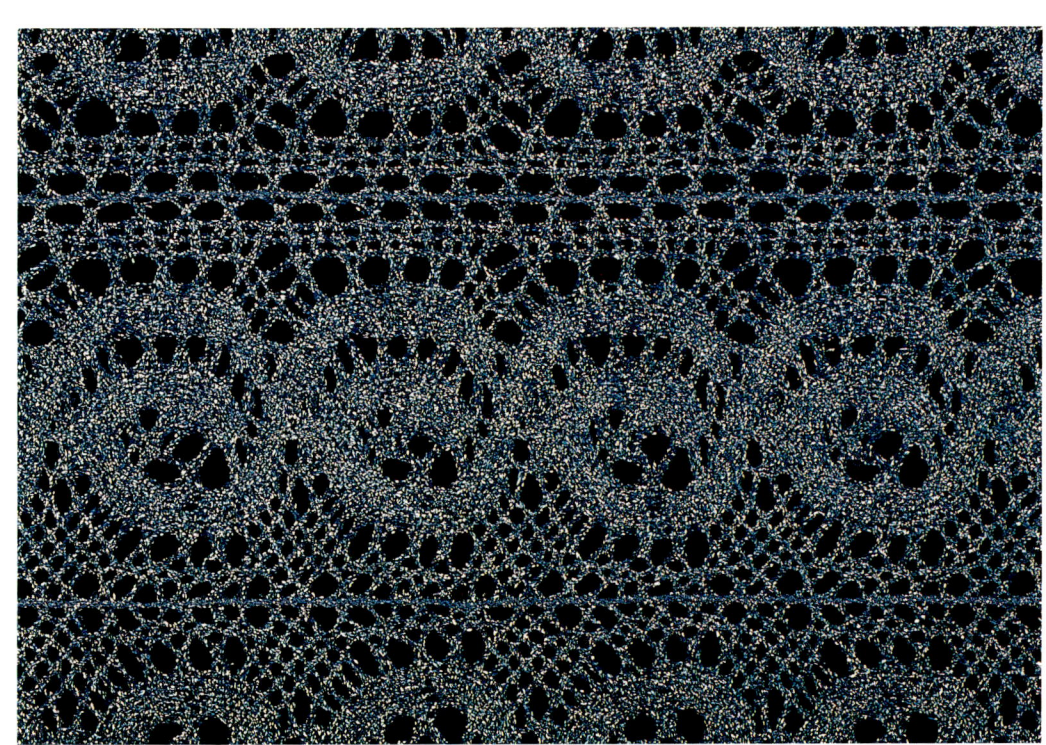

Blue and silver lace. Japan, 1960s.

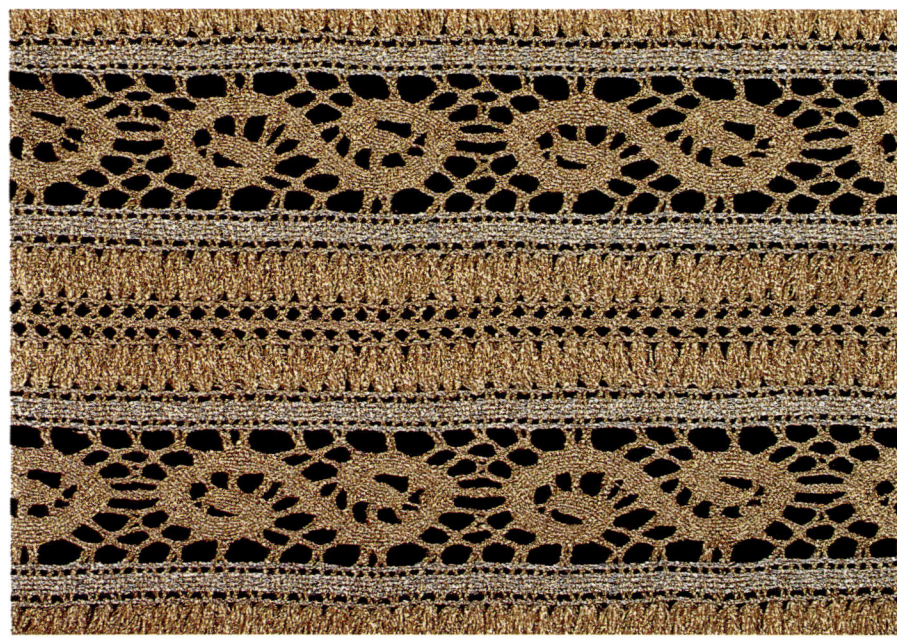
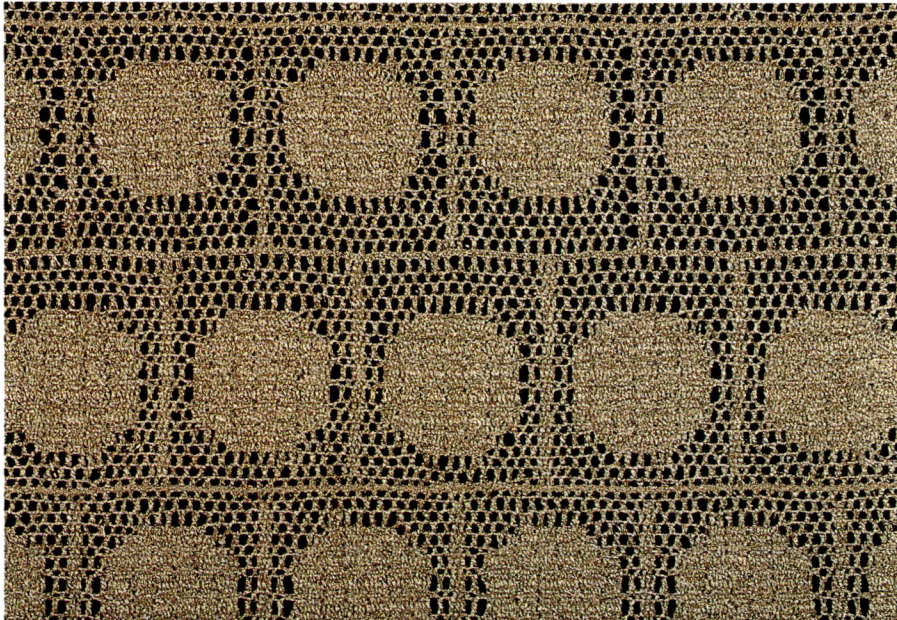
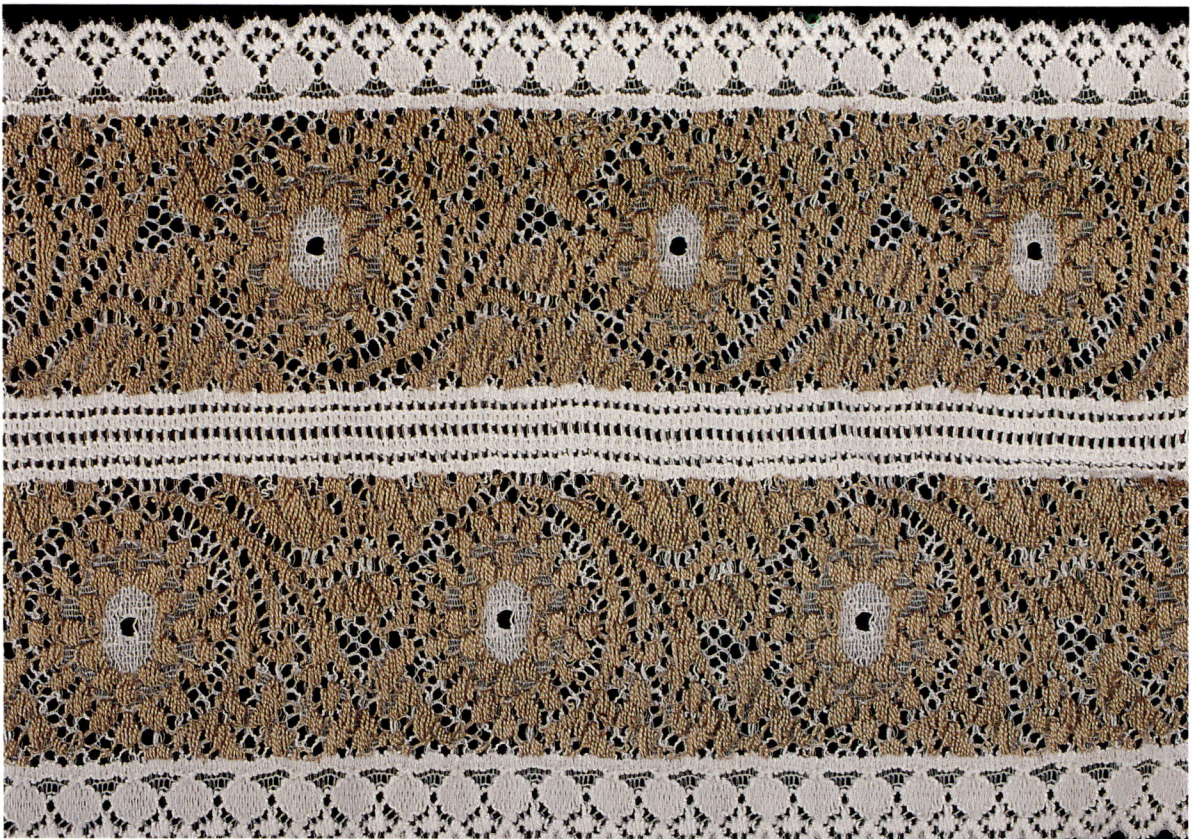

Top left: Fringed gold and silver lace. Japan, 1960s.

Top right: Gold lace with circles-and-squares pattern. Japan, 1960s.

Bottom right: Gold and white lace. *Courtesy of Desseilles Textiles, Calais, France.*

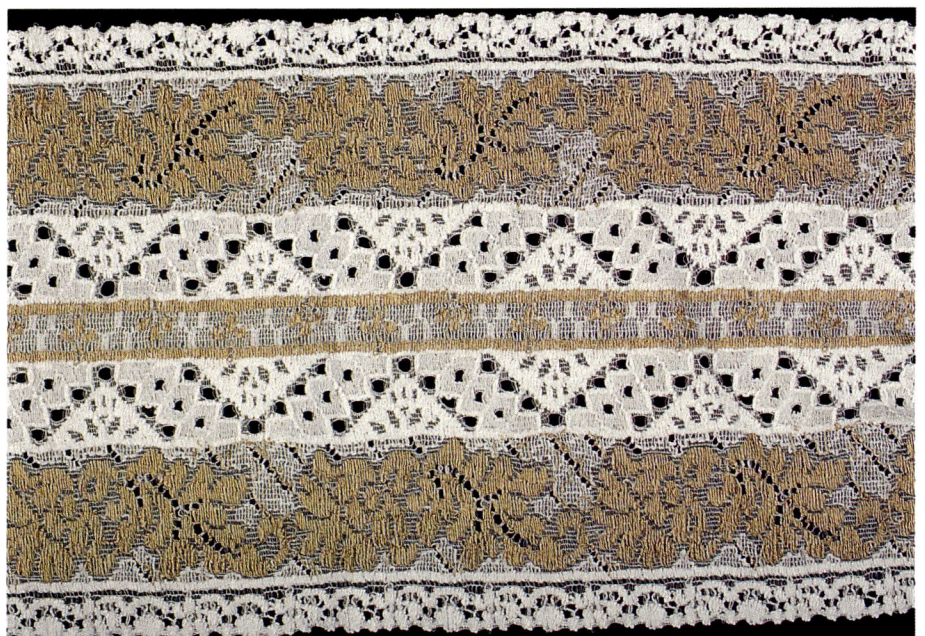

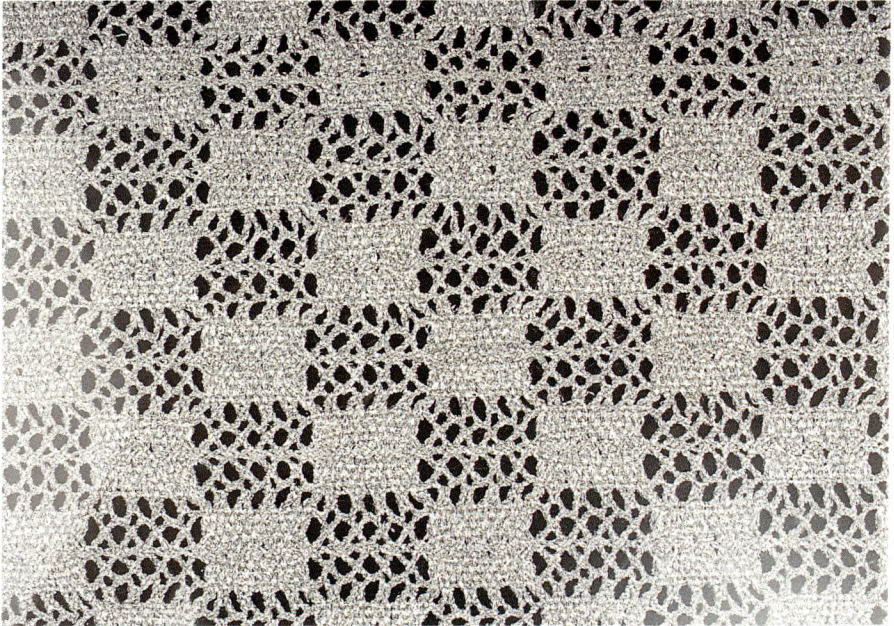

Top left: Gold and white lace. *Courtesy of Desseilles Textiles, Calais, France.*

Top right: Shimmery, pearled white lace. Japan, 1960s.

Bottom left: Copper and white lace. *Courtesy of Desseilles Textiles, Calais, France.*

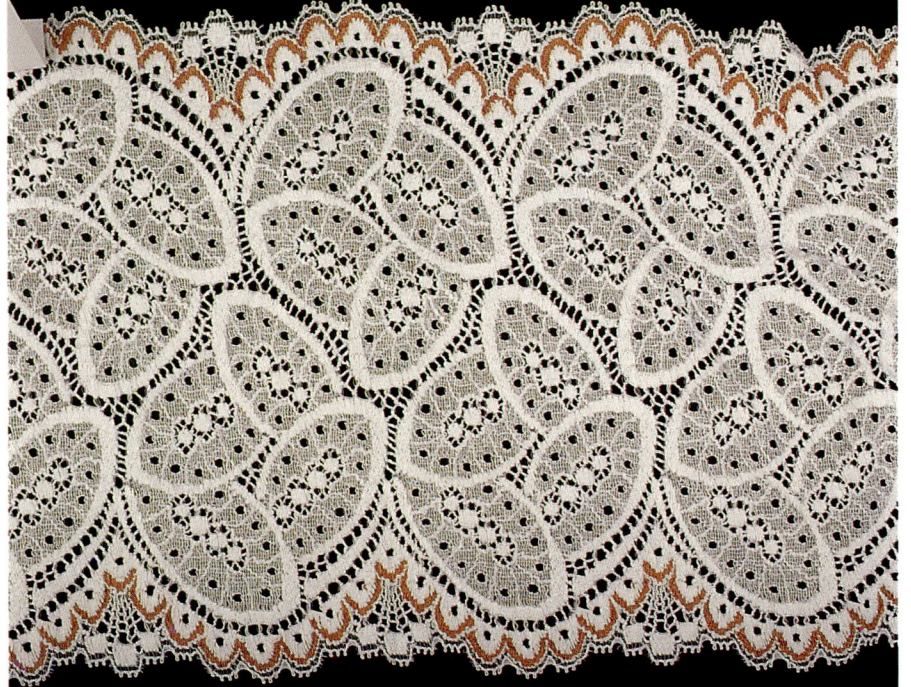
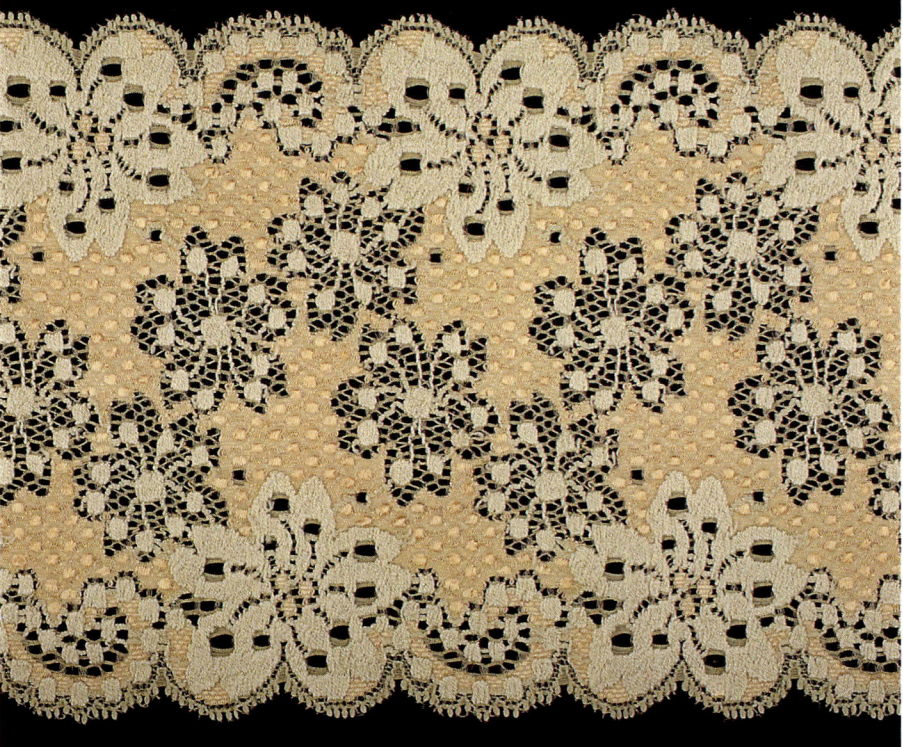

Top left: Copper and white lace. *Courtesy of Desseilles Textiles, Calais, France.*

Top right: Mint green lace with gold. *Courtesy of Houlé Dentelles, Calais, France.*

Bottom left: Gold and silver circles in lace framework. Japan, 1960s.

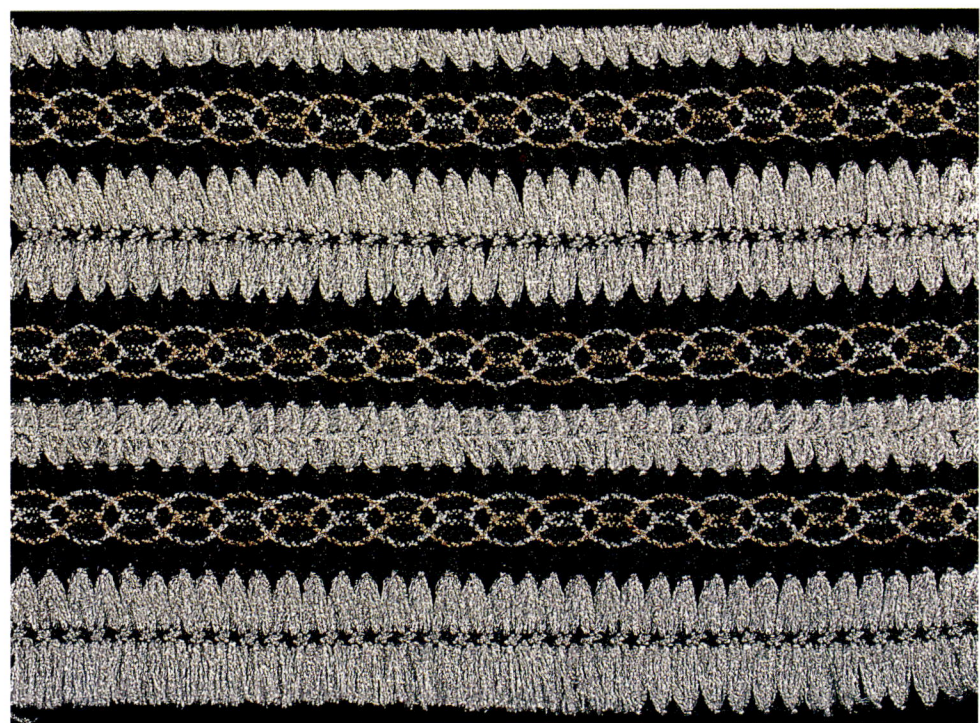

Fringed silver, black, and gold lace. Japan, 1960s.

Black floral pattern on gold. *Courtesy of Tessitura Taiana Virgilio, Olgiate Comasco, Italy.*

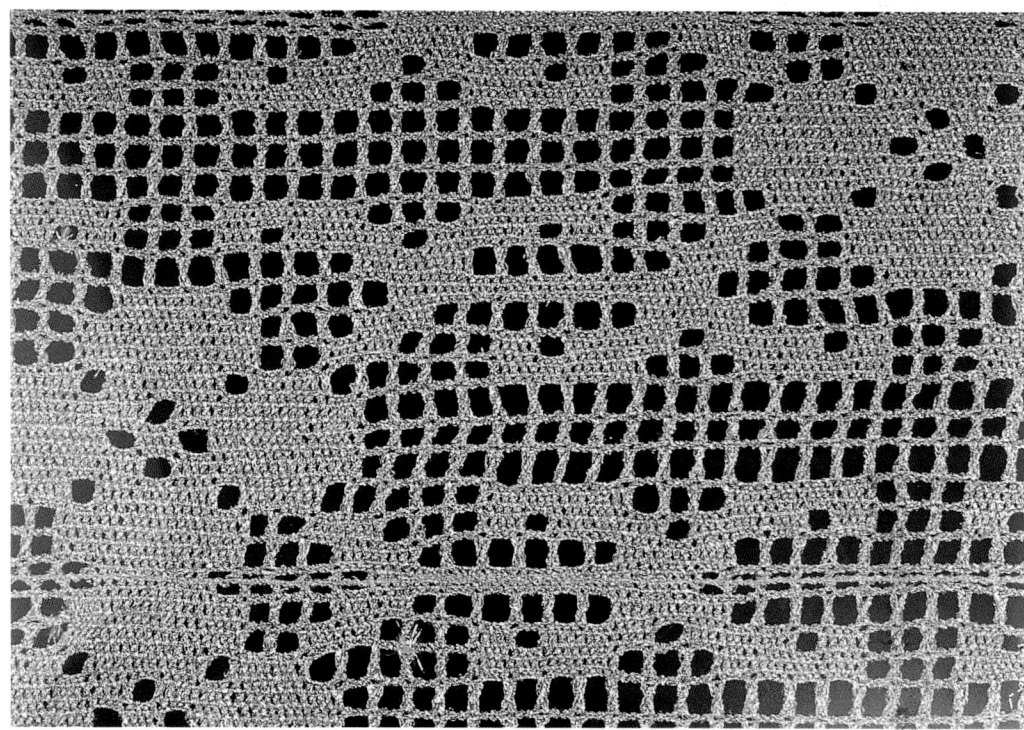

Silver lace suggestive of floral pattern. Japan, 1970s.

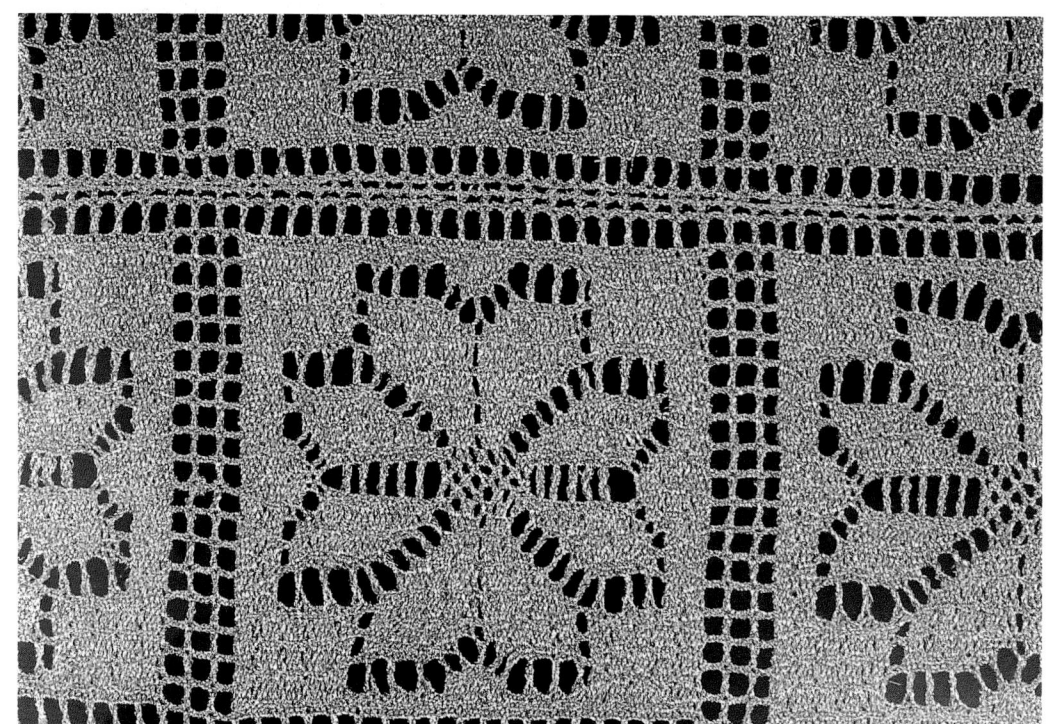

Flowers in check pattern. Japan, 1970s.

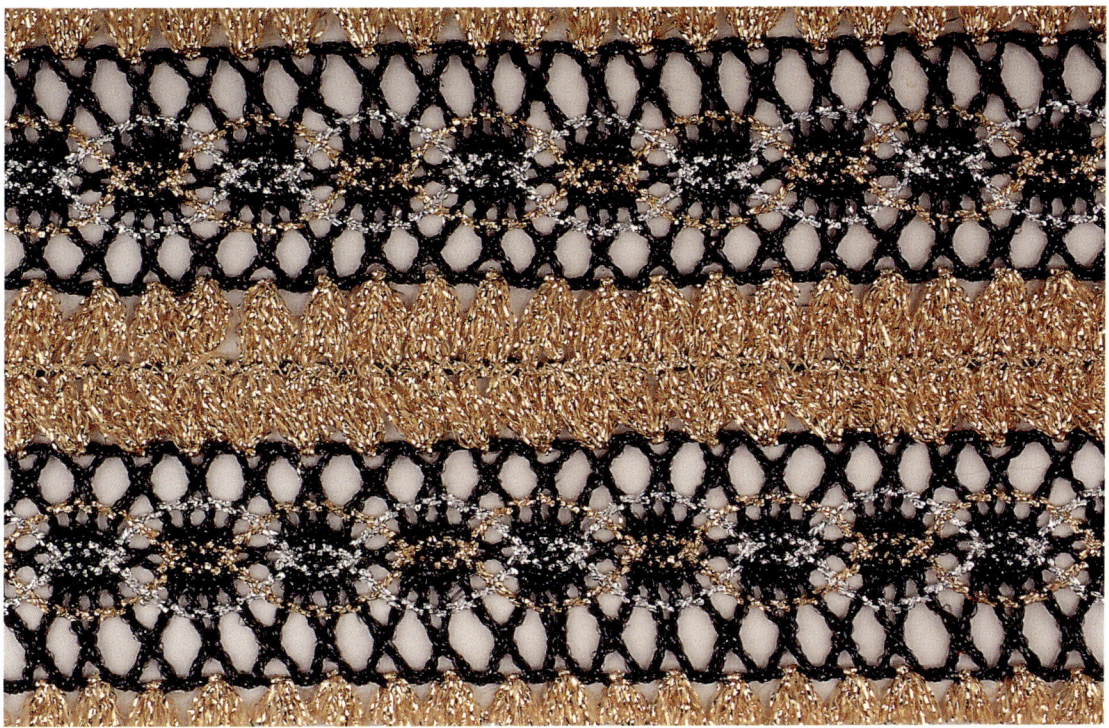

Gold and black fringed lace. Japan, 1960s.

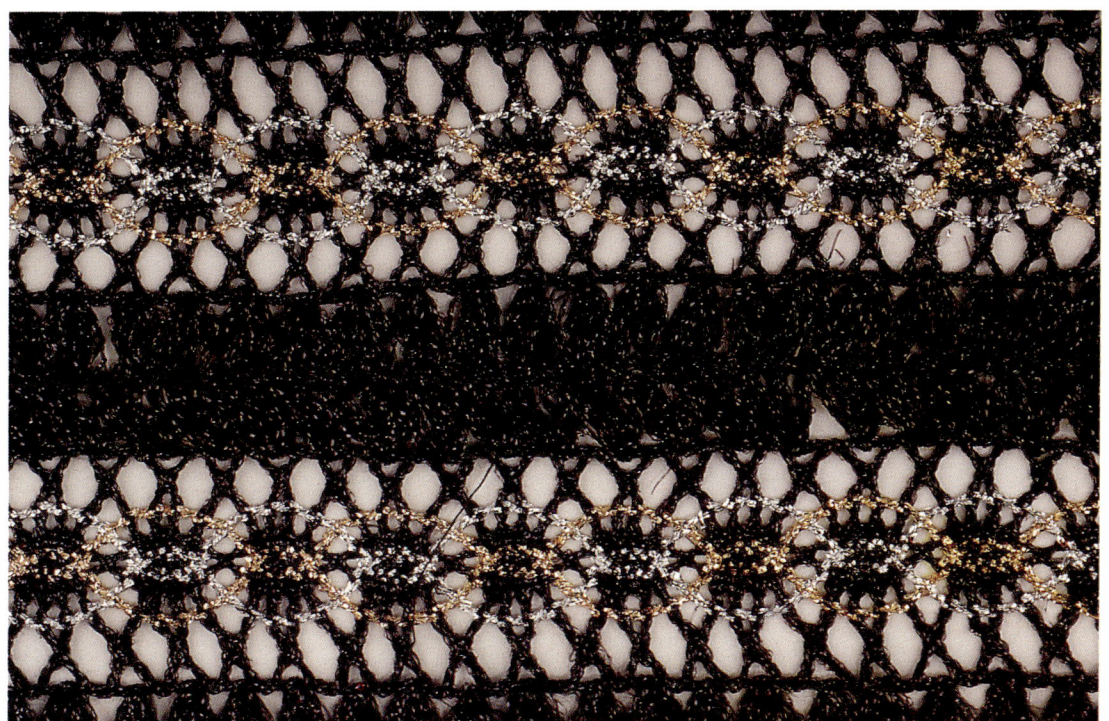

Black and gold fringed lace. Japan, 1960s.

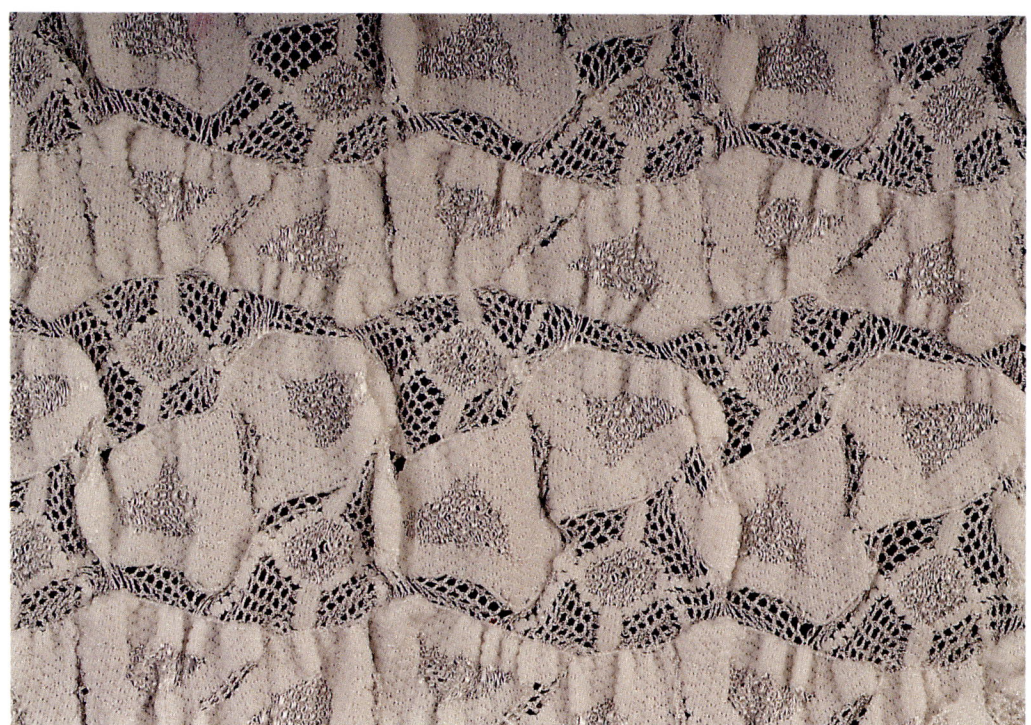

Stretch lace with silver highlights. Nylon/rayon. *Courtesy of Gartex International, Busto Arsizio, Italy.*

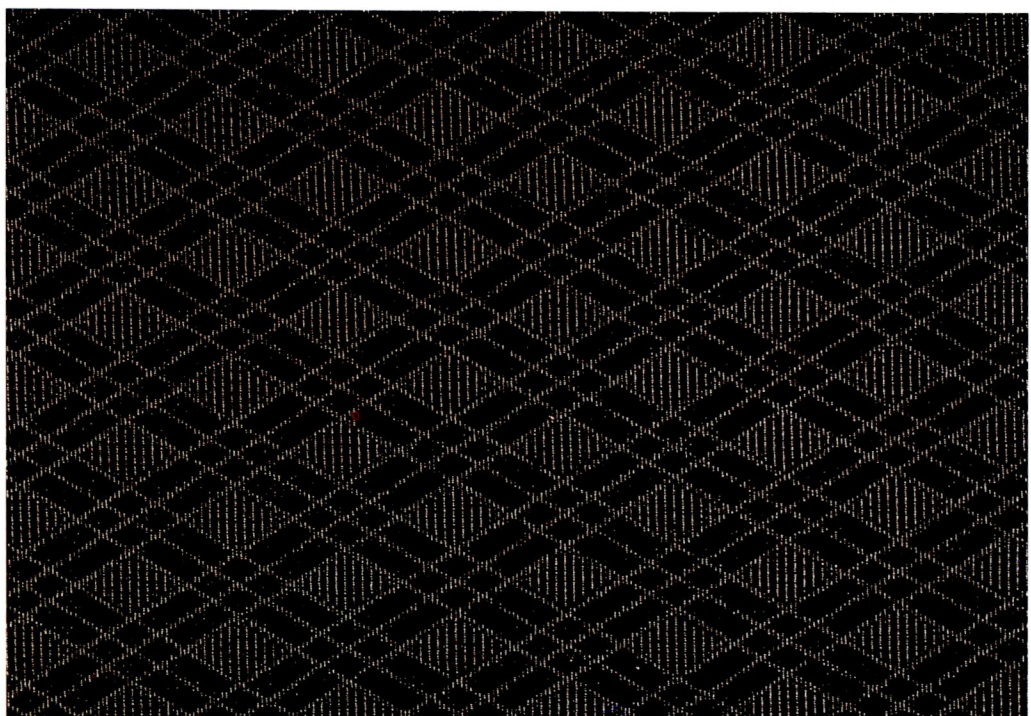

Black harlequin pattern with gold. *Courtesy of Tessitura Taiana Virgilio, Olgiate Comasco, Italy.*

Chapter Nine

MISCELLANEOUS

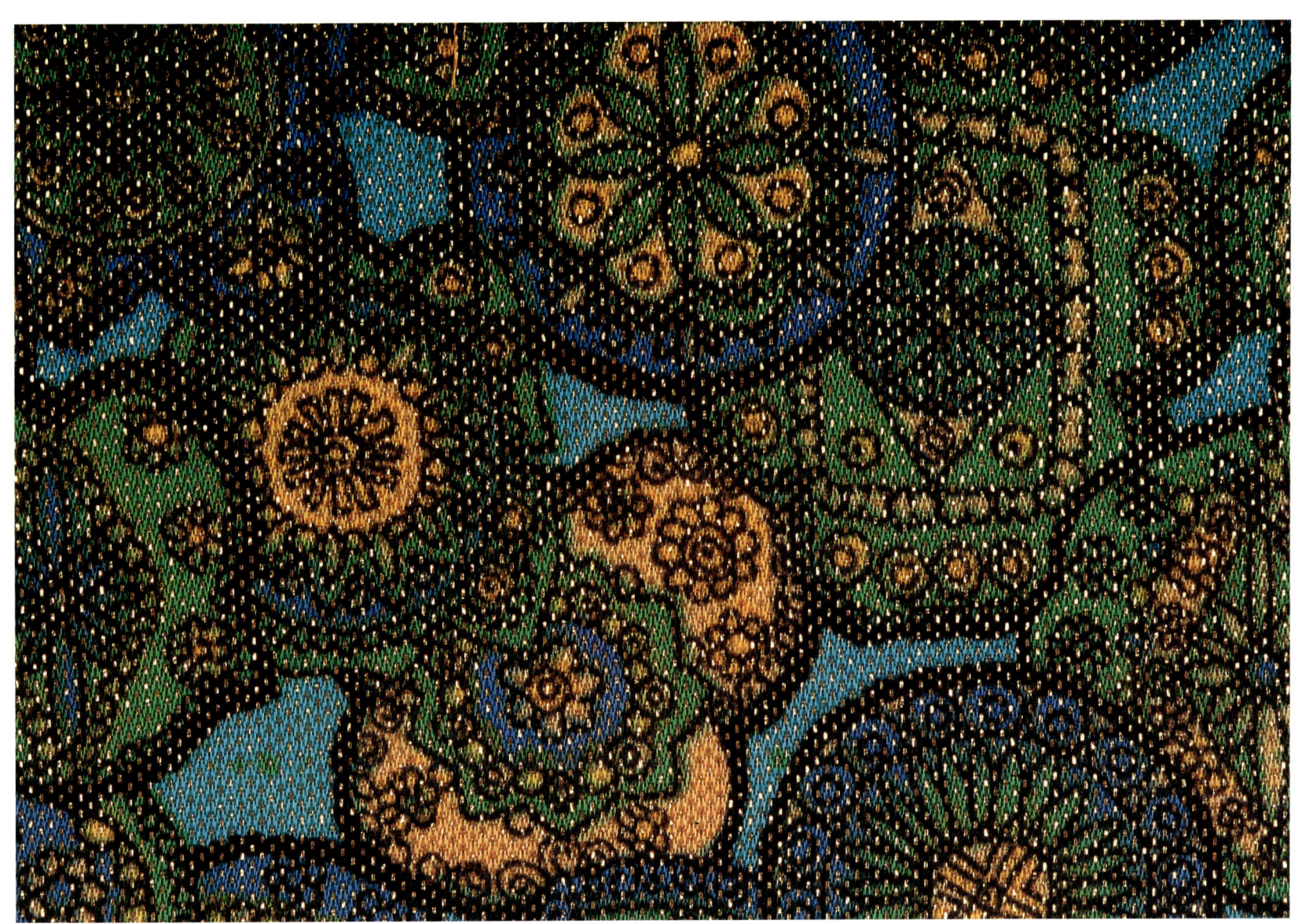

Gold highlights with stylized flowers. Cotton/polyester, France, 1963.

Gold and yellow weave with black and white print. Nylon polyester fused to acetate, France, 1967.

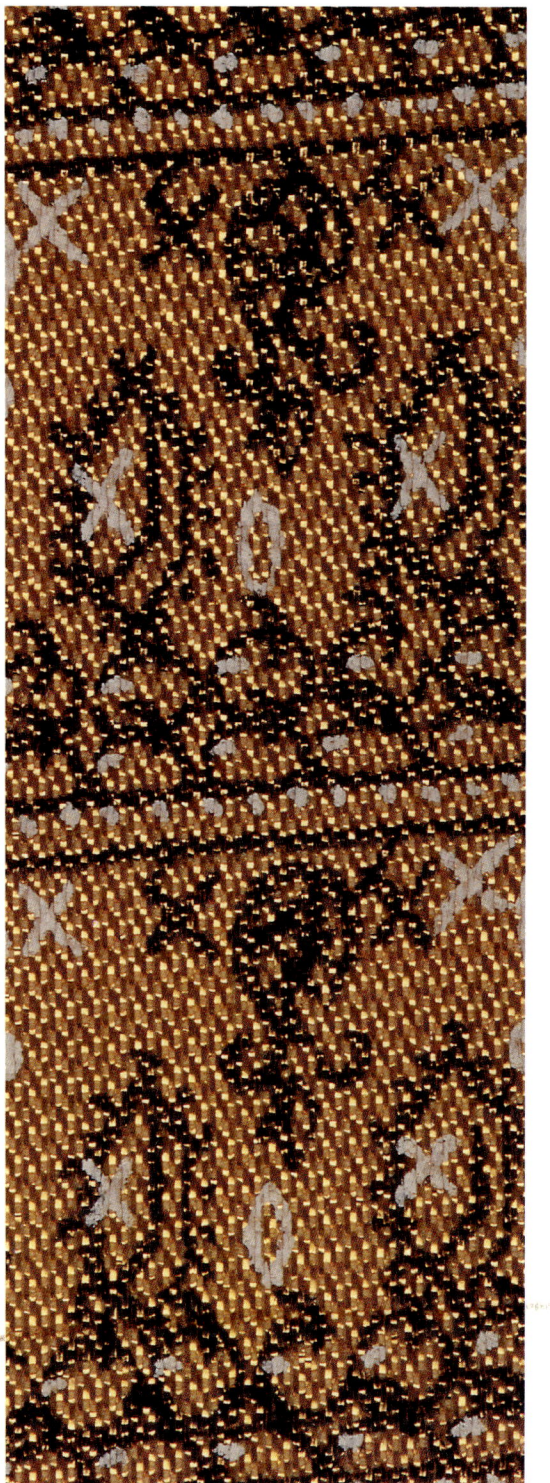

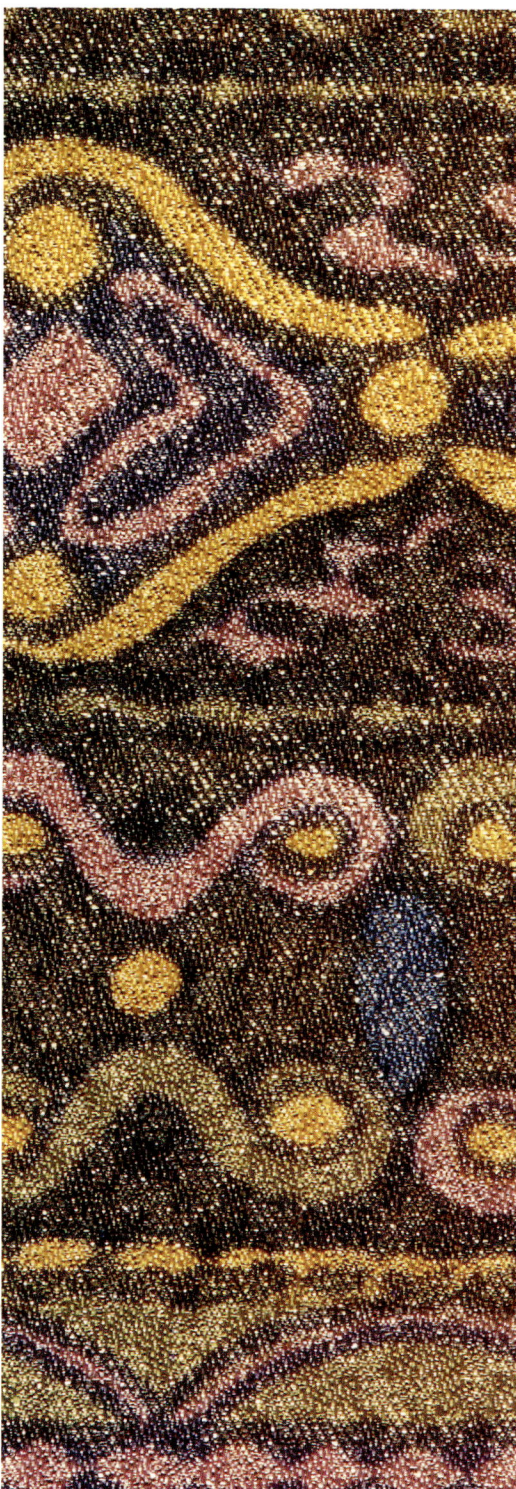

Gold highlights dark green ground with pink and green striped print. Acetate polyester, France, 1967.

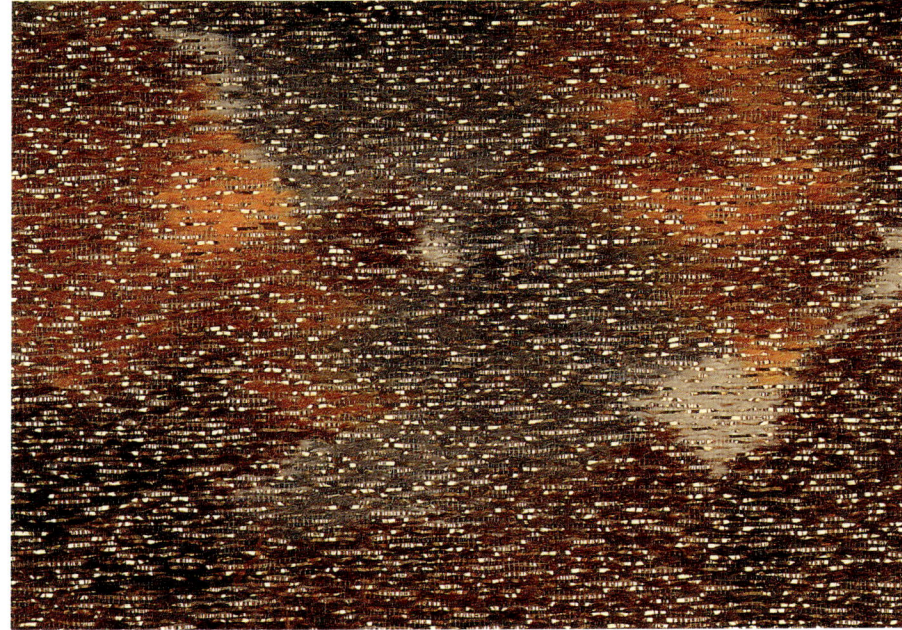

Natural tones with gold. Wool/nylon, France, 1961.

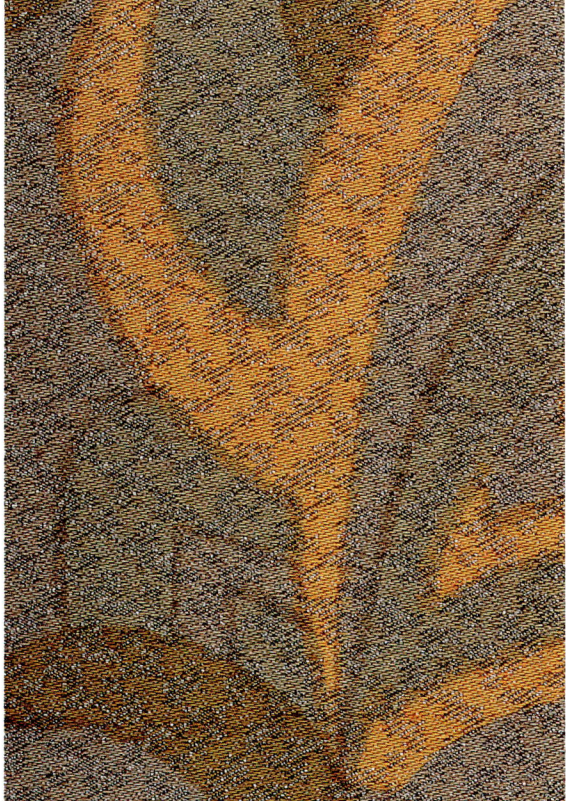

Loose harlequin pattern of silver highlights over orange, mauve, and greens. Acetate Polyester, France, 1967.

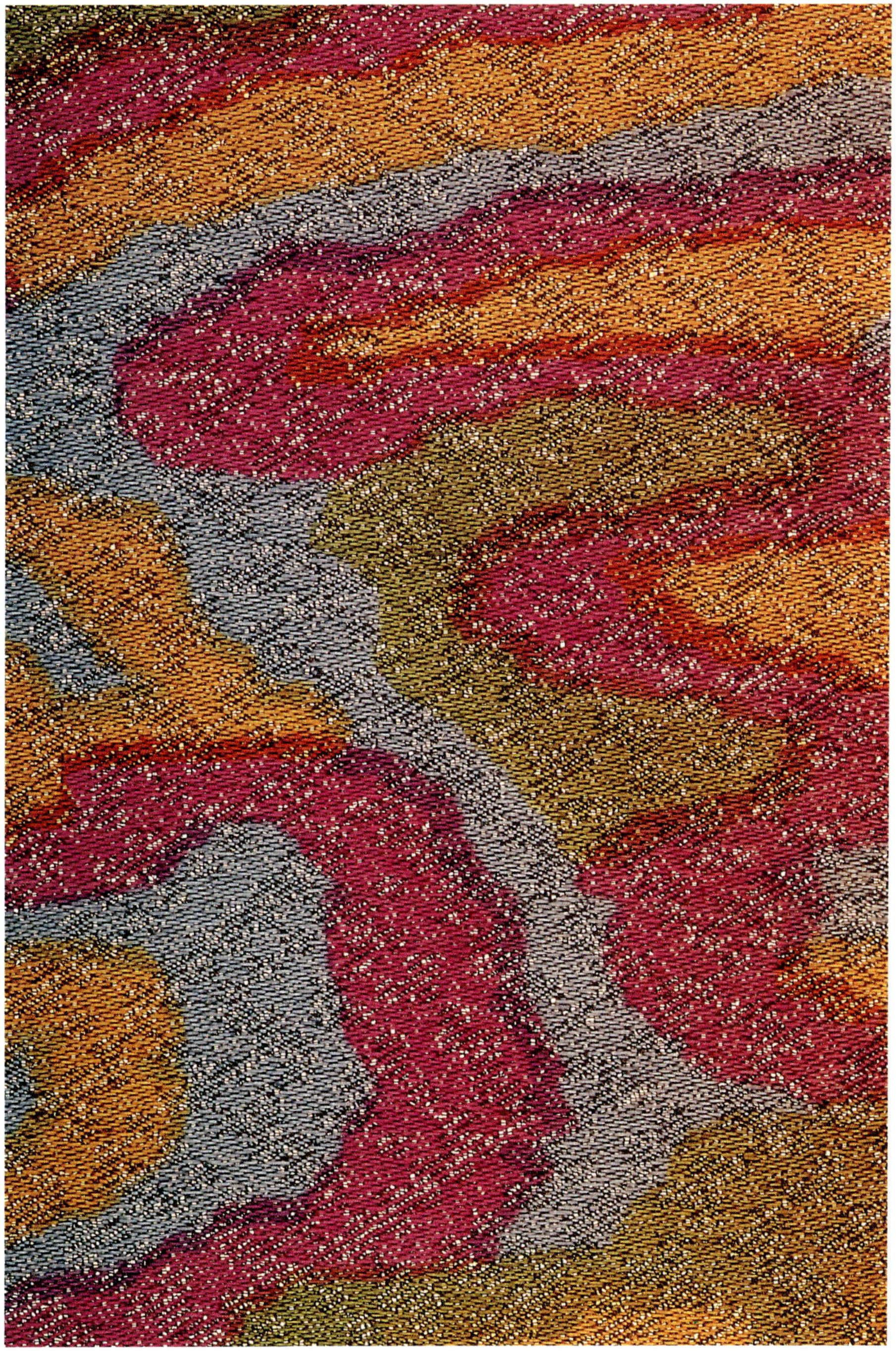

Loose harlequin pattern of gold over hot pink, light blue, yellow, and green. Acetate polyester, France, 1967.

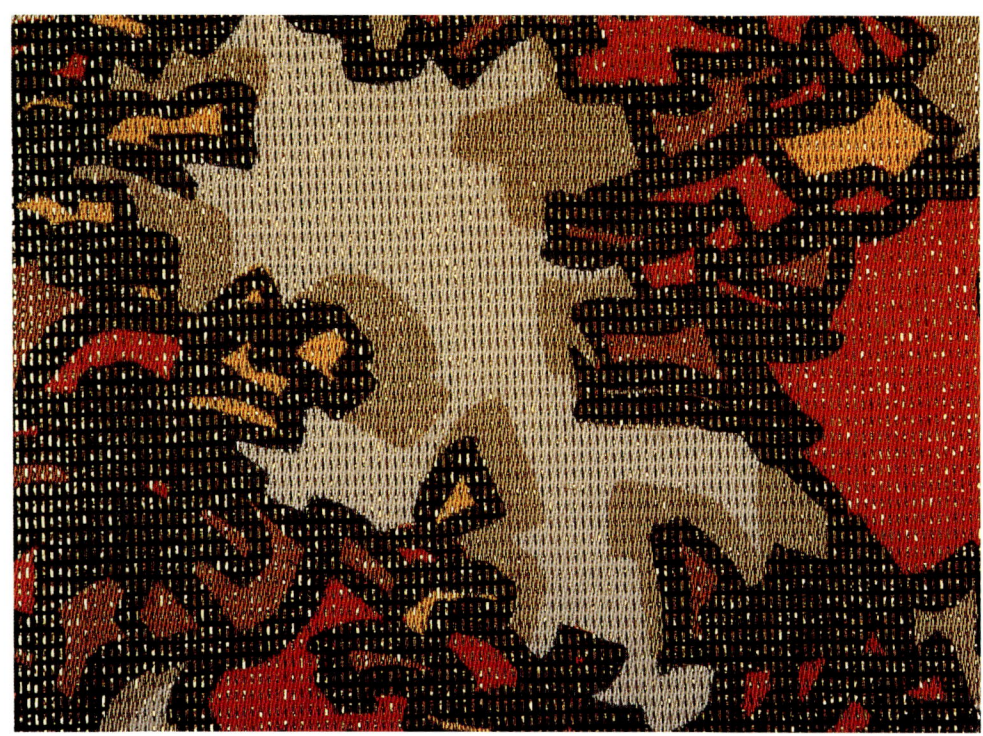

Vertical gold threads in orange, black, and taupe print. Polyester blend, France, 1961.

Gold threads run vertically, adding sparkle to abstract black and white. Rayon/cotton/polyester, France, 1963.

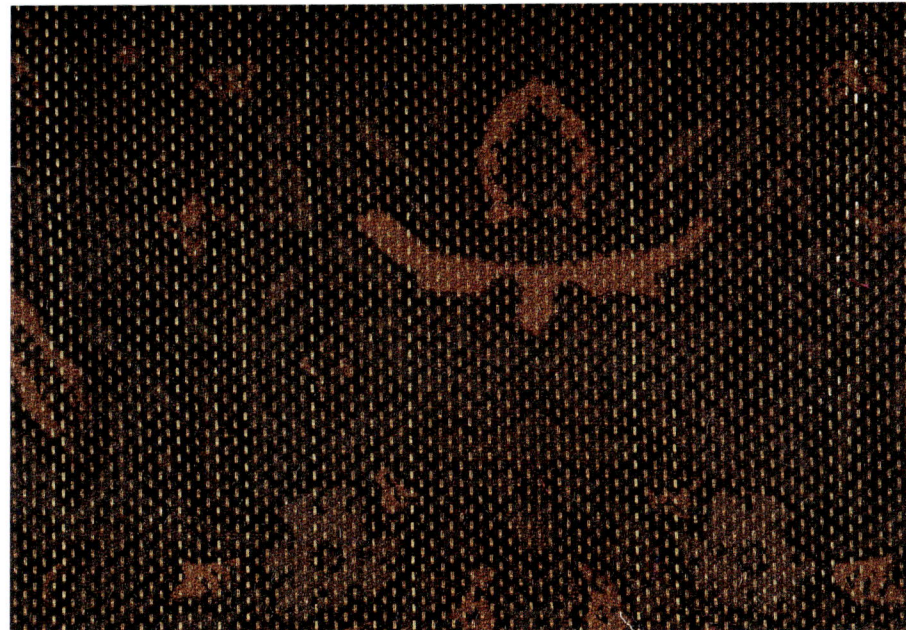

Dark tones with vertical gold threads. Wool blend, France, 1961.

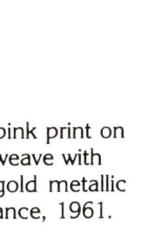

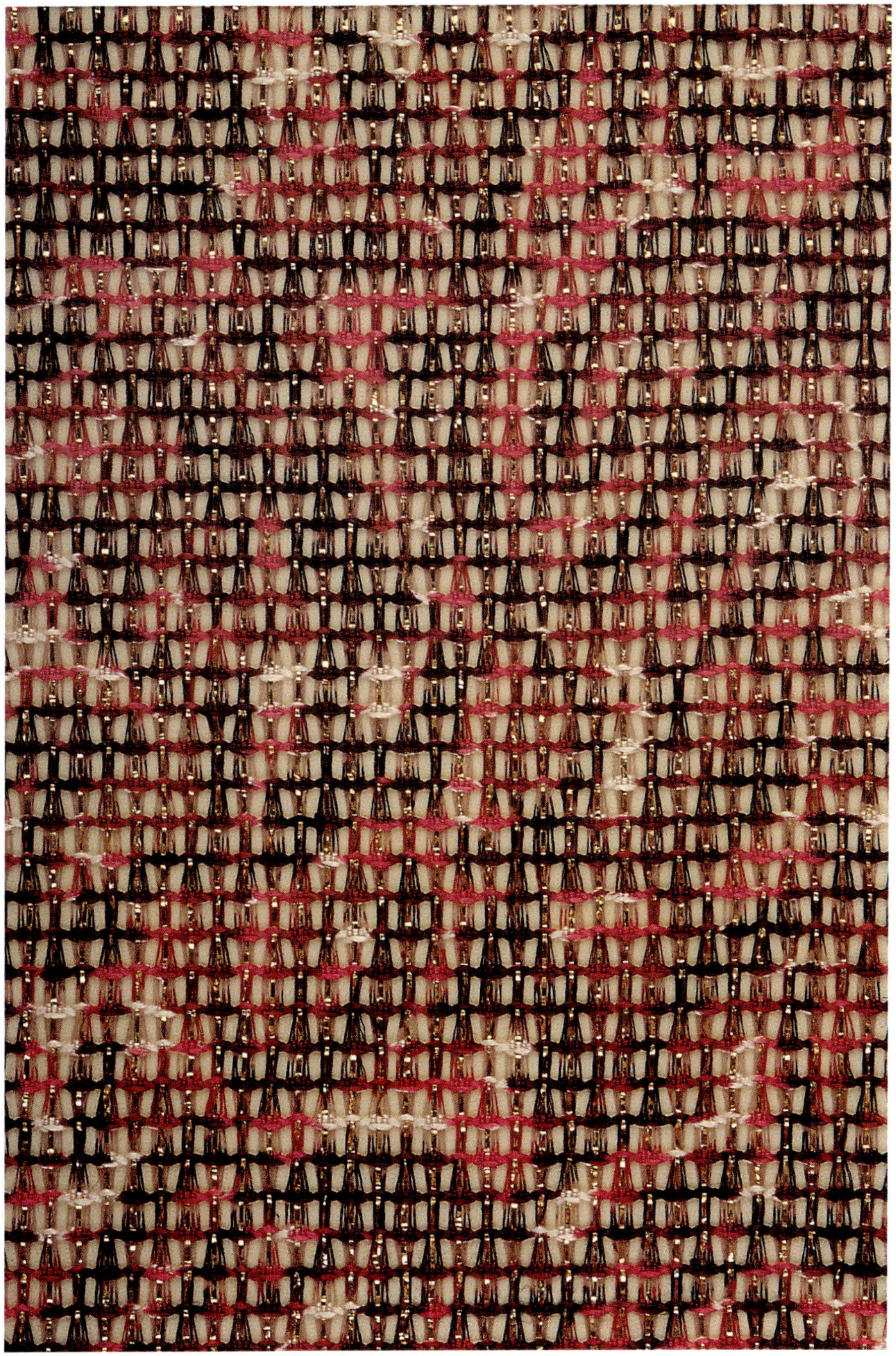

Black and pink print on lacy, open weave with horizontal gold metallic threads. France, 1961.

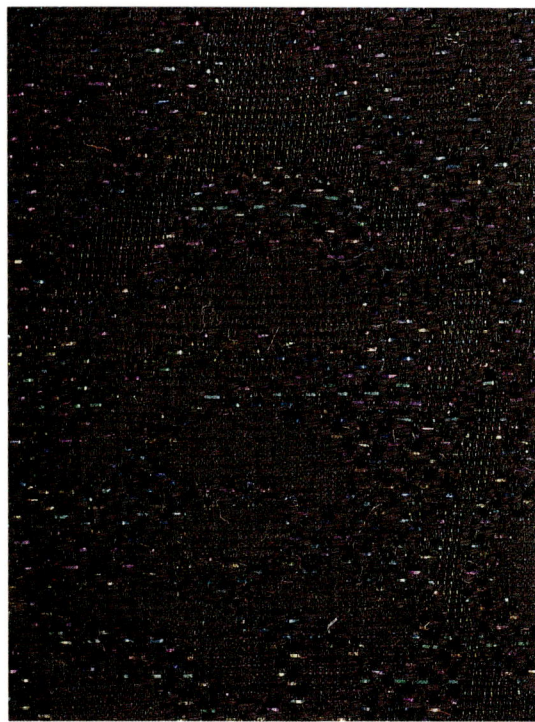

Colorful metallic threads spark black brocade. France, 1964.

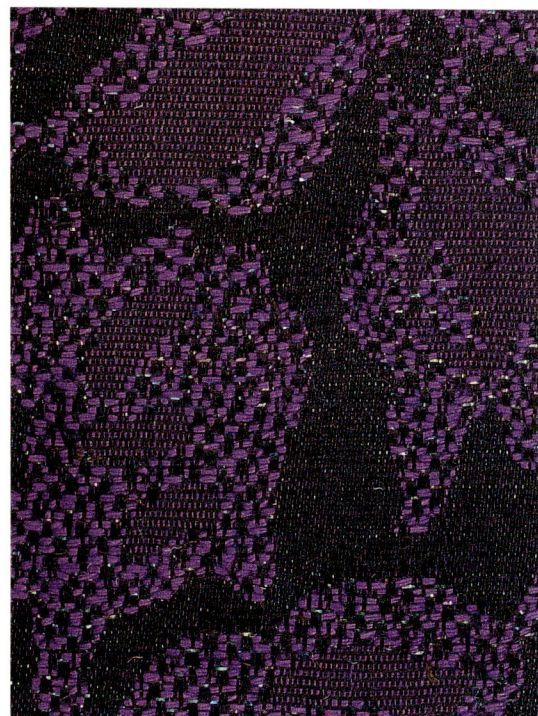

Black metallic threads in purple brocade. France, 1964.

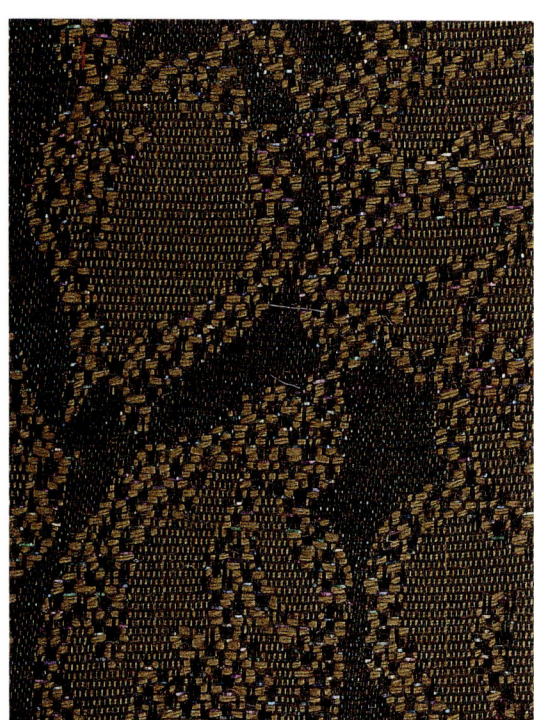

Black and colored metallic threads in green and black brocade. France, 1964.

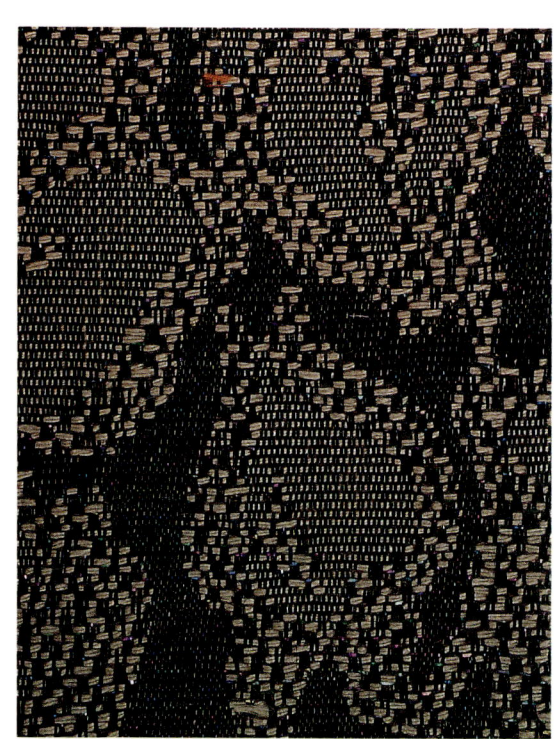

Black and colored metallic threads in black and taupe brocade. France, 1964.

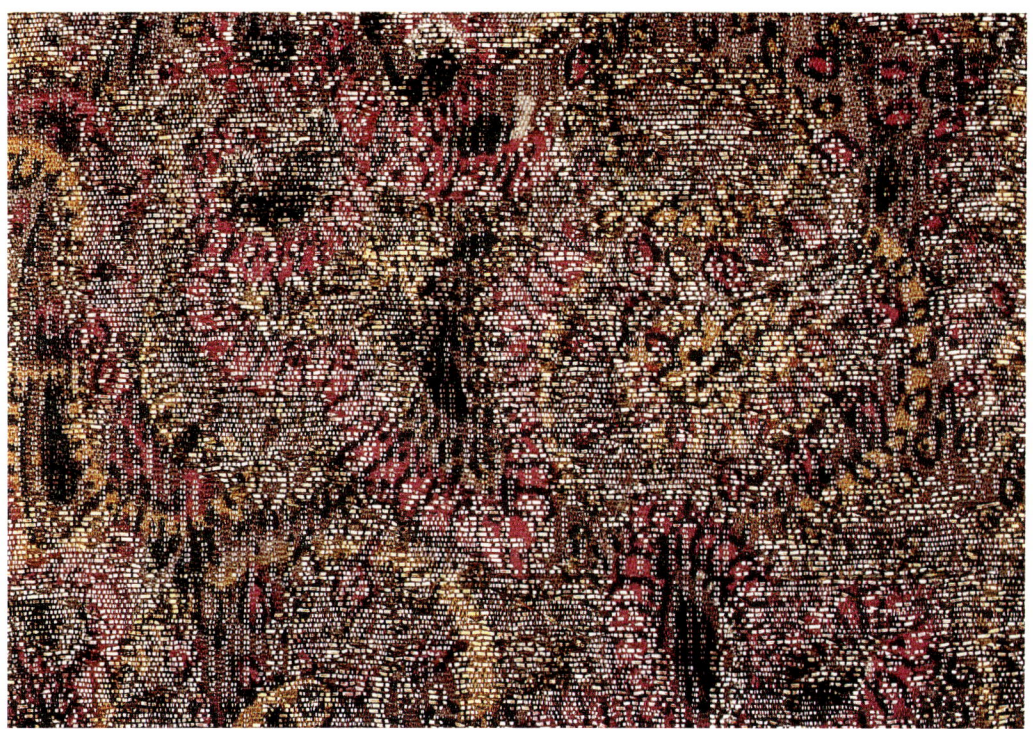

Abstract brown, pink, and gold design gets sparkle from horizontal gold threads. France, 1965.

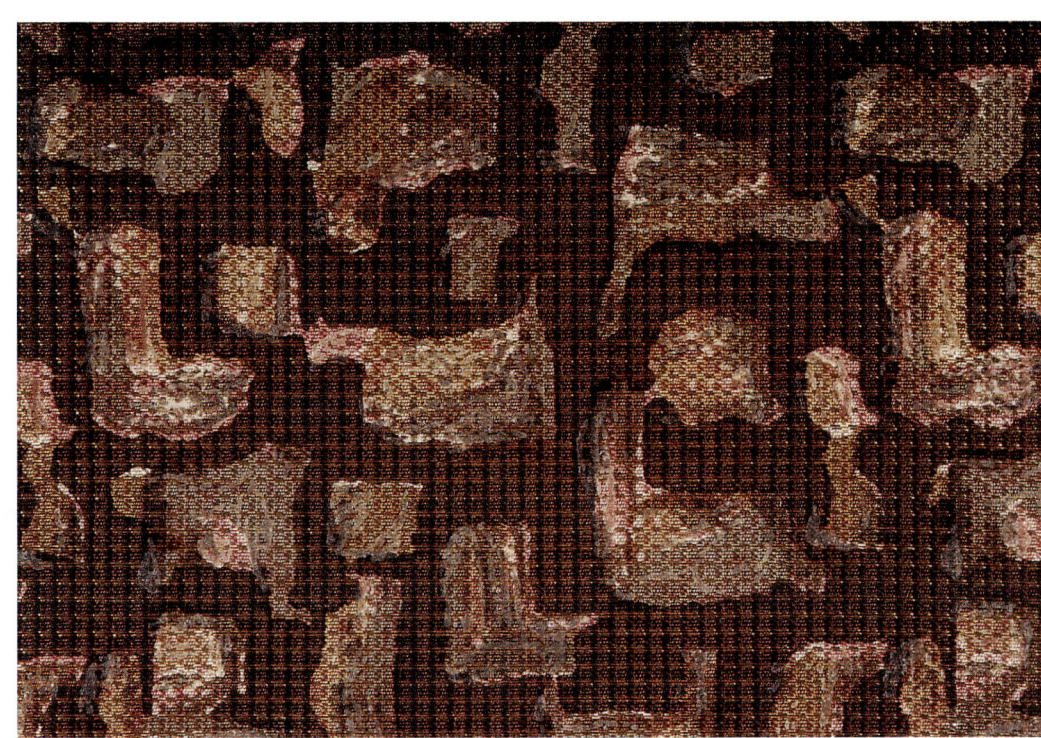

Horizontal gold woven with rich brown overprinted with painterly blocks of color. France, 1961.

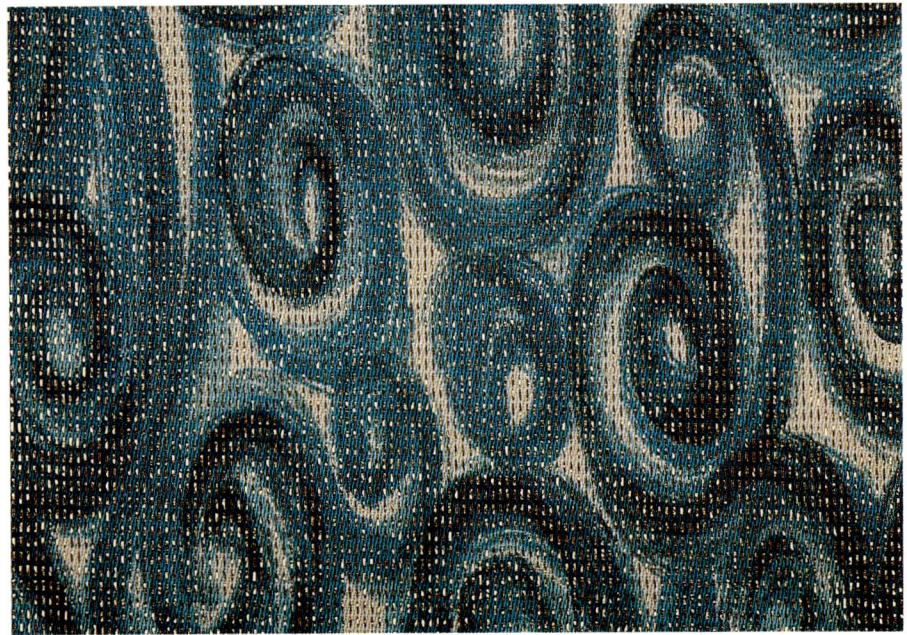

Vertical gold threads with blue swirl print. Cotton/acetate, France, 1962.

Vertical gold with purple and orange over white. Polyester blend, France, 1961.

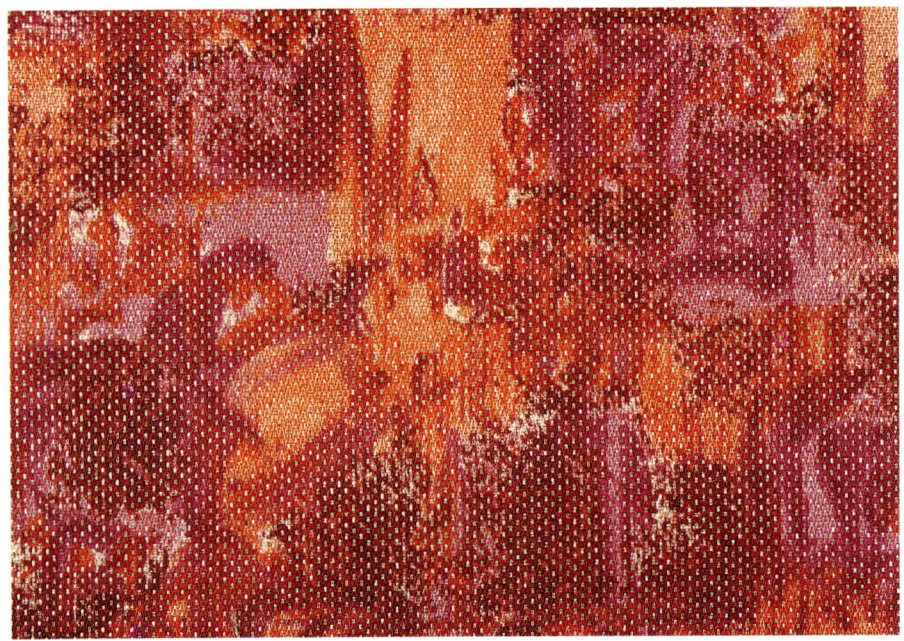

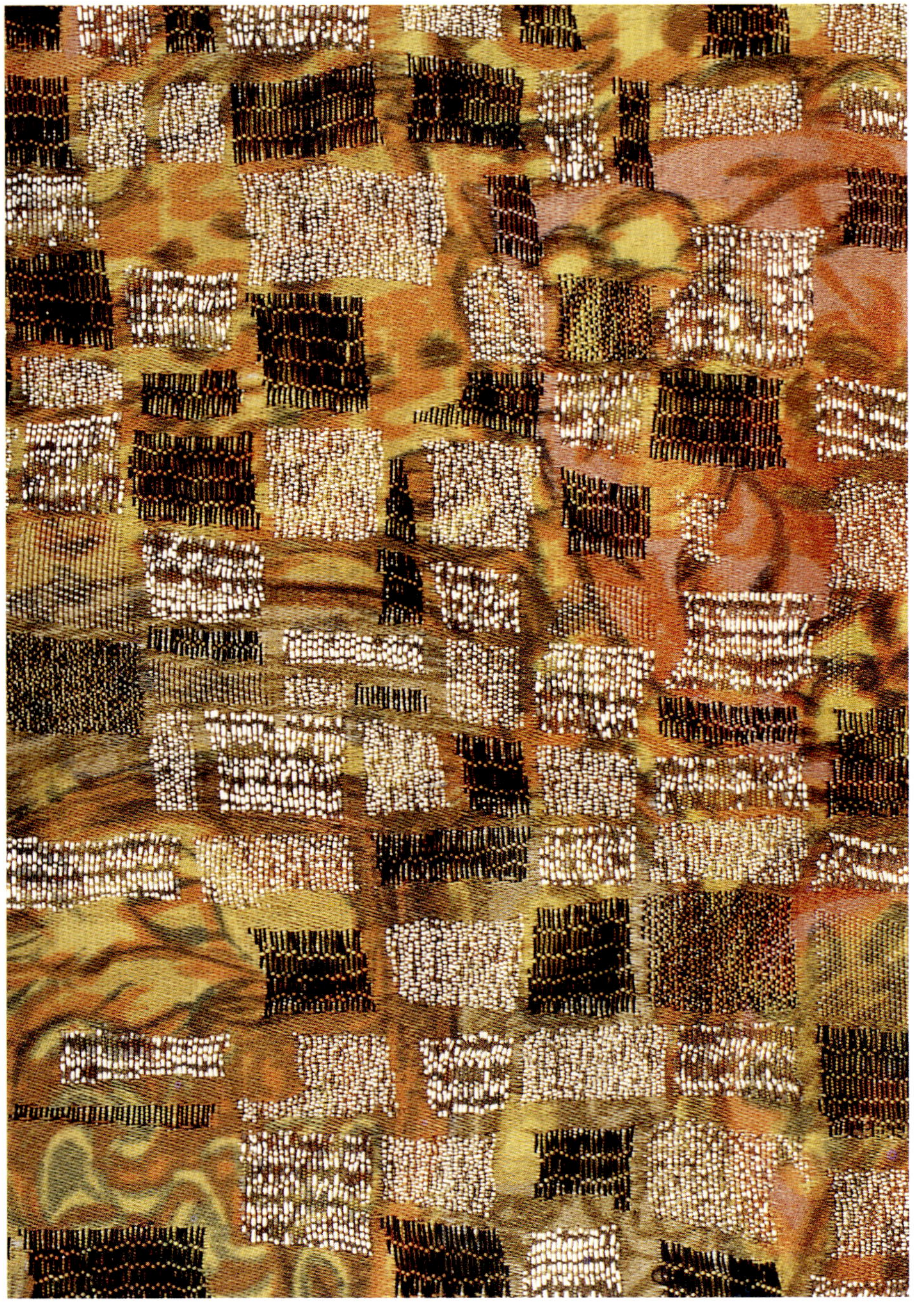

Blocks of black and gold plastic threads on green and peach abstract ground. Rayon blend, France, 1963.